"Our passport to Kauai!" – LB, Durango, CO

San Francisco Chronicle:
"An incredible source of information about . . . what tourist traps to avoid and where to find the best values."

Los Angeles Times:
". . . filled with information on beaches, restaurants and things to do and see. Lenore Horowitz's love for Kauai comes through in her writing."

Vancouver Courier:
"A little gem of a book that each and every traveler should have in hand."

Travel-Age West:
"A downhome commentary on the best beaches, restaurants, and activities..."

"...It's like having our own tour guide!"– JH, Hartford, CT

"The best investment I made!"
– GM, Freeport, TX

"It's the only travel guide you'll ever need!"
–CM, Boston, MA

Los Angeles Times:
"Our vacation became an adventure the day we discovered the *Kauai Underground Guide!*"

Seattle Post Intelligencer:
"I can't imagine riding around the island without this book resting on the dash of my rental car."

San Francisco Chronicle:
"Our constant companion! This book opened our eyes to delights we would otherwise have missed."

"A fabulous book! We saw places we've ignored because we didn't know they existed."
– EW, Milwaukie, OR

"I found beautiful beaches that showed me what Hawaii was like years ago."– DC, Coos Bay, OR

"You've been our valued companion, through your book, on all our trips since 1988."
– TM, El Cerito, CA

'the bible!' – *Travel & Leisure*

'Everything you need to know'– *Hawaii Magazine*

'Distinctive, thorough, & helpful!'
– Jeff Phillips, Senior Travel Writer, *Sunset Magazine*

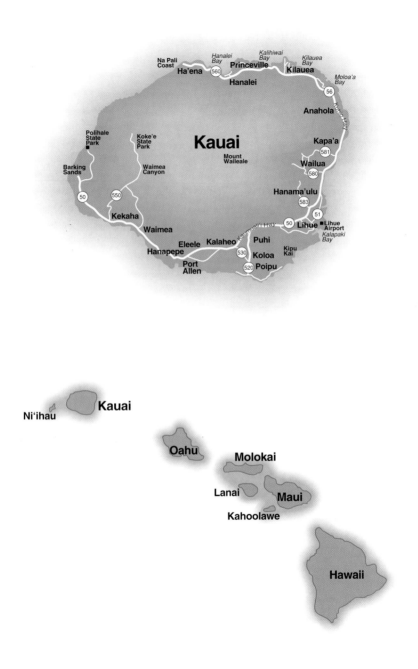

Kauai Underground Guide

Lenore W. Horowitz

Mirah A. Horowitz

17th edition

Papaloa Press

© 2004 by Papaloa Press, a Division of LCH Enterprises Inc.

First edition:	1980
Second edition:	1981
Third Edition:	1982
Fourth edition:	1983
Fifth edition:	1984
Sixth edition:	1985
Seventh edition:	1986
Eighth edition:	1987
Ninth edition:	1988
Tenth edition:	1989
Eleventh edition:	1990
Twelfth edition:	1992
Thirteenth edition:	1995
Fourteenth edition:	1996
2nd printing	1997
Fifteenth edition:	1998
Sixteenth edition:	2000
2nd printing	2002
3rd printing	2003
Seventeenth edition	September, 2004

ISBN 0-9745956-0-8
ISSN 1045-1358
Library of Congress Catalog card 82-643643

Original Line Drawings by Lauren, Mirah, Jeremy &
Mike Horowitz, Devon Davey & Tara French
Historic Petroglyph Drawings by Likeke R. McBride
Photographs by Lenore W. Horowitz

*Special thanks to Mirah, Jeremy, Mike, Lauren, & Larry
for their invaluable help with the research, writing,
illustration, and design of this seventeenth edition
& mahalo nui loa to Keali'i & Fred
& special thanks to David, Andy, Marvis, Megan, Jason & Wailea
and in fond remembrance of John Akana*

Printed in Canada
by Kromar Printing Ltd., Winnipeg, Canada

Contents

Planning Ahead

Beach Adventures

Activities & Discoveries

by Robert Trent Jones, Jr.

Adventures

Restaurants

$\mathcal{P}$reface

Kauai is a very different island than the one we wrote about in our first edition of the *Kauai Underground Guide* in 1980, when sixteen typewritten pages were enough to give advice on what to do and see. Today, you can still enjoy the Hanama'ulu Tea House, Barbecue Inn, Hanalei Dolphin, Kountry Kitchen, Bull Shed, Beach House–but the island has changed dramatically. And so has our Guide, growing to 240 pages, turning into many colors, spanning the desktop revolution in computer technology, and moving onto the internet.

To celebrate this milestone, we've arranged for a special Hawaiian Music CD Sampler featuring songs by Keali'i Reichel, whose first album *Kawaipunahele* took the music world by storm in 1994 and is now the bestselling album of Hawaiian music. Keali'i joins us in doing something special for Kauai. We've created the *Kauai Underground Guide 'Campaign for Kids'* to raise money from our book sales and to encourage matching donations from 'community partners' to benefit non-profit agencies helping Kauai's children–for health and welfare, education, literacy and the arts (see page 238).

We've been writing *The Kauai Underground Guide* for more than twenty years– through two hurricanes, and as an important phase in the island's history draws to an end. Sugar is no longer a real factor in the island's economy: the MacBryde Sugar Company has closed on the westside; Grove Farm Plantation has been sold to Steve Case of AOL; Lihue Plantation lands at Kealia are being developed into vacation estate sites. The island's appearance is changing, as fields of sugar cane are replaced by fields of coffee and macadamia nuts, as well as vacation homes with impressive views and high prices. The determining factor in the island's future may well turn out to be not a longer runway for the Lihue Airport but a wider pipeline on the information highway. As broadband becomes more accessible, Kauai seems less remote than before – an island in transition, as the new millennium gets underway.

The Kauai we will try to describe to you in our *Guide* is not what you would see from a tour bus, but the rare and special place we have discovered during more than twenty years as vacationers and homeowners. We want to share with you our favorite adventures – at the beaches, in restaurants, on tours and expeditions. We do not describe every restaurant or shop, only those we have visited, and our opinions are shaped by a preference for peace and quiet, privacy and natural beauty.

In many ways our *Guide* is unique. As a family of six, we can offer advice on beaches and activities based on having taken children to Kauai at all ages. For adults with that enviable freedom to go off by themselves, we describe adventures and what one can expect to find in many island restaurants. Even a single year brings dramatic change to this island, and our working vacations keep us busy tracking what's new, what's different, and what's still as lovely as ever. You may find that in some cases prices, policies, even managements may be changed, so do your research carefully when making decisions and keep us posted about what you find out. It's been great fun hearing from people all over the country who have explored Kauai with our *Guide,* and want to help update the next one.

So as we go to press with this 17th edition, we want to thank all the readers who have helped make our *Guide* a storybook success. Who would have thought that our first edition would grow into a book which has sold more than 200,000 copies! Or that our oldest child, Mirah, would arrange such a spectacular send-off by handing our first edition to a friend she made on the beach. He turned out to be Chandler Forman of the *Chicago Sun-Times*, and when his story about Kauai–and our book–was syndicated nationwide, more than 700 letters arrived at our door, and we had to rush to press with a new edition.

When she arranged this PR spectacular, Mirah was a gregarious six-year-old with two baby brothers. The more observant of our readers may notice that her name now joins mine on the title page, as the torch, or rather the pen, is passing to the new generation! Our boys have changed too, their love for sandcrabs and rainbow shells giving way to a passion for surf, which they indulge in between law cases. Our youngest is the only one left in college, and arrives on the island with her east coast friends who love to try new adventures and share what they find out.

Watching our children change so dramatically over more than twenty years helps put the development of Kauai in perspective. With children and with islands, change brings the excitement of new opportunities and at the same time the loss of what was precious. The roads we travel today are certainly more congested, but our destinations seem far more interesting. Once perfect for our family with small children, Kauai is also perfect for a family with young adults, with definite and sometimes contradictory interests. And as we explore their newest horizons, we see this wonderful island unfold in fascinating new possibilities.

Like an old friend, Kauai gets better with each visit. New adventures take us to new places, and at the same time we rediscover with deeper affection what we have loved in the past. We hope you will feel the same way about this special place and return again soon!

www.explorekauai.com

Lumahai Beach on the spectacular north shore

Exploring Kauai

Kauai is like an America in miniature, with rolling hills and valleys to the east and majestic mountains to the west. On the eastern shore, sand as fine as sugar rings half-moon bays fringed with stately ironwood trees. These are the best beaches for walking and hunting for shells and driftwood. On the south shore, the island's flat, leeward side offers protected swimming almost all year round under sunny skies and gentle breezes. We love the north shore, where magnificent cliffs reach to touch the sky, and the foaming, churning surf crashes against the rocks. Here, rain showers freshen the air, dance among the flowers, and make the coastline sparkle. Or go west to Kekaha, for great walking beaches, or all the way to the end of the road, to Polihale Beach, with cliffs like the exotic towers of some lost civilization, and golden sand stretching as far as the eye can see. Kauai will never bore you, because a half-hour drive, at the most, can take you to a beach that almost seems to belong to another island.

Almost circular in shape, Kauai has three main tourist areas: Princeville & Hanalei to the north, Poipu to the south, and the 'Coconut Coast' between Lihue and Kapa'a to the east. Each has its own character, and all are wonderful. Take a virtual tour with panoramic photographs at www.virtualguidebooks.com.

North Shore

By far the most spectacular, the north shore combines rugged mountains with beautiful beaches and green vistas – the Kauai of post-cards. As the windward shore, the north also gets the most rainfall, particularly in winter months, when surf at the beaches is also stronger and more unpredictable. No matter the season, many people love the north shore for its rural tranquility and magnificent beauty, and come here to 'get away from it all,' to wind down to 'island time' in an area made remote by one lane bridges occasionally washed out in winter storms.

The major resort area on the north shore is *Princeville*, perched high on an ocean bluff overlooking Hanalei Bay. Princeville includes private homes and condos, two championship golf courses, and the *Princeville Hotel*, with elegant rooms and service, gourmet dining, and a magnificent cliffside setting. A small beach at the base of the cliff, which you reach by elevator, offers marvelous views and, when seas are calm, swimming and snorkeling. Starwood Hotels; from $405/nite (plus $15/day for parking) 800-325-3589; www.princeville.com. Nearby, the *Hanalei Bay Resort* combines the conveniences of a condominium with hotel amenities. Quintus hotels: from $185/nite/room and $350/nite/suite. 800-827-4427; www.hanaleibayresort.com). You don't have to stay at a hotel! Surrounding Princeville's golf courses are a host of condos and private homes

Spectacular Hanalei Bay in summer, the view from the Princeville Resort. In winter, surf can reach twenty feet, and boats take shelter in the south.

Princeville Resort overlooks Hanalei Bay

offering astonishing ocean views, particularly at sunset, though getting to the beach may be difficult, requiring a hike down the cliff to one of the small beaches (hotel guests have elevator privileges).

Outside Princeville, you can get closer to the ocean, for example in the town of Hanalei, near one of Kauai's finest beaches. You'll also find privacy on or near the beach in the lovely residential areas of Kalihiwai, Anini, Wainiha, and Ha'ena. The *Hanalei Colony Resort* in Ha'ena offers beachfront condos from $185/nite (800-628-3004; www.hcr.com).

South Shore

The south shore, at Poipu, on the island's leeward side, has drier weather and generally calmer swimming conditions year round. It's also flatter, with vegetation more dry. For swimming, there is wonderful Poipu Beach, and for sheer beauty, spectacular Maha'ulepu.

You have many choices for lodgings, including two resort hotels–the *Hyatt Regency* and the *Sheraton Kauai*. The *Hyatt Regency* offers spacious rooms and elegant dining in an architecturally beautiful resort. The beach is beautiful, but has strong surf and intimidating currents. Instead, the 600 room Hyatt offers guests an elaborate swimming water-way, with riverpools, waterfalls, and 150 foot waterslide, as well as a 5 acre meandering saltwater lagoon with islands. From $340/425, plus $15/

At the Hyatt Regency in Poipu, a popular waterway complex features a salt water lagoon and a 150-ft waterslide.

nite 'resort fee.' 800-233-1234; www.kauai-hyatt.com. Nearby, the *Sheraton Poipu Beach* has 413 comfortable rooms located right on beautiful Poipu Beach, great for swimming in all seasons. From $325, plus $23/nite 'resort fee' (800-782-9488; sheraton-kauai.com). The *Waiohai is* now a Marriott timeshare. Rates from $249 (808-742-4400 or 800-228-9290; www.marriott.com).

Poipu's condominium resorts offer the convenience and space of an apartment along with many hotel amenities. The best location on Poipu Beach is the *Kiahuna,* managed by 3 competing companies: Outrigger's *Kiahuna Planta-*

Poipu Beach

tion has 115 units from $169/nite (800-688-7444; www.outrigger.com). Castle Resorts has 95 units from $225/nite (800-937-6642; www.castleresorts.com). *Kiahuna Beachfront* has the best beachfront units (only 13) from $300/nite (800-937-6642; www.kiahuna.com). *Poipu Kai,* set back from the beach, is managed by Aston (800-922-7866; www.aston-hotels.com) and Suite Paradise (800-367-8020; www.suiteparadise.com). The *Embassy Resort* has the most luxurious suites, but fronts a beach too rough for easy swimming. From $384/nite (800-535-0085; www.embassykauai.com).

Choose from many condos and charming B&B's, many in walking distance of Poipu Beach Park, with excellent protected swimming and snorkeling all year round. See *Kauai Vacation Planner* (800-262-1400) or the Poipu Beach Organization (742-7444; www.poipu-beach.org).

Westside

Largely undeveloped, the west side is still 'local' Kauai. The weather is sunny, dry, even arid, which you'll appreciate when other parts of the

Kauai Marriott–great location on Kalapaki Beach

island have rain. Just west of Poipu and Koloa, you'll come to the town of Hanapepe and Salt Pond Beach Park, a beautiful spot enjoyed primarily by local people. The Green Garden Restaurant and a host of art galleries make the nearby town of Hanapepe fun to explore. Further west, you'll love the long, sandy beach at Kekaha, great for swimming, surfing, and beachwalking. Beyond that is the awesome expanse of sand and cliffs at Polihale. Choose from vacation homes, apartments, and B & B's in the towns of Kekaha and Waimea. *Waimea Plantation Cottages* offers hotel services with oldstyle charm in vintage plantation cottages & Kauai's first free wireless internet access. Rates from $100 (waimea-plantation.com; 800-9-WAIMEA). The best swimming beach, however, is at Kekaha.

Eastern Shore

The eastern shore, from Lihue (where the airport is located) to Wailua and Kapa'a–the "Coconut Coast"– has location as its main advantage. It's about midway between Poipu and Hanalei and about a half-hour drive from each, so you can explore the island in either direction, depending on the weather and your inclinations.

You'll find hotels, condos and B & B's, many of which can accurately be described as 'beachfront.' You should ask careful questions, however, because eastern shore beaches can have tricky currents, and swimmers must be very cautious. Beachfront at its best? The *Kauai*

The Kauai Marriott pool, one of the largest resort pools anywhere, features an island and four jaccuzzis.

Marriott fronts the magnificent sandy swimming beach at Kalapaki Bay in Lihue, a spectacular hotel with more than 880 acres of golf courses and waterways. Rooms may be smaller than the Hyatt's, but you can't beat the beach or the hotel's circular pool ringed by jaccuzzis, one of the state's largest. From $270 (800-220-2925; www.marriotthotels.com/LIHHI).

The Coconut Coast near Wailua offers moderately priced hotels as well as condo resorts and B & B's. Some excellent beachfront condos include *Lae Nani* (877-523-6264), *Wailua Bay View* (800-882-9007), *Lanikai* (808-822-7700), *Kapa'a Sands* (800-222-4901), *Kapa'a Shores* (808-822-3055). The *Aloha Beach Resort Kauai* is great for families, close to Lydgate Park's rock-rimmed pools and wonderful playground From $135/nite (888-823-5111; www. abrkauai.com). For modest rates try *Islander on the Beach* (800-847-7417; www.astonhotels.com) and *Kauai Coast Resort* (877-977-4355) formerly the Beachboy, and now a timeshare with suites. Recently renovated *Kauai Coconut Beach Resort* (808-822-3455) is operated by Marriott. On a budget? Try the newly remodeled beachfront bargain, *Hotel Coral Reef* (800-843-4659).

Before You Go

　　* **Call the Kauai Visitor's Bureau** (800-262-1400) and request the *Kauai Vacation Planner.*

　　* **Contact Resort Associations** on Kauai. The *Poipu Beach Resort Association* represents south shore accommodations and activities: PO Box 730 Koloa, HI 96756 (808-742-7444 or www.poipu-beach.org). For Princeville and information on the north shore: *Princeville Resort*, PO Box 3069, Princeville HI 96722 (800- 826-4400 www.princeville.com).

　　* Go surfing! The internet changes faster than the weather, but here

are some sites for a start. View the interiors of actual hotel rooms, condos, homes, B & B's. Compare beach locations, pools, facilities; schedule activities and adventures, find internet discounts. For the online Kauai Yellow Pages, visit www.ad-venturespublishing.com (and get 5 free minutes). Download maps at www.kauai-beaches.com.

Helpful Kauai links

Kauai vacations	www.kauaivisitorsbureau.org
	www.kauaivacation.com
Kauai County homepage	www.kauai-hawaii.com
Facts, Information, & Links	www.gohawaii.about.com
Garden Island Newspaper	www.kauaiworld.com
Kauai calendar	www.kauaiworld.com/calendar
All-island calendars	http://calendar.gohawaii.com
Surf & weather	www.surf-news.com
Kauai Yellow Pages	www.ad-venturespublishing.com
Local Kauai links	www.kauaistyle.com
	www.trykauai.com/Lilikoi_Links.htm
Poipu Beach Association	www.poipu-beach.org
B & B's, condo rentals	www.kauaivacationresorts.com
	www.kauaivacationrentals.com
Hawaiian music	www.mele.com www.tropicaldisc.com
Hawaiian music postcard	www.nadobra.com/postcards
Keali'i Reichel MP3s	www.kealiireichel.com
Hawaiian culture, language	www.geocities.com/~olelo
Kauai beaches & maps	www.kauai-beaches.com
Kauai hiking	www.hawaiitrails.org
Kauai sites of interest	www.hawaiiweb.com/kauai/html/sites

Renting a Private Home or Condo

The Kauai Vacation Planner lists vacation condos and homes (800-262-1400), as do classified ads in publications like *Hawaii Magazine* or *Sunset Magazine*. Some internet sites offer an accommodation overview, with links to individual owners: kauaivisitorsbureau.com, travel-kauai.com, kauaivacationresorts.com. kauaivacation.com, poipu-beach.org, bestplaceshawaii.com. Contact island rental agencies: *Kauai Vacation Rentals* (800-367-5025; KauaiVacationRentals.com), *Garden Island Properties* (800-801-0378), *Prosser Realty* (800-767-4707;

prosser-realty.com). Some agencies specialize. **South shore**, contact the *Poipu Beach Association* for a detailed member list (P.O. Box 730, Koloa, HI 96756 or 808-742-7444; www. poipu-beach.org for links to properties). Agencies: *Grantham Resorts* (800-325-5701 grantham-resorts.com), *R & R Realty* (800-367-8022), *Poipu Connection* (poipuconnection.com; 800-742-2260), *Poipu Beach Travel* (800-3-ALOHA-3), *Garden Island Properties* (800-801-0378; kauaiproperties.com), *Garden Island Rentals* (800-247-5599), *Suite Paradise* (800-367-8020; poipu-kai-condos.com).

North shore agencies include: *Na Pali Properties* (800-715-7273; napaliprop.com), *North Shore Properties* (800-488-3336; kauai-vacation-rentals.com), *Harrington's Paradise Properties* (808-826-6114), *Blue Water Rentals* (800-628-5533), *Hanalei Aloha Management* (800-487-9833), *Oceanfront Realty* (800-222-5541), *Anini Beach Rentals* (800-448-6333; www.anini.com). Expect to pay at least $100 per night ($180 for a condo at or near a swimming beach). Advance deposits and one week minimum stays are usual. For popular months (December– March; August), reserve well in advance and check cancellation policies.

Bed & Breakfasts

B & B's are plentiful on Kauai and come in all prices (from $45, with $70 as the average) and types, from a beachfront cottage to the spare room-with-bath in a home with gregarious host, even a river estate (808-826-6411; riverestate.com). Individual owners are listed in the *Kauai Vacation Planner*. Many link to larger sites like kauaivacation.com, poipu-beach.org, kauaivacationresorts.com, or bestplaceshawaii.com.

Two agencies on Kauai represent many individual owners, as well as small hotels, inns and condos. *Bed & Breakfast Hawaii* (800-733-1632 www.bandb-hawaii.com) has listings on all the islands, and *Bed & Breakfast Kauai* (800-822-1176; www.BnBKauai.com) has an exclusive focus on Kauai. Single travelers receive special consideration from both agencies, and can also call Edee Seymour of *Victoria's Place* in Lawai (808-332-9465). For women travelers, *Mahina's Guest House* (808-823-9364; www.mahinas.com). Questions to ask: What's for breakfast (continental, full meal, or stocked kitchen)? What kind of beds (length,

---

Internet: Local access numbers: AOL 245-4284. Earthlink 482- 2916 or 855-0020. Arrange local dial-up for $10/2 weeks (no set-up charge) with Hawaiian.net. 800-536-5162 /245-4598; accounts@hawaiian.net. Visit Kauai's internet cafes (p.233). Share the free wireless at Waimea Plantation Cottages if you come for lunch or dinner.

width, etc.)? What degree of interaction with host and other guests (How friendly or private do you want to be?)

Most require a deposit and a minimum stay. Ask about cancellation policy. Many are booked 2 to 3 months in advance, so plan ahead.

Rustic Retreats

If you like hiking and camping (yet amid relative comfort), you can rent cabins in some of Kauai's loveliest wilderness areas. In the Koke'e forest region, you can rent a cabin with stove, refrigerator, hot shower, cooking and eating utensils, linens, bedding, and wood burning stove at bargain rates, only $35-$45/night (maximum stay of 5 nights during a 30 day period). Contact *Koke'e Lodge,* Box 819, Waimea HI 96796 (808-335-6061). To explore Kokee, visit www.aloha.net/~kokee. Also in Koke'e, *YWCA Camp Sloggett* offers hostel accommodations ($20/pp) and platforms for tent camping ($10/pp). Reservations: YWCA Kauai, 3094 Elua St., Lihue HI 96766. 808-245-5959; www.campingkauai.com.

On the north shore, *YMCA Camp Naue* in Ha'ena offers beachfront camping in bunk houses (or your own tent). $12/nite. YMCA of Kauai, Box 1786, Lihue HI 96766 (808-246-9090). Kapa'a's *International Hostel* costs $20/nite/bunk (808-823-6142; www.hostels.com/us.hi.ka.html). In Kapa'a, private units from $40 (www.kkbedbath.com; 800-615-6211).

Beachfront & Oceanfront

If you want to be located on or close to a swimming beach, become a connoisseur of words. 'Ocean front' probably means a rocky place, or at least marginal swimming, but even 'beachfront' can be a misleading term. The so-called 'beach' could be rocky or unswimmable due to dangerous currents and strong surf. A property as a whole may be accurately described as 'beachfront,' but actually be shaped like a pie wedge, with the tip on the beach and the wide end (where *you* may end up being situated) back on the road. Or it may be technically adjacent to a beach, but with a building, a swimming pool (or even a road) in between.

Key questions: What will I see when I open up my sliding glass door? How far do I have to walk (or drive) to get to the nearest sandy swimming beach? If you have children, ask about the closest 'child-friendly' swimming beach. Ask about the swimming pool, as pools vary in size and location, and yours may end up being a tiny kidney next to the parking lot. Ask how far you have to walk to reach it, a crucial point if you have toddlers and all their paraphernalia to carry.

What to Pack

When two suitcases disappeared during one flight home, we learned some lessons the hard way about packing. Now we pack a change of clothes, bathing suit, and toilet articles for each family member, as well as any prescription drugs, in a carry-on bag just in case someone's suitcase is lost temporarily. We also distribute everybody's belongings in every suitcase, so that no one person is left without clothes if a suitcase is lost permanently. And we label each bag clearly *inside* where the label can't be accidentally detached. A replacement-cost rider on our Homeowner's insurance policy turned out to be a wise investment, for the airline's insurance limit is $1,850 per passenger. Airlines typically subtract 10% of the purchase price for each year you have owned an item, exclude cameras and jewelry, and may take up to six months to process a claim. If your luggage is missing or damaged, save all baggage-claim stubs, boarding passes, and tickets, and be sure to fill out an official claim form at the baggage supervisor's office *before* you leave the airport. Most clearly tagged luggage makes its way to the owner within 24 hours (and they deliver). Call daily for an update.

Vacation days are too precious to spend on line in stores. We try to cut down on clothes (except for swim suits and T-shirts) and use space for other essentials – beach sandals, walking shoes, snorkel gear (that fits), extra film, sunscreen, hat with brim, sunglasses, beach bag or back pack, frisbee, tennis ball or beach ball. Island restaurants are informal – no tie or jacket. A light sweater in winter is a good idea.

Flying to Kauai

The typical travel plan involves a flight first to Honolulu International Airport on Oahu and then a connecting flight to Kauai's Lihue Airport. This can turn into a full day of travel, particularly on the return trip to the mainland, when the clock moves ahead of you. You can gain back some vacation time on that return trip if you take the latest evening flight out of Honolulu, leaving Kauai around dinner time to make the connection. United and American, and also ATA offer non-stop flights between Lihue and Los Angeles, or between Lihue and San Francisco. Charter discount fares may save you money, but can also cost you time – if there's a problem with your flight, you'll have no way to change carriers. Major airlines with frequent daily flights give you more options in case someone gets sick, or you need to go home earlier, or (even better) later!

After you land in Honolulu, you will take a connecting flight on Hawaiian or Aloha Airlines for your twenty-minute flight to Kauai. Airline regulations require a minimum 70 minute layover in Honolulu to allow passengers and baggage to be transferred to inter-island connecting flights. However, you can beat the system and minimize time wasted in the airport. After landing in Honolulu, go directly to the Inter-island Terminal, a ten-minute walk (inside security) or short bus ride (outside security). Go to your airline's ticket counter, and try to get on an earlier flight to Lihue, even as a stand-by. (The computer data is often wrong, and stand-bys can usually get seats). Your luggage will remain on your originally scheduled flight, but you will be in Lihue with a head start – to fill out forms for your rental car while waiting for the baggage. On long travel days, especially with children, this saved time can be a lifesaver.

On your inter-island flight, you may be asked to check your carry-on luggage because of size, as some inter-island aircraft have small overhead bins. Keep your jewelry, camera, prescription drugs, and favorite stuffed animals in a small bag you can pull out of that carry on, if necessary.

Hawaiian Airlines: 800-367-5320; www.hawaiianair.com; 835-3700
Aloha Airlines: 800-367-5250; www.alohaair.com; 484-1111

Traveling with Children

If you are traveling with babies or toddlers, you can request bulkhead seating (but not exit rows, which can be assigned only to adults) in advance. Be sure to get an assigned seat in the computer in advance too, so that your seats have priority if the flight is overbooked. Enroll in the airline's Frequent Flyer Program – the kids too. You should bring along your child's car seat, which can go into the baggage compartment with your luggage, as Hawaii state law requires them for children under three. Airlines now permit use of the child's restraint seat on board the aircraft, but that requires the child to have a paid seat on crowded flights. (Staying a week or more? Save money and help kids. The YWCA can help you buy a car seat to use on Kauai, have it ready for you at the rental car agency, then pick it up as a donation when you leave). Call Nancy (808-245-6362).

Families who fly to Kauai from the east coast might consider staying overnight in California to help children make the difficult time adjustment in stages, particularly on the long trip home. After flying from Kauai to California, the kids can run around in the hotel, have some ice cream, and stay up as late as possible in order to push their body clocks ahead three hours while they sleep. If you book a late morning flight out of California the next day, the kids can sleep late in the morning, and if you're lucky, they will wake up fresh for the second day's flight, ready to adjust their body clocks another three hours. Traveling through multiple time zones is no snap, but this plan can make it easier.

On that journey home, bad weather might delay your connecting flight from Lihue to Honolulu, and so you might consider taking a flight earlier in the day, before the inter-island flights get backed up. In fact, it's a good idea to see if you can get on as a stand-by on *any* earlier flight to Honolulu once you're in the Lihue airport, and well worth it if you are traveling with young children and can't afford to miss your mainland connection.

Kite flying at Hanalei Bay

To amuse little ones during the long flight, pack lots of small toys, crayons, books, paper dolls, and an "airplane present" to be unwrapped when the seatbelt sign goes off. Ask the cabin attendants for "kiddie packs" or cards right away as supplies are often limited. Pack a secret snack or toy for those awful moments when one child spills coke on another. Keep chewing gum handy to help children relieve the ear-clogging which can be so uncomfortable, even painful, during the last twenty minutes of the descent when cabin pressure changes. Sucking on a bottle will help a baby or toddler.

To save shopping time, we stuff as many beach and swimming toys into suitcase corners as possible. 'Swimmies' (arm floats) are great for small children to use in the pool, as are goggles and masks, toy trucks for sand-dozing, frisbees, inflatable beach balls, and floats. Boogie boards, by far the best swimming toy, can be brought home in the baggage compart-ment after your vacation (packed in a pillowcase!). Best choices are at the M. Miura store (Kapa'a), Progressive Expressions (Koloa), or even K-

Mart and Wal-Mart. Boogie boards are better balanced than the cheaper imitations. Caution: they can be hazardous in a pool; a small child who tips over in deep water can be trapped underneath.

Rent children's equipment at *Ready Rentals* (823-8008 or 800-599 8008; www.readyrentals.com). $15 delivery. To protect a baby's delicate skin, bring a hat with a large brim, socks for feet, and a strong, waterproof sunblock (re-apply frequently).

Weathering Kauai

If you dial 245-6001 for the weather report on Kauai, you will probably hear this 'forecast': "Mostly fair today, with occasional windward and mauka (mountain) showers. Tonight, mostly fair, with showers varying from time to time and from place to place." Except for storms, Kauai's normal weather pattern is mostly sunny, with showers passing over the ocean, crossing the coastline and backing up against the island's mountainous interior. Like all the Hawaiian islands, Kauai's sunny side varies with the winds. Normal trade winds blow from the north and northeast, bringing rainfall to these 'windward' shores and creating the 'lee' of the island in the south, at Poipu, and west, at Kekaha and Polihale. When the clouds back up against the mountains and bring showers to the north shore beaches, Poipu and Salt Pond may have sunny skies! However, sometimes the winds blow from the south and west, and these 'Kona winds' create the lee in the north and northeast. The north shore may be spectacular while the eastern and southern shores have rain.

Careful planning can make the most of any weather, however, since Kauai has 'micro climates' and a 20 minute drive can take you from rain to sun. On Kauai, no matter where you stay, be prepared to drive to the sun – all the way west to Polihale if necessary! Plan your adventures with an eye to the weather. If it's clear up north, visit the north shore, for these beaches are by far the most spectacular, and if your stay is only for a few days, you may not get another chance. Rain outside? Drive south to Poipu or west to Salt Pond or Kekaha, where it's usually drier. With heavy rain, Polihale might be your best–even your only–dry option.

Only an island-wide storm should send you indoors to rent a movie, so check the weather and surf report before deciding whether to go north to Hanalei, south to Poipu, or west to Kekaha. Try www.kauaiworld.com/weather. Or call merchants who have agreed to be your weather tipsters:

Nukumoi Beach Center, Poipu (742-8019*); Wrangler's Steak House,* Waimea (328-1218); *Pedal & Paddle,* Hanalei (826-9069).

Weather patterns vary with the seasons. Showers are more frequent in winter and spring, while summer months are warmer and more humid, fall months clearer and more dry. Temperatures range between 60's at night & mid-80's most days, and in summer can reach the 90's. The beaches also change their moods with the seasons. In summer, the water may be calm and clear, but winter surf at the same beach can foam and crash like thunder. Some north shore beaches disappear entirely under winter surf, and may even be officially closed for safety reasons.

For Visitors with Disabilities

Kauai County provides a 'Landeez' all-terrain wheelchair at lifeguard stations at Poipu Beach Park, Lydgate Park and Salt Pond Beach Park. These parks, and Kalapaki Beach (parking directions on p.31) have the most accessible facilities and pathways. At Kalihiwai and Anini Beach (North shore) and Hanama'ulu Beach (Eastside), parking is flat and close to the water. Some companies make a special effort to help: Greg Winston at *Watersports Adventures* (whose efforts were much appreciated by 8-year-old Jeffrey Barrett) 821-1599; Chuck Blay of *Kauai Nature Tours* 888-233-8365, and Debra Hookano at *Liko Kauai Cruises* 338-0333. For rental of equipment 24/7, including Landeez chairs and ramps, and helpful island advice, call Clyde Silva at *Gammie Home Care* (632-2333; www.gammie.com). For help, talk with Christina at the ADA Office (mayorsada@kauaigov.com or 808-241-6203 (V/TTY). Visit www.state.hi.us/health/dcab for statewide information. For non-hotel lodging options: *Bed and Breakfast Hawaii* (800-733-1632), or *Bed and Breakfast Kauai* (800-822-1176). For transportation, call ahead to the Kauai Bus (808-241-6410), and bring your valid ADA paratransit ID card, as well as your parking placard to park in accessible parking stalls.

Driving on Kauai

No matter where you decide to stay, you can easily explore the rest of the island by car. Except for the wilderness area in the northwest quadrant, Kauai is nearly encircled by a main two-lane highway, with sequentially numbered 'mile markers' to make tracking easy. You can drive from Lihue to Kapa'a in about 10 minutes, from Kapa'a to Hanalei in about 30 minutes, from Lihue to Poipu in about 20 minutes, and from Poipu to Polihale in about 35 minutes.

Kauai is still rural as far as the infrastructure goes – just two-lanes, all around the island! Increasing traffic has prompted the creation of 'bypass roads.' You'll see the first one as you leave the airport; it merges with Rt. 56 or Kuhio Highway, the island's main two-lane road, just north of Hanama'ulu. Traffic moves easily as you continue north – until you reach the town of Wailua, where three little traffic lights can cause unbelievable congestion during rush hour. A bypass road behind Wailua winds through cane fields, then comes out near the center of Kapa'a, offering you a view of sugar cane rather than the rear bumper of the car in front of you! You'll see the turnoff on the left, just north of the traffic light at Wailua Family Restaurant and just south of the Coconut Plantation Marketplace. It brings you to the center of Kapa'a about two blocks behind the ABC Store.

A third bypass road connects the center of Koloa with eastern Poipu and the Hyatt Regency Hotel. Turn left off Rt. 520 (Maluhia Road) just before you reach Koloa (at the athletic fields), then follow the signs to Poipu. On the fourth bypass road, you can take a scenic route between Nawiliwili Harbor and Puhi, avoiding the center of Lihue. In Nawiliwili, near the small boat harbor, take Niumali Road to Halemalu Road, and follow it past the Menehune Fish Pond to Puhi Road which reconnects with Rt. 50, and from there you can continue on to Koloa and Poipu.

While driving your rental car on Kauai, keep this in mind: speed limits are strictly enforced. It's illegal to make a U-turn in a "business district," even if it doesn't look like much of a business district.

The best places to explore on Kauai are accessible by either paved roads or established dirt roads in the cane fields which are maintained as 'rights of way' to the beaches. So pack a picnic lunch and some beach mats, sunscreen, a good book and your Keali`i Reichel music CD, and explore some of the island's most beautiful hidden beaches! Plan your adventures according to the weather and the season. In winter, the surf is more unpredictable and dangerous on the beaches to the north and northeast, while the best and safest swimming is on the south shore. In summer, the surf may be up on the south and west, with north shore beaches beautiful for swimming. Whatever the season, follow this simple rule for swimming safety: don't swim alone or too far out at any beach whose currents are unfamiliar to you. Read *'Beach Safety'* carefully (p. 76). When you park, be sure to lock up and store your valuables in the trunk, to guard against theft as you would at home.

On Kauai, it's a two-lane lifestyle. So polish your left hand turn skills, avoid driving between 4 and 6:30, and be patient. Remember, you're on vacation!

Beach Adventures

*Kalapaki Beach, a family favorite for swimming & playing – and
exploring the Marriott Hotel afterwards. Page 30.*

Eastern Shore Best Bets

Beaches

Ninini Beach 31
Kalapaki Beach 30
Hanama'ulu 31
Lydgate Park 32
Wailua Bay 34
Kealia Beach 34
Donkey Beach 36
Anahola Beach 36

Hotels

A Marriott Courtyard
B Islander on the Beach
   Kauai Coast Resort
C Kauai Sands
D Aloha Beach Resort
E Radisson Hotel
F Marriott, Kauai Lagoons

Shopping

Lihue, Wailua 37
Kapa'   aa 38

Anahola Bay
for great
beachwalks
and family fun

For island tastes,
visit Farmer's
Markets in Lihue
and Kapa'a (p. 86)

Scuba anyone? Lessons are
fun and can begin a great
adventure! (p. 108)

Wailua River, Kauai's only navigable
waterway. Great for kayak explora-
tions (p. 130) or water-skiing (p. 116)

Zipline (p. 118)
Tubing (p. 116)
Adventures

Long beachwalks along Wailua
Beach south of Lydgate Park

Lydgate Park
has snorkeling
and rafting for
the whole
family

Kauai's main traveled roads: Rt. 56
(Kuhio Hwy) travels north from Lihue
to Wailua, Kapa'a and Anahola. Rt. 56
curves to the west towards Kilauea and
then Princeville, Hanalei & Ha'ena. Rt.
50 connects in Lihue and goes south to
Poipu and west to Waimea.

Kayaking on the Hule'ia River
and Alakoko (Menehune)
Fish Pond (p.131)

www.explorekauai.com

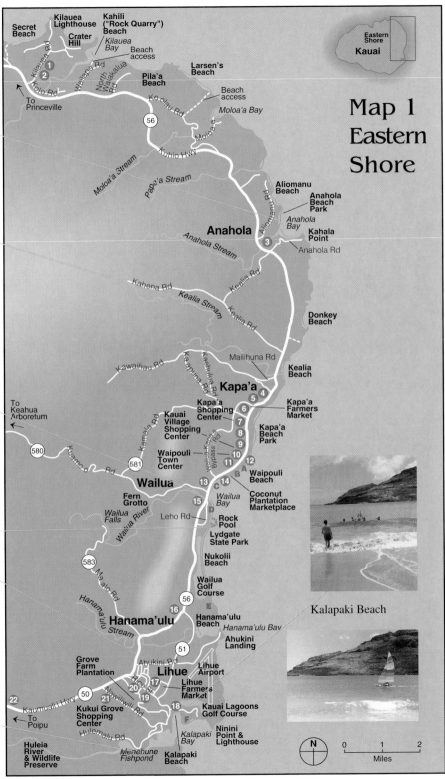

Map 1
Eastern
Shore

Kalapaki Beach

Eastern Shore Funfinder

Activities

Water ski on the Wailua River 116
Hike Sleeping Giant Mountain 100
Horseback Riding 102
Golf 94
　　Grove Farm Golf Course 96
　　Wailua Golf Course 96
Windsurf, catamaran, kayak,
　　snorkel, body board rental 111
Sport fishing 111
Scuba 107
Snorkeling 109
Surfing 114
Tubing 116
Zipline 118, 131
ATV 80

Tours

Helicopter tours 120
Boat tours 126
Kayak tours
　　Wailua River to Fern
　　　　Grotto 130
　　Hule'ia River 131
　　Kipu Falls 131
　　Sea kayak 132
Grove Farm Plantation Tour 133
Kauai Museum 134
Gay & Robinson Tour 134
Kapa'a History Tour 135
Movie Tours 135

Family Fun

Lydgate Park 32
Kalapaki Beach 30
Body board & kayak rental 111
Tubing 116

Restaurants 144

Kilauea
1　Lighthouse Bistro 198
2　Kilauea Bakery 195
　　Pau Hana Pizza

Anahola
3　Ono Char Burger 175

Kapa'a
5　Kountry Kitchen 168
　　Wasabi's 183
6　El Cafe 173
　　Ono Family Rest 175
　　Mermaids Cafe 172
7　Sukothai 179

Wailua
8　King & I 165
9　A Pacific Café 176
　　Coconuts 152
　　Lemongrass 170
　　Papaya's Café 178
　　La Playita Azul 169
　　Ba Le 147
10　Waipouli Deli 183
12　Bull Shed 149
13　Kintaro 166
　　Mema Thai Cuisine 171
　　Caffé Coco 150
14　Hukilau Lanai 161
　　Al & Don's 145
15　Wailua Marina 182

Hanama'ulu
16　Hanama'ulu Tea House 159

Lihue
17　Okazu Hale 172
18　Duke's 154
　　JJ's Broiler 162
　　Kalapaki Beach Hut 163
　　Portofino Cafe 151
　　Tokyo Lobby 180
　　Kauai Chop Suey 163
　　Aromas 145
　　Whaler's Brew Pub 184
19　Barbecue Inn 147
　　Ma's 170, Kiibo 164
　　Hamura's Saimin 158
　　La Bamba 168
　　Garden Island BBQ 156
20　Oki Diner 174
21　Deli & Bread Connection 186
22　Gaylord's at Kilohana 156

The beautiful Wailua coastline along the 'coconut coast'

Favorite Beaches

* Our favorite swimming beach is **Kalapaki Beach**, wonderful for swimming, skim boarding, and when the surf is right, boogie boards. The sand is perfect for playing ball or frisbee, running, or simply sunning. Rent a catamaran or kayak, if surf conditions are calm.

* **Lydgate Park** in Wailua is perfect for families – an enormous lava rock-rimmed pool offers wonderful swimming and snorkeling, with a smaller rock-rimmed pool just right for toddlers. Beyond the pools, the beach is great for long walks. Lydgate also offers the best playground on Kauai, the Kamalani Playground for the climbing and swinging set, and the beach is a great spot to watch glorious golden sunrises.

* For water activities, try **Wailua**. Wailua Beach is popular with local surfers, and on the Wailua River, you can water ski, or explore upstream towards the Fern Grotto by kayak (p. 130).

* Surfers will love **Kealia Beach**, where wonderful, even rollers can give great rides when conditions are right.

* For picnics and beach walks, visit beautiful **Anahola Bay.**

* Hungry? For inexpensive lunch in Lihue, try Hamura's Saimin, Barbecue Inn, Kalapaki Beach Hut. Spend a bit more and enjoy Duke's Barefoot Bar, Gaylord's, Aromas, or Whaler's Micro Brewery.

Great Days on the Eastern Shore

Day 1 (Wailua/Kapa`a). Breakfast at Kountry Kitchen (p. 168). Morning: water-ski or kayak on the Wailua River (p. 130), or hike Sleeping Giant Mountain (p. 100). Lunch: Ba Le (p. 147). Afternoon at Lydgate Park, great for kids or long beachwalks (p. 32). Dinner: Hukilau Lanai (p. 161), or Kintaro (p. 166).

Day 2. (Lihue) Breakfast at Tip Top (p. 180). Morning: kayak trip up the Hule'ia River (p. 131); or tour Grove Farm Plantation (p. 133), or try a zipline (p. 118) or tubing (p. 116) adventure. Lunch at Kalapaki Beach Hut (p. 163) or Hamura's Saimin (p. 158). Afternoon: relax or sail at Kalapaki Beach. Dinner: Bull Shed (p. 149), Aromas (p. 145), or Duke's Canoe Club (p. 154).

Kalapaki Beach

Kalapaki Bay is unforgettably beautiful. Almost enclosed by craggy green hillsides, this natural harbor has a wide sugar sand beach with some of the best swimming on the island. The waves roll to shore in long, even swells and break in shining white crests which are usually great for swimming and rafting. At times, surf is very rough, but even if you can't swim, you can enjoy beautiful views. On one side, the green mountains have the contours of a giant animal sleeping in the sun, while on the

Sail a catamaran on Kalapaki Bay

opposite side, houses on stilts perch so precariously on the sheer cliff that you wonder what combination of faith and hope keeps them standing.

Fronting this beach is the spectacular Marriott Resort at Kauai Lagoons, a headline-maker from the time it opened in the late '80's as a Westin Hotel because of its lavish design and elaborate collections of far eastern art and tropical birds and animals. Here you'll find Kauai's largest swimming pool, its tallest high-rise, its only two-story escalator.

Kalapaki Beach is a favorite family spot. The firm sand is perfect for games and hard running, and the waves can at times break perfectly for boogie boards. Build sandcastles, play beach volleyball, rent a kayak or catamaran, or try your hand at windsurfing. Heed any high surf warnings, however, for at certain times, particularly in winter months, the waves can break straight down with enormous force, and every so often a really big wave seems to come up out of nowhere to smash unwary swimmers.

Directions: Take Rice St. through Lihue, and turn left into the main entrance of the Kauai Marriott. Pass the main lobby, and turn right at the first street, follow it down the hill to the beach access parking lot. The hotel maintains a restroom accessible to people with disabilities. Map 1

Ninini Beach

The drive to this tiny beach, "Running Waters," is more interesting than the destination. You wind along a cane road right next to the airport runway, so close, actually, that the jets taking off and landing almost make you want to duck! Turn off Kapule Rd. just south of the Lihue airport at the marble gates (once the limo entrance to the old Westin) and follow it through brush and rustling grasses, then through the hotel grounds, always bearing towards the water, until you reach the lighthouse at Ninini Point. Near the lighthouse, you'll have a gorgeous view of the coastline, a great spot to watch surf crash onto the rocks. The beach is not safe for swimming. Come instead for the view and the seclusion. Map 1

Hanama'ulu Beach

A perfect crescent of soft shining sand, the beach at Hanama'ulu Bay is perfect for building sandcastles and hunting sunrise shells. In summer, the waves are gentle enough for children to enjoy. Rolling to shore in long, even swells only about a foot or two high, they break into miniature crests which turn to layers of white foam flecked with sandy gold, like the lacy borders of a lovely shawl. Even the occasional "wipe-outs" are not serious because the sandy bottom slopes very gradually.

Hanamaʻulu Beach

Kids can chase lots of tiny sandcrabs, and there is plenty of shade for babies beneath the tall iron-wood trees which fringe the sand. Behind the beach, the Hanamaʻulu Stream forms shallow pools as it winds toward the bay, and they can hunt for tiny crayfish and other creatures with nets. The deep gold of the river is shaded by trees so tall and dense you can hardly see the sky, and the dark green leaves trail into the water behind stalks of laven-der water hyacinths, their petals streaked with the colors of peacock feathers. A picnic pavilion faces the river, and other tables look out over the beautiful curve of the bay. Everything is uncrowded, as this beach is frequented by few tourists. Unfortunately, it is also in the path sometimes used by helicopters returning to the airport from their scenic tours. Try to ignore the noisy choppers, and plan your visit for the morning, as the mosquitoes get hungry about 4 pm!

Directions: Turn off Rt. 56 towards the sea at Hanamaʻulu, between the 7-Eleven and the school. Bear right at the fork which has a sign to the Beach Park. The road ends at the park. Restrooms, playground. Map 1

Lydgate Beach Park

Lydgate Park just south of the Wailua River is a favorite spot for families. A rock-rimmed pool provides safe swimming for babies and toddlers, even in winter months. Adjacent is an enormous rock-rimmed pool which breaks the surf into rolling swells excellent for swimming, rafting, and floats of all kinds. The pool is one of the best year–round snorkeling spots on the island, for families of brightly colored fish feed along the rocky perimeter, so tame they almost swim into your hands. The rocky wall protects snorkelers and swimmers from surf and dangerous currents. You can also fly a kite, play frisbee on the wide, sandy beach, and collect shells and driftwood. Lydgate has a lifeguard and showers.

Kids will love the Kamalani Playground, 16,000 square feet of funland, with mirror mazes, a suspension bridge, lava tubes and circular slide. The beach south of the lava rock pools is ideal for long walks, very beautiful and almost deserted. Continue past the rocky point in front of Kaha Lani Condominiums, and you can walk along the section of beach-front called Nukoli'i towards the Radisson Hotel. The sand is firm and fine, perfect for walking, and you'll have spectacular views of the coastline, particularly beautiful when sunrise or sunset paints the sky with gold and orange, and deepens the blues of the ocean, bright with shining foam. The patterns of foam crossing the sand are the most lovely we have

Lydgate's rock rimmed pools

ever seen. You'll probably find only one or two people, probably fisher-men checking their lines. Swim with caution, however, for the surf can be rough and currents powerful; Lydgate's pools are much safer.

Directions: If you are driving north on Rt. 56, turn right onto Leho Rd. just past the Wailua Golf Course. The right turnoff to the park is clearly marked. Follow this road to the Park and the rock pools. If you are driving south on Rt. 56, you must turn left onto the Leho Road just across the bridge over the Wailua River, at the Aloha Beach Resort. Map 1

Wailua Bay

Wailua Bay's long, curve of golden sand is perfect for walking. In the middle is the mouth of the Wailua River, sometimes shallow enough to ford, but at other times deep and treacherous. Swimming in the brackish, calm water of the river can be fun, although parents of young children should not let them stray from the edges because the water can become deep very quickly. Swimming where the river empties into the bay is not recommended because currents can be dangerous and unpredictable. South of the river, local kids congregate at a popular spot for surfing and body boarding, particularly in summer. A lifeguard is usually on duty. For surfing lessons, see p. 115.

The Wailua River offers many activities: water skiing (p. 116), kayaking (p.130), or touring Fern Grotto (Smith's Boat Tours 822-4111).

Directions: On Rt. 56, just north of the bridge over the Wailua River.

Kapa'a Beaches

A white sandy beach, which runs almost the length of Kapa'a town, offers relatively safe swimming and fun for families with small children. An offshore reef breaks the surf and wind chop, creating a quiet lagoon, except in winter months when an eastern swell can make a strong current flow out of the channel. Usually, however, the water is calm, filled with children splashing while babies play in the shaded sand.

Directions: Take Rt. 56 through Kapa'a. Turn towards the water at Niu St. by Kapa'a ballpark. Map 1

Kealia Beach

North of Kapa'a on Rt. 56 and just past a scenic overlook turnout, you will see spectacular Kealia Beach, a long, wide curve of golden sand ending in a rocky point. When the surf is up, lots of surfers ride the long, even rollers. During summer months, the waves can be gentle enough for children at the far end of the beach where lava rocks extending into the sea create a cove where the water is quieter. Kealia has long been one of Jeremy's and Mikey's favorite beaches for surfing and body boarding. The sandy bottom slopes so gradually that you can walk out to catch some wonderful long rides, though at times the waves can be too powerful for children (even adults). Exercise caution, particularly in winter. Surf near

Body board fun for kids at Kalapaki, Kealia, Anahola, Lydgate, and Hanama'ulu.

the body boarders, and not the hard board surfers who are looking for the bigger thrill. Watch out for the small, blue 'men o' war' jellyfish, which wash ashore, in certain seasons, after high surf. If you see them on the sand, they are probably also floating in the water. They pack a nasty sting, so go to another beach for the day. Firm, level sand makes this a perfect walking beach, and children will enjoy playing in shallow pools behind the beach where a stream flows into the ocean. Strong rip currents near the river mouth, however, can make ocean swimming hazardous.

Directions: Drive north of Kapa'a on Rt. 56. Between mile markers 10 and 11, turn off to the right where you see all the cars parked. Map 1

Donkey Beach

Donkey Beach is a lovely and peaceful spot, a long curve of sand which ends in piles of rock on both sides. Surf and currents are strong, even in summer, making swimming risky and only for experts. Waves rise slowly; curl in long, even swells; crest with gleaming foam, and break straight down with thunderous explosions of spray. The rhythm is hypnotic–you could watch them form and crash for hours. We saw no one in the water, though – our first hint that Donkey Beach was for sun-worshipers rather than swimmers. In fact, it has for years been a place where nude sunbathing was the rule. Times are changing, however, as the land once devoted to sugar is developed into homesites, and security patrols help folks remember the rule to cover up.

Directions: A scenic public bike and walking path follows the cane road from Kealia Beach to Donkey Beach. Or park in the public lot just off Rt 56 between the mile 11 and 12 markers.

Anahola Bay

The beach at Anahola Bay is so long that to walk from one end to the other may take you nearly an hour. The colors are magnificent, particularly as the sun is rising, or in late afternoon as it moves to the west over the dark green mountains, deepening the blue of the water and the gold of the sand while brightening the tall white puff clouds until they glow with light.

While the walking is spectacular, swimming can be risky, for the surf near the center of the bay can be strong and currents powerful most of the year. The southern end of the bay is more sheltered, and local families come for snorkeling and picnicking at the park near the end of Anahola Road. You can also drive to the northern end of the bay, where the Anahola stream flows into the sea. Children will love playing in the large shallow pools formed by the stream as it winds toward the bay, which is sometimes filled with tadpoles just slow enough to be netted by the younger set. The tiny river fish were harder to catch but fun in the trying, as were the small shrimp we discovered hiding by the grasses near the bank. The children also enjoyed making voyages of discovery on their boogie boards where the stream is deeper.

Anahola Bay is a favorite place for the whole family, and a good choice on weekends when other, more well-known beaches become crowded. Watch out for the small, blue 'men o' war' jellyfish which are sometimes washed ashore after a storm. If you see them on the sand, go to another beach for the day, for they're probably in the water too, and the sting can be very painful. A short drive (or long walk) north of the river will take you to Aliomanu Beach, popular with local families because its extensive offshore reef is terrific for fishing and seaweed harvesting. Snorkeling is for experts only, who should venture out if tradewinds are light and the current from the river is not strong. It's a great spot for a picnic, with little sandy 'nooks' along the road perfect for two. You can walk a long way along the sand, climbing some rocks, passing homes that peek out from the vegetation, listening to the sound of waves. Phone in a picnic order to Ono Char Burger for great burgers (with avocado, bacon, cheese, tomatoes, pineapple - you name it! 822-9181).

Directions: Turn off Rt. 56 at the Aliomanu Road just north of Duane's Ono Burger and the Anahola Store and follow it to the mouth of the stream. To get to the beach park at the southern end of Anahola Beach, take Anahola Road (just south of Ono Burger) towards the water. Restrooms, outdoor showers. Map 1

Eastern Shore Shopping Stops

At KILOHANA about a mile west of Kukui Grove on Rt. 50, you can visit a historic sugar plantation homestead and browse shops from the elegant to the cute. *Kahn Galleries* has works by respected Hawaiian artists. *The Country Store* and *Hawaiian Collection Room* feature island crafts and jewelry, while *Kilohana Galleries* has work by Hawaiian artisans working in wood, glass, fabric, ceramics, and papers. Just behind the plantation house, visit *Kilohana Clothing* for beautiful designs, made by Melody, with fine fabrics and careful finishing. Her aloha shirts are a family favorite! You'll love the colorful pottery at *Kilohana Clayworks*.

In LIHUE, *Kukui Grove*, Kauai's most 'modern' shopping center, includes major department stores like *Macy's* and *Sears*, as well as a host of specialty shops including the *Kauai Products Store*, which has original crafts, clothing, and jewelry by Kauai artists. Near *K-Mart*, *Borders Books & Music* has Kauai's largest selection of books and music, and you can listen to CDs by Kauai musicians like Ka'awa, the McMasters and the Shakers (p. 106). *Borders Espresso Cafe* offers excellent 'food for the body' – as well as the mind. Nearby, at *Anchor Cove*, visit *Crazy Shirts* for great tee-shirt designs, and a host of interesting shops.

In LIHUE town, the *Kauai Museum* has a wonderful shop for books, maps, as well as island crafts and memorabilia, including Ron Kent's fine, almost translucent wood bowls and authentic Ni'ihau shell leis. You won't have to pay the museum entrance fee to visit the gift shop. Stop at *Hilo Hattie's,* at the corner of Kuhio Highway and Ahukini Road in Lihue, for aloha wear, souvenirs, and hats at factory-direct prices. *Discount Fabric Center* nearby has the island's best supply of Hawaiian print fabrics. (Now you can order online at www.gotfabric.com). *Wal-Mart* features island coffees, candies, nuts and gifts at excellent prices. North of Lihue, in HANAMA'ULU, don't miss *Kapaia Stitchery* for beautiful handcrafted clothing, quilts and sewing supplies, Hawaiian fabrics.

Woodworkers and furniture lovers will appreciate the finely crafted pieces at *Kama'aina Cabinets.*

In **Wailua**, *Goldsmith's Kauai* in Kinipopo Shopping Village is a must stop for original designs crafted of gold, silver, beautiful pearls and precious gems by award-winning artists Dana Romsdal and her goldsmith partners. Visit www.goldsmiths-kauai.com to see their fine workmanship. We ordered a beautiful pearl birthday pendant and tracked the progress of the design on its own web page! Next door, *Kinipopo Fine Art Gallery* features fascinating works by members of the Kauai Society of Artists.

Just north of Wailua, the *Coconut Plantation Marketplace,* has lots of shops. In *Hawaiian Traditions*, you'll find Hawaiian quilts in beautiful traditional patterns. Kids will love *Chicks Who Rip*, a local company with dynamite designs in T-shirts, sweat shirts, sunglasses, Rosie the Riveter posters. Ask for a free sticker (www.chickswhorip.com). At *Gecko Store*, geckos appear in shirts, jewelry, pens and pencils, stickers, glasses, cups, even hats! *Plantation Stitchery* will solve all your crafts and sewing needs. Try *Island Surf Shop* for great fashions–including teen magic brands like Roxy and Quicksilver. *Bodacious* features a wide selection of stylish clothes and cute island gifts. Kauai Village in Wailua has a variety of clothing and souvenir shops, *Waldenbooks,* and the wonderfully stimulating *Kauai Children's Discovery Museum* for kids of all ages.

In **Kapa'a**, a family favorite is *M. Miura Store*, for the latest surfing-shirts, shorts, and aloha shirts, even boogie boards. Visit *Jim Saylor* and see his jewelry designs with precious stones– lovely rings, necklaces, and bracelets. Jim loves designing, sketching deftly as he talks enthusiastically about a unique ring or pendant just for you! *At Kela's,* Larry Barton displays contemporary glass art by more than 35 artists, including beautiful shell designs, elegant vases, colorful fish (822-4527; www.glass-art.com). Next door at *Kebanu*, you'll find fountain art, photographs, and other treasures, while *Hula Girl* has a great selection of aloha style shirts, dresses, and clothing and gift items with hula motifs. Across the street, *Island Hemp and Cotton* features comfortable beach clothes.

Shop online at www.shopping-hawaii.com and www.maikaihawaii.com.

North Shore Beaches

Kilauea Lighthouse has a bird's eye view of Secret Beach.

North Shore
Map 2

North Shore Kauai

Ke'e Beach

Tunnels Beach

Ha'ena Beach Park

Kepuhi Beach

560

C

Pali Ke Kua ("Hideaways") 7

Pu'u Poa Beach 6

5

Hanakapiai Beach

Kalalau Trail

Wet Caves

Ha'ena

Wainiha Beach

Lumahai Beach

Hanalei Bay

Hanalei Pier

Limahuli Stream

Manoa Stream

Wainiha Powerhouse Rd

Wainiha River

Lumahai Stream

Waikoko Beach

Wai'oli Beach Park

Ching Young Village

3 4

Hanakapiai Stream

Limahuli Falls

Kuhio Hwy

Hanalei Center

2

Hanalei

Wai'oli Stream

Honoiki

Liholiho

Weke Rd

Hanakapiai Falls

Hotels
A Princeville Hotel
B Hanalei Bay Resort
C Hanalei Colony Resort

Hike the Na Pali trail to Hanakapa'ia 98

Princeville Hotel – come for sunsetl

Hanalei Bay

Lumahai Beach

Kauai's main traveled roads: Rt. 56 (Kuhio Hwy.) travels north from Lihue, becomes Rt. 560 at Princeville, continues west to road's end at Ke'e Beach.

Kilauea Lighthouse

Beaches

Restaurants

Most Na Pali boat tours now depart from south and westside harbors 126

Sharing the wave at Kalihiwai

Kalihiwai Bay, a jewel on the North Shore

Favorite Beaches

* Spectacular **Hanalei Bay**, an unforgettable image of Kauai for those rainy evenings back home! Great for swimming and surfing, running and walking (p. 82), and sunset music at Hanalei Pavilion (p. 106). Start with breakfast at *Cafe Hanalei* Princeville Hotel (p. 191). Incredible view!

* Our favorite family beach is **Kalihiwai,** which combines spectacular beauty with wonderful summertime swimming, as well as firm golden sand, perfect for running. In winter, surf is up, to the delight of our boys, and even spectators can have fun watching the surfers catch spectacular rides. Kids will love the brackish pools behind the beach for fishing, swimming, and playing with a rope swing (p. 49).

* **Anini Beach** is gentle enough for children, and a popular spot for snorkeling and windsurfing (p. 51).

* For long, solitary beachwalks, try **Larsen's Beach** (p .45) or **Moloa'a Bay** (p. 43).

* Adventurers love hiking to **Secret Beach**, both secluded and spectacular, with magnificent views of the northern coast (p. 48).

* The best snorkeling, when surf is calm, is at **Tunnels Beach** (p. 56) In summer months, **Ke'e Beach** (p. 58) has excellent snorkeling as well.

* From Keʻe Beach, you can hike the cliffside trail through the Na Pali wilderness to **Hanakapiʻai Beach** (p. 98), magnificently beautiful, though too dangerous for swimming. Try the first quarter-mile climb to a spectacular point overlooking Keʻe Beach and the Haʻena reefs. For sunset watching, don't miss the view from the Princeville Hotel, or from **Tunnels Beach, Keʻe Beach** or, in summer months, **Anini Beach** (p. 112).

Great Days on the North Shore

Day 1: Breakfast at Café Hanalei (p. 191) or Postcards (p. 200), morning at Hanalei Bay (p. 53). Relax on the beach, or rent a kayak and explore the Hanalei River (p. 132). Picnic on Kalihawai Beach (p. 49) with sandwiches from Kilauea Farmer's Market (p. 185). Watch the sunset, listen to Kauai's talented entertainers at Princeville Hotel's Living Room (p. 106). Dinner at Neidie's (p. 199).

Day 2: Breakfast at Zelo's or Hanalei Wake Up Cafe. Drive to the end of the road to Keʻe Beach (p. 58). Hike the cliff trail to the Keʻe Beach overlook (p. 98), or on to Hanakapiʻai Beach. Or, instead, visit lovely Limahuli Gardens (p. 137). Pack a picnic lunch. Spend the afternoon snorkeling (or resting!) at Keʻe Beach or Tunnels. Sunset watching, music (p. 106) and dinner at Bali Hai (p. 189).

Day 3. Breakfast at Kilauea Bakery (p. 195). Hike to Secret Beach (summer) or trail ride (p. 102). Lunch at the Princeville Golf Course (p. 201) or Tropical Taco (p. 187). Lazy afternoon beach walk at Larsen's Beach or Moloaʻa. Dinner at Postcards (p. 200).

Moloaʻa Bay

At the end of a well-graded, semi-paved road winding for several miles through the lush green countryside, Moloaʻa Bay's lovely curve of sandy beach is discovered by few tourists. As you follow the road through this quiet, rural landscape, you can hear wonderful sounds – the breeze rustling in the leaves, the chirping of insects, the snorting of horses grazing in tree-shaded meadows. At road's end, you will find a gate attached to an unfriendly looking fence intended to discourage parking along the shoulder of the road. Walk through the gate and cross a shallow stream, where our children often discovered tadpoles apparently not informed that frog's eggs had hatched a month earlier everywhere else.

At this point the bay, hidden by the half dozen homes which ring the beach, suddenly comes into view—an almost dazzling half-moon of shining golden sand and turquoise water. The long, wide beach ends in grassy hills and piles of lava rocks on the left, and a sheer cliff on the right. To the left, the rocks are fun to climb and search for shells and trapped fish, although this windward side of the bay is usually too rough for swimming, and the bottom is very rocky. To the right of the stream, the bay is more sheltered, the water gentler and the bottom more sandy. In summer, snorkelers can swim out through the sandy corridor to the rockier part of the bay, or float in the shallow water close to shore and dig in the sandy bottom for shells. In times of heavy surf, however, this bay, like all windward beaches, can have dangerous currents. During these times, Moloaʻa Bay is a beautiful place for walking. The peaceful solitude is filled with the sound of waves. The crystal blue water, traced with the shadowy patterns of the rocks below, stretches out to the distant horizon where pale clouds fade into a limitless sky. At 5 pm you might see a dozen horses, wandering home after another difficult day of grazing, stop at the stream for a drink or a roll in the shallows—a spectacular sight with the light glistening on the water and the horses darkening slowly to silhouettes.

Directions: Take Rt. 56 to Kuamoʻo Road, a half-mile north of the mile

Moloaʻa Bay

16 marker. Turn right at Moloa'a Road and follow it to the end. About 16 miles north of Lihue; 30 miles from Poipu; 6 miles from Kapa'a.

Larsen's Beach

Road to Larsen's Beach

Getting to Larsen's Beach is half the fun. A right-of-way-to-beach road wanders through pastureland, where horses grazing peacefully seem sketched into a landscape portrait of silvery green meadows with waving dark green grasses, trees and mountains, and masses of white, shining clouds. At the end of the well-graded, sandy road is a small parking area and a gate leading to the top of the cliff, where the beach below seems a slender ribbon of white against the dark blue water. Although a second, smaller gate seems to direct you to the right, walking through it takes you to a steep path ending in rocks.

Instead, walk down the hillside to the left on a well worn path with a gentle slope. Even when our children were small, they had little difficulty managing the descent or the climb back up. A five-minute walk down the slope brings you to a long, lovely beach curving along the coastline and disappearing around a distant bend—perfect for lazy afternoons of beachcombing and exploring. Although a rocky reef extending about 70 yards offshore seems to invite snorkeling, Larsen's Beach is one of the most dangerous on the island.

Before you begin the hike down, observe the ocean carefully and locate the channel through the reef, just to the left of the rocky point where you are standing. The churning water caused by the swift current makes the channel easiest to see from this height, and once noted, it can be recognized at sea level. Once you see this channel, you can also pick out the smaller channels which cut through the reef at several other points. Swimmers and snorkelers should avoid going near any of these channels, particularly the large one, because currents can be dangerously strong and even turn into a whirlpool when the tide is going out. Remember, Larsen's Beach has no lifeguard, and help is not close by. Currents can be exceptionally treacherous at *any* time, but particularly in winter months, and four years ago two experienced local fishermen drowned here. The watchword is caution: swim in pairs, never go out beyond the reef, try to

Larsen's Beach, a great spot for beachwalking and shell collecting, even if winter surf is too strong for safe swimming.

stay within easy distance of the shore, and examine the surface of the water carefully to avoid swimming near a channel. If you snorkel, don't get so absorbed in looking at the fish that you lose track of where you are, and don't go out at all if surf conditions don't seem right to you.

A trip to Larsen's Beach does not require swimming or snorkeling. If you bring reef-walking sneakers to protect your feet, you can walk around in the shallow water and watch colorful fish who don't seem afraid of people. Or walk for miles along the magnificent coastline of this picture-perfect beach. Hunt for shells, or simply lose yourself in the spectacle of nature's beauty. You will probably encounter only another person or two. The drive back is wonderful, with spectacular views of the rolling hills, lined by fences and stands of trees, and beyond them the dark and majestic mountains reaching to touch the clouds.

Directions: From Kapa'a, turn right off Rt. 56 onto Kuamo'o Road just a half-mile past the mile 16 marker (If you pass the old dairy farm, you've missed the turn). Bear left at the Moloa'a Road turnoff, go about 1.1 miles and look for a dirt road on the right. The right turn marked 'beach access'

will be very sharp and angled up an incline. Then another beach access sign
will mark the left turn onto the long, straight road to the beach. From
Hanalei, turn left off Rt. 56 at the mile 20 marker, and left again at the
beach access road. Drive to the end of the beach access road, park, lock up,
walk towards the cliff, and down the trail on the left. About 7 miles east of
Princeville; 20 miles north of Lihue; 10 miles north of Kapa'a. Map 2.

Kilauea Bay

If you've ever had the fantasy of searching through the jungle to find a
remote and hidden paradise, Kahili Beach at Kilauea Bay should be your
destination. The road to this unspoiled beach tests the mettle of both car and
driver with challenges at practically every turn. Deeply rutted, even gouged
in places by ditches and holes, it can turn into a quagmire in rain, but in dry
weather, it can be navigated without too much difficulty by a careful driver
even in a rented subcompact. Pick a dry day, and the road will add the zest
of adventure and heighten the excitement of discovering, just down the hill
from the parking area at road's end, a bay shaped like a perfect half-moon,
the deep blue water sparkling with light, and the golden sand outstretched
between two rocky bluffs like a tawny cat sleeping in the sun.

At the northern end is the Kilauea stream. One year it may be shallow
enough for small children at low tide; the next, too deep. The width can
vary from a few yards to fifty. To the left of the stream, the beach ends
abruptly in an old rock quarry, a great spot for pole fishing. To the right of
the stream, the sandy beach extends a long way before ending in piles of
lava rocks which children will enjoy climbing and exploring for tidal pools.
Chances are you'll encounter only another person or two and can watch in
solitude as the waves roll towards the beach in long, even swells, break into
dazzling white crests, and rush to shore in layers of gold and white foam.

Surf can be dangerously strong and the currents treacherous at certain
times, particularly in winter when the beach may almost disappear beneath
the crashing waves. We found the swimming safe enough in summer for our
seven and ten-year-olds to surf on their boogie boards in the shallow water,
although even close to shore the pull of the undertow made us watch them
closely. The tiny blue Portuguese 'men o' war' are sometimes washed
ashore here after a storm, so if you see any on the sand, go to another beach,
for these small jellyfish pack a giant sting!

Behind the beach, the stream forms brackish pools where children can
swim safely, except near the stream's entrance into the bay where the
current can be swift, particularly at high tide. One August, the pools were
wider than we had ever seen, like a shallow lagoon, and our family had a

great time netting tadpoles. Our children loved this beach because of the variety of things they could do and the challenge of ripping the leaves off the branches that scraped the sides of the car as we maneuvered around the gullies on the way down and back. We love the beach because we have had it, sometimes, all to ourselves.

Directions: Just south of Kilauea, turn towards the ocean at Wailapa Road (between mile markers 21 and 22) and after .4 of a mile, turn left onto a dirt road and follow it (only in dry weather) for about a mile until you reach the beach. 25 miles north of Lihue; 39 miles from Poipu. Map 2

Secret Beach

Secret Beach is one of those rare and special places where the world can be forgotten, where you can feel, for a few hours, as if you were alone at the beginning of time. The colors are brilliant, the breeze fresh and tangy with salt. The ocean reaches out to touch the sky at an endless horizon, and the crashing of waves is all you can hear. As you walk, you may leave the only footprints on warm, golden sand shining in the sun.

Nestled at the base of a sheer cliff just north of Kilauea, Secret Beach is well off the beaten track for good reason. You must hike down (and back up!) a rocky trail which zigzags through trees, gullies, and brush. You can drive only to the trail's beginning at the top of the cliff. From here, you can hear the waves crashing below—apparently not very far away—as you look down on a trail which seems to disappear into a tangle of jungle. The path is steep in places — sneakers are a good idea — but branches, roots, and vines offer plenty of handholds, and in a pinch, you can always resort to the seat of your pants!

The walk down will take about seven minutes, and it is pretty much straight down. As the path makes the last sharp plunge before leveling off to the sand, you can see, at last, through a screen of trees and hanging vines, a magnificent stretch of golden sand and a shining turquoise sea. In rainy times, this enormous triangle of sand may be partly covered by a lagoon fed by a stream winding down behind the beach. Towards the left, you can climb a rocky outcropping and find a small beach ending in a steep cliff. Towards the right, you can see the Kilauea lighthouse and walk a long way across the sand.

Secret Beach is not a place to come alone, for the obvious reason of its isolation. Swimming is not a good idea. The surf is rough, and the current strong and unpredictable; you'd never find a lifeguard if you were caught in a current. In fact, during the winter, this beach, enormous as it is, can disappear almost entirely under huge, crashing waves. Instead of swimming, walk along the water, hunt for shells, and forget everything but the feel of wet sand between your toes.

The walk back up the cliff will give you time to adjust to the world you left behind—just about 10 minutes of mild exertion, with the air cool under the trees and the leaves speckled with sunlight. This would not be pleasant in the mud, though, so plan your adventure with an eye to the weather and don't go after a soaking rain. By the time you reach your car and remember that you have to stop at the store for milk, the peaceful solitude you left behind will be as hard to recapture as a wave rippling on the sand. But for a few moments, you were lost to your working-day world. This may be the secret of Secret Beach, a secret worth keeping!

Directions: Drive north of Kilauea on Rt. 56 about a half mile. Turn right onto Kalihiwai Road. Bear left, then turn right onto a dirt road which looks like a broad red gash in the landscape. Follow towards the water till it ends. Park, lock up and walk down the trail. The rest is up to you! Note: One reader discovered another secret about this beach, when she and her family reached the bottom of the trail and ran into "a long-haired young man wearing nothing but a guitar!" So be prepared for strange music! Secret Beach is about 25 miles north of Lihue; 39 miles from Poipu; 15 miles from Kapa'a. Map 2

Surfing at Kalihiwai on a summer day

Kalihiwai Bay

You'll catch your first glimpse of Kalihiwai Bay as you drive down the narrow road carved into the side of the sheer cliff which encloses it on one side. From this angle, the bay is a perfect semi-circle of blue, rimmed with shining white sand and nestled between two lava cliffs. Ironwood trees ring the beach, just about

Sea changes

Kalihiwai—our favorite family beach on the north shore. In summer, the ocean can be calm, almost like a lake (below) while in winter, thundering surf can crash onto the sand (above).

completely regrown after being sheared of their branches by Iniki's winds. A clear, freshwater stream flows into the bay near the far end, so shallow and gentle at low tide that small children can splash around safely. It becomes deep enough behind the beach for kayak adventuring up-river.

One of our favorite family beaches, Kalihiwai Bay offers wonderful summertime fun for people of all ages. Little ones will love the shallow pools behind the beach where they can fish or float on rafts, while older kids will enjoy the rope swing. Ocean swimming can be terrific too! The waves rise very slowly and break in long, even crests over a sloping sandy bottom, perfect for wave jumping and boogie boarding. One summer day we watched a dozen children celebrate a birthday with a surfing party. In winter, the surf and currents in the bay can become formidable. Even experienced surfers may have difficulty managing the currents which can be particularly strong when a swell is running. Even if the surf is too rough, Kalihiwai is a lovely beach for walking or running, with firm sand and magnificent views of the cliffs. Note: Nearest public restrooms are in Kilauea at the ball field behind Farmers Market (next to home plate!)

Directions: A yellow siren atop a pole just south of the beach is a re-minder of the *tsunami* or tidal wave of 1957 which washed away the bridge originally linking the two roads leading from Rt. 56 to the bay. Both are still marked Kalihiwai Road at their separate intersections with Rt. 56. Either one will take you to the bay, although, if you choose the Kalihiwai Road just north of the long bridge on Rt. 56, you'll have to wade across the stream's mouth in order to reach the beach. The Kalihi-wai Road south of the bridge and just northwest of Kilauea is the prefer-able route. It winds through a rural residential area before curving down the steep cliff on the southern edge of the bay. Kalihiwai is about 25 miles north of Lihue; 39 miles from Poipu; 15 miles from Kapaʻa. Map 2

Anini Beach

At the edge of Anini Road, you will find miles of white sandy beach protected by a reef. At some places the beach road is so close to the water that you could almost jump in! A beach park offers restrooms and picnic facilities, although you can turn off the road at almost any spot, park, and find your private paradise. The reef creates a quiet lagoon, great for summertime snorkeling, and for windsurfing at any time of year. During high surf, particularly in winter, the current running parallel to the beach can become strong enough to pull an unwary swimmer out through the channel in the reef at the west end of the park. Stay inside the reef.

Across from the Beach Park, the Kauai Polo Club hosts polo matches on summer Sunday afternoons. Continue along Anini road through a quiet residential area all the way to its western end, where a sandbar extending quite far out invites wading and fishing. Children enjoy the quiet water and the tiny shells along the waterline, and you'll love the amazing combination of sounds— the roar of the surf breaking on the reef far offshore, and near your feet, the gentle rippling of the sea upon the sand.

In summer months, you can watch the sun set into the ocean at Anini Beach, a glorious sight which can be yours in perfect solitude. The tall ironwood trees darken to feathery silhouettes against a pale gray and orange sky, filled with lines of puff clouds. The water shimmers gold as the sun's dying fire fades slowly to a pearl and smoky gray, to the songs of crickets and the lapping of gentle waves.

Directions: Drive north on Rt. 56, pass Kilauea, and turn towards the ocean at Kalihiwai Road (the northern one, between mile markers 25 and 26). Bear left at the fork, following the road as it winds downhill past the park and continues to the base of the cliffs at Princeville. Anini is about 1 mile east of Princeville. Map 2

Pu'u Poa Beach, Princeville

Tucked beneath the Princeville Resort Hotel's ocean bluff perch is a sandy beach set inside a reef. When you look down from the hotel, you can see the rocky bottom that makes swimming less than perfect. This same reef can make for good snorkeling in calm summer seas, but you must negotiate your way carefully through one of the small sandy channels into the deeper water. In winter, waves crash against the outer reef, and it becomes a challenging surfing spot.

Public access is available through a cement path leading from the left of the gatehouse entry to the Hotel. Be forewarned: on the way down the cliff, you'll have to descend nearly 200 steps (and then come back *up* those same steps later on)! You can explore the beach more easily if you visit the hotel for breakfast or lunch, both wonderful meals in a spectacular setting. After dining, take the hotel elevator down to the beach level, where lovely gardens frame the sand. Bring a camera! Map 1

Directions: Drive Rt. 56 north, enter Princeville at the main entrance (pick up a free map) and stay on Ka Haku Road until the end. Park in the hotel visitor's lot if you're going to the hotel for lunch. If not, try the small public lot just in front and to the right of the hotel entry gate.

Pali Ke Kua or 'Hideaways' Beach

At the base of the cliff near the Pali Ke Kua Condominiums in Princeville is a lovely sandy beach set inside a reef, where you can watch the sun sparkle on the waves in near solitude. It is a peaceful spot, secluded and beautiful, actually two beaches connected by a rocky point. Swimming is not the best because of the coral bottom and the offshore rocks, but snorkeling can be very good in calm summer seas. Be cautious. As on all north shore beaches, snorkeling can be risky and is advisable only in a calm ocean; when the surf is up, currents can become dangerous. In winter, waves can cover the beach entirely. It's called Hideaways for good reason. It's hard to get to, popular primarily with surfers or with people staying at Pali Ke Kua who can use the condominium's improved concrete pathway down the cliff. The public right-of-way is much more difficult, half of it made up of steep steps with a railing, and the rest dwindling to dirt path. It can be slippery, even treacherous, when wet. The trek down will take about ten minutes, and the way up, as you can imagine, somewhat longer.

Directions: Enter Princeville, drive to the hotel and park in the lot. The hotel staff usually doesn't mind if you take one of the back spaces nearest the cliff, where you'll see the top of the steps down to the beach. Map 2

Hanalei Bay

A long half-moon of sandy beach carved into the base of a sheer cliff on one side and narrowing into a rocky point on the other, Hanalei Bay is simply spectacular. Take almost any road in Hanalei leading off Rt. 560 and you will come to Weke Road, which runs east to west along the bay. Turn right to get to Hanalei Pavilion Beach Park (showers and restrooms), where each night at 6 pm, Doug & Sandy McMaster play traditional Hawaiian slack key guitar music (826-1469). At the end of Weke is the Hanalei Pier. Several Trans-Pacific Cup Races from California to Hawaii end in this beautiful bay, and during summer, gaily colored boats rock gently at anchor. The boats are moved out of the bay, however, by mid-October, and by winter, twenty-foot waves are not uncommon.

Looking for surf? You'll find the biggest breakers near the center of the curving coastline, where surfers come to hunt the perfect ride. During winter months, when the surf can become dangerous, Hanalei Bay is still wonderful— the wide sandy beach firm and level for hard running. Walk west to where the Wai'oli Stream, icy cold from mountain water, flows into the bay. Sometimes it's shallow, at other times the current is formi-

Hanalei can be peaceful and calm in summer, but winter waves can reach 20 feet, and boats move to safer harbors on the south shore and westside.

dable, but at all times it's a beautiful, peaceful spot, with waves crossing from different directions in foam glistening with gold.

West of the town, you can explore almost any road turning off Route 560 towards the water. At the westernmost curve of the bay, near the mile 4 marker, you'll find a calm, protected beach where the water is relatively quiet even when most of the north shore is too rough for safe swimming.

Directions: Drive Rt. 560 north, pass Princeville, and enter the town of Hanalei (mile 3 marker). Aku Road (or any other right turn) will take you to Weke Road, which runs along the bay from east to west. Turn right on Weke to go to Hanalei Pavilion Park (showers, rest rooms, lifeguard) or past it to the pier. Turn left onto Weke, and you can choose several 'right of way to beach' streets leading to the Bay. Showers, restrooms available at Ama'ama Rd., called 'Second Parking Lot.' About 33 miles from Lihue, 47 miles from Poipu; 23 miles from Kapa'a. Map 2.

www.explorekauai.com

Lumahai Beach

The setting for the Bali Hai scenes in the movie *South Pacific*, Lumahai Beach is stunningly beautiful, a curve of white sand nestled at the base of a dark lava cliff, with a giant lava rock jutting out of the turquoise sea just offshore. Getting there requires a trek down from the road, possibly through slippery mud (showers are frequent on the north shore), and the trip back up is even worse, especially if you have to carry a tired child. If there are toddlers in you family, you might consider hiring a babysitter or buying a postcard!

Swimming at Lumahai Beach can be very dangerous, particularly during winter months. Without a reef to offer protection from unpredictable currents and rip tides, Lumahai Beach is one of the most treacherous spots on the island, and people drown here almost every year. Beware of climbing that spectacular offshore rock for a photograph, as a sudden powerful wave can easily knock you off!

At the western end of Lumahai, about a mile further on Rt. 560, is a beach with wide golden sand and breakers and currents which can be big enough to make swimming dangerous. Children will love playing in the stream flowing into the sea, ice cold from mountain rainwater.

The stream meets the ocean at a huge rocky bluff, a spectacular place to sit quietly and watch the waves crash against the rocks, sending dazzling spray into the air. It is also a beautiful beach for walking, although the coarse sand is hard-going near the waterline, and you must cross a vast expanse of hot sand to get from the parking area to the sea, so bring sandals! Hunt for striped scallop shells shining in the sun, or wander all the way to the other rocky bluff that separates this part of Lumahai Beach from the part pictured in all the postcards. Trying

Lumahai Beach, one of the island's most dangerous

to cross the rocks would be hazardous, however, even at low tide, because an occasional 'killer wave' can come up suddenly out of nowhere and smash you into the rocks. A small cave etched into the base of the cliff, with powder soft, cool sand invites daydreaming and wave-watching.

Directions: Pass Hanalei on Rt. 560 to the mile 4 marker. You'll see cars parked on the shoulder just past a 25 m.p.h. sign. Park on the right, lock up, and begin the hike down. No restrooms. To get to the western end of Lumahai, drive to the mile 5 marker, look for an emergency telephone by the road. Across the street is the entrance to a sandy parking area. About 34 miles from Lihue; 49 miles from Poipu; 24 miles from Kapaʻa. Map 2

Tunnels

Makua Beach, popularly known as Tunnels Beach, has a large lagoon perfect for swimming because it is protected by two reefs, the outer reef favored by surfers for perfect arcs, and the inner reef filled with cavities and crevices for snorkelers to explore for fish and sea life. Divers love the outer reef for its tunnels, caverns and sudden, dramatic drop off. Tunnels is about the only beach on the north shore that is usually calm enough for those trying to snorkel for the first time, although even here you may find rough surf and treacherous currents during winter months.

Listen to the surf reports, and plan any winter visits for times when surf is manageable, and preferably at low tide. In calm conditions, bring the kids and let them paddle about on boogie boards while the older ones try their luck with mask and snorkel. Bring a plastic baggy of fish food, or even a green leaf, swish it in the water and you'll be surrounded by fish! Swimming through the coral formations of the reef, which is almost like a maze of tunnels, can be great fun when the water is quiet. Enter the reef through one of the small sandy channels or the large one on the right, and dozens of fish in rainbow colors will swim right up to your mask. If the showers which frequent the north shore rain on your parade, you can take shelter under the ironwood trees—or under your boogie board! If you see a monk seal lying on the beach, give it a wide berth. It's probably exhausted, sleeping before heading out to sea. Seals don't trust humans and need privacy to rest.

Warning: Even when the area between the two reefs may look calm enough for safe swimming, watch out for these danger signs: high surf on the outer reef or fast moving ripples in the channel between the reefs. These indicate powerful, swift currents that could sweep you out through the channel into open ocean. Instead of swimming, hunt for shells on the beach, or walk around the rocks to the east, where you may find sunbathers with very dark tans in all the best places.

The reefs at Makua Beach, or Tunnels, can be great for snorkeling.

Directions: Drive west of Princeville on Rt. 560, and go 1.1 miles west of the Hanalei Colony Resort. You will pass the mile 8 marker and the turnoff to the YMCA camp. Parking is nearly impossible due to opposition by local residents; cars parked along Rt.560, a state road, will be ticketed. Drive ahead to Ha'ena Beach Park, park, and walk back along the beach, or try parking along the county road leading to the YMCA campground (Parking is legal on any county road). No public facilities.

Ha'ena Beach Park

An icy stream winds across this lovely golden sand beach curving along the coastline. The water is a dazzling blue. Reefs bordering both sides of the beach, named 'Maniniholo' after the large schools of striped convict fish feeding on the coral, provide summertime snorkeling, when the waves are gentle enough for swimming and rafting. During winter months, however, large waves can break right onto the beach, making swimming, even standing, a hazardous activity. Restrooms, showers, picnic and barbecue facilities, and a lifeguard are available, as well as camping by permit. You can walk a long way in both directions, with spectacular views of the towering cliffs and shimmering sea.

Directions: From Princeville, follow Rt. 560 west and pass the mile 8 marker. Ha'ena Beach Park will be on your right, about 40 miles from Lihue; 54 miles from Poipu; 8 miles from Princeville. Map 2

Ke'e Beach

When you can drive no further on the main road along Kauai's north shore, you will discover a beach so beautiful you won't quite believe it to be real. The Na Pali cliffs rise like dark green towers behind the golden sand, and a reef extending out from shore creates a peaceful lagoon ideal for summertime swimming. As you walk along the shining sand, new cliffs come into view until the horizon is filled with their astonishing shapes and you begin to imagine captive princesses in enchanted castles.

Like all beaches on the north shore, the surf at Ke'e Beach varies with the seasons. Winter surf can reach 20 feet, when the ocean roars with crashing waves and churning foam with undercurrents far too strong for safe swimming. In summer, the turquoise water can be perfectly still and so clear that bubbles on the surface cast shadows on the sandy bottom.

Snorkeling can be spectacular alongside the reef, where the water, though warmed by the sun, will feel ice cold along the surface from

Ke'e Beach's lagoon (at left in this photograph) is great for summer swimming, but thunders with surf in winter.

rainshowers. If the tide is not too low, you can snorkel on top of the reef itself. Be careful: The coral reef may look shallow enough to walk on, but you won't want to take a chance on coral cuts. Be careful of unpredictable currents in the channel to the left of the reef, as they can be strong enough to pull a swimmer out of this sheltered area into the open sea. A lifeguard is usually on duty to keep swimmers out of the channel.

Large trees at the beach provide shade for babies and protection from the occasional rainshowers which cool the air and make the coastline sparkle. The dark sand can be very hot, so you'll need your sandals. Small children can play and swim safely in the shallow water or climb over the rocks at low tide. Bring nets and pails for small fishermen.

Sometimes you can walk west across the rocks and around the point. From this vantage point, the Na Pali cliffs are truly magnificent – jutting into the cobalt blue ocean in vivid green ridges, the surf crashing in thundering sprays of foam. This walk can be dangerous in any but the calmest sea, and you must watch the direction of the tide carefully so that your return trip does not involve crossing slippery rocks through crashing waves. Ke'e Beach, lovely as it looks, can have treacherous currents and unpredictable surf, and so extra caution is a must. For a spectacular, bird's eye view of Ke'e Lagoon, consider climbing the first quarter-mile of the hiking trail to Hanakapia'i Beach. If possible come early and come midweek, for parking at this lovely and popular spot is hard to come by, especially in summer. Public restrooms and showers.

Directions: Follow Rt. 56 north to Princeville and then continue (The road becomes Rt. 560) to the very end. Park alongside the road, as close to the beach as you can get. Or turn right at the dirt road by the showers and restrooms, and look for a space (if you are lucky) under the trees. About 40 miles from Lihue; 54 miles from Poipu; 30 miles from Kapa'a. Map 2

North Shore Shopping Stops

In KILAUEA, stop by at *Kong Lung* and explore a wonderful collection of works by local artists, as well as antiques, jewelry, souvenirs, beautiful gourmet cookware and tableware, and Hawaiian style shirts and dresses, including a special section of toys for children. Browsing is a treat!

PRINCEVILLE Shopping Center is slated for a new look. You'll find some interesting shops, like *SanDudes* for beachwear. Heading for the beach? Check out the beach and picnic gear at *Ace Hardware.* Try the *Paradise Music* kiosk for Hawaiian music CDs (ask for Keali'i Reichel). On Rt. 56 closer to Hanalei you'll find *Ola's*, where Doug and Sharon Britt display an eclectic collection of handcrafted puzzles, glass, jewelry, wooden bowls, baskets, and furniture, each piece almost a collage of extraordinary and interesting bits and pieces. Next door, *Kai Kane* has great beachwear. In HANALEI village, island artists exhibit at *Evolve Love Gallery,* and you'll love to browse the interesting shops, like *Yellowfish Trading Company* for vintage hula gear, postcards, and collectibles, and *Hanalei Surf Company* for wonderful beach & surf gear, *Rainbow Ducks* for children's clothes, *Tropical Tantrum* and *Hot Rocket* for fashions. Across the street *The Back Door* features skateboards and surf gear; *Spinning Dolphin* has custom hand-screened clothing, and *Hanalei Video* is a great place to 'talk story' about Hawaiian music. Across from *Zelo's* check your email at an internet café (p. 233). Find inexpensive jewelry and crafts at the weekly farmers' markets just north of town (p. 86).

You may see a monk seal lying on almost any Kauai beach. Give it a wide berth — it's probably exhausted, resting before heading back out to sea. State law requires a 'safe distance' of 50 feet from the seal. If you try to get closer, you run the risk of provoking a nasty bite, or perhaps frightening the animal into the water before it has fully rested. The Hawaiian Monk Seal is on the list of endangered species.

South Shore Beaches

Maha'ulepu

Favorite Beaches

When it's raining up north, you may want to travel south (even west) to find the sun! In the island's lee, south shore beaches offer relatively calm swimming conditions all year, except during a south shore 'swell.'

* **Poipu Beach Park** is perfect for families, the rock rimmed pool a safe place for small children, and the snorkeling at the other end of the curving beach is wonderful for older ones and their parents (p. 68).

* Our favorite hidden beach (though increasingly popular), is **Maha'ulepu Beach** east of Poipu. Wild and beautiful (p. 65).

* Enjoy lunch with a slice of ocean at *Brennecke's* (p. 208), or dinner and enjoy the colors of sunset. Great lunches are a short drive away in Kalaheo: *Camp House Grill* (p. 210) and *Brick Oven Pizza* (p. 209).

Restaurants

1 Carving Stone
2 Hanapepe Cafe 229
3 Green Garden 229
4 Camp House Grill 210
5 Brick Oven Pizza 209
6 Kalaheo Steak House 215
7 Pomodoro 221
8 Beach House 207
9 Pizzetta 187
   Tomkats Grill 227
10 Taqueria Nortenos 225
11 Keoki's Paradise 216
   Roy's Poipu Grill 223
   Pattaya 218
12 Plantation Gardens 219
   Shells 224
   Naniwa 218
   Casablanca 211

13 Brennecke's Broiler 208
14 Casa di Amici 212
15 Hyatt Regency Hotel:
   Poipu Bay Clubhouse 220
   Tidepools 225
   Dondero's 213

Hotels

A Kiahuna 13
  Sheraton 13
B Poipu Kai 13
C Embassy Resort
  at Poipu Point 13
D Hyatt Regency 11

Beaches

Kipu Kai 64
Maha'ulepu 65
Shipwreck Beach 66
Brennecke's Beach 67
Poipu Beach Park 68
Salt Pond
  Beach Park 71

Rt. 50 Kaumuali'i Highway heads west from Lihue to Kalaheo, Hanapepe, Kekaha, & Waimea.
Rt. 520 connects Rt. 50 with Koloa, & from there south to Poipu.

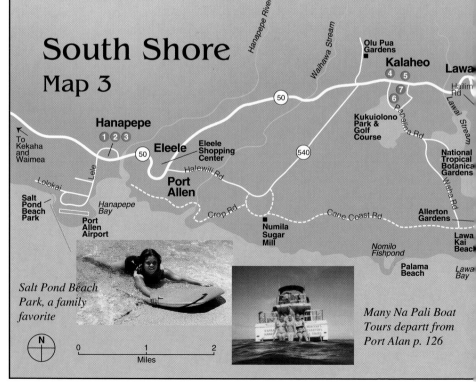

South Shore
Map 3

Salt Pond Beach
Park, a family
favorite

Many Na Pali Boat
Tours departt from
Port Alan p. 126

The wild beauty of Maha'ulepu.

Heliconia blooms at NTBG Gardens, Lawai. (p. 135)

ATV adventure p. 80

Poipu Beach Park

Kahili Mountain Park

To Lihue

50

Tree Tunnel

520

Maluhia Rd

530

Omao Rd

loa Rd

Waita Reservoir

Koloa

Weliweli Rd

9

Waikomo Rd

520

Koloa Poipu Bypass

Camp Rd

8

Lawai Rd

Prince Kuhio Park

10

Kiahuna Golf Course

Hoonani Rd

Poipu Rd

11

Poipu Shopping Village

Koloa Sugar Mill

Poipu

CJM Stables

Kawailoa Bay

Poipu Bay Resort Golf Club

Gillin's Beach

Ha'ula Beach

Maha'ulepu Beaches

Kipu Kai

Long Beach

Kukui'ula Small Boat Harbor

Spouting Horn

Lawai Beach

Koloa Landing

12 13 14 15

A B C D

Hoone

Poipu Beach Park

Brennecke's Beach

Keoniloa Bay

Shipwreck Beach

Kauai
South Shore

Great Days on the South Shore

Day 1. Breakfast at Tomkats, Koloa (p. 227). Take a boat cruise (p. 126) along the south shore to Kipu Kai (winter) or Na Pali Coast (summer). At the end of the day, head to Mahaʻulepu Beach for great walking (p. 65). Sunset dinner at Beach House (p. 207). Or watch the sky glow at sunset from Poipu Beach Park (p. 113) and dine at Brennecke's (p. 208). Stroll through the beautiful Hyatt Resort after dinner (free valet parking).

Day 2. Visit Kauai's National Tropical Botanical Gardens (p. 136), or bike to Mahaʻulepu (p. 81) or trail ride (p. 102). Then snorkel at Poipu Beach Park. Before dinner, enjoy Hawaiian music at Hyatt's Seaview lounge. Dinner at Roy's (p. 223). Stroll through the Kiahuna and Sheraton grounds after dinner.

Kipu Kai

You can only get to Kipu Kai by boat, for the private road crossing the gap in the mountains between Rt. 50 and the south shore is deeply rutted and gouged, suitable only for the sturdiest 4 wheel drive vehicles. Some boat companies offer day trips to this lovely section of Kauai's coastline (p. 126).

Kipu Kai is actually three beaches which share a rocky peninsula shaped like an alligator. Long Beach is, as you would expect from the name, stretches out in a long line of fine sand in the shape of a half moon, nearly enclosed by outcroppings of rocks at each end. Set at the base of the rocky mountains behind Kipu Kai, Long Beach is special among south shore beaches, combining the favorable weather of the south with a rugged beauty more characteristic of the north shore. As if this weren't enough, the ocean is relatively gentle due to the rocky points which embrace the beach, breaking the surf and creating a protected lagoon.

A wonderful old rambling ranch house sits atop Turtle Beach, so named for its shape. The house was built in stages by the Waterhouse family using orders of wood and supplies floated ashore from cargo ships. From the veranda overlooking the bay, Jack Waterhouse used to communicate with the "rest of the world" by signals. According to his will, the Waterhouse family descendents retain use of the land until the end of the next generation, when Kipu Kai Ranch is destined to become a state park.

Maha'ulepu

At the end of a dusty drive through winding sugar cane roads, you will find a beautiful sandy beach carved into a rocky point. This part of the south shore can be very dry and very hot — and you'll soon find a thin red film on every surface inside your car, including you! But it's worth the dust to reach a beach astonishing in its wild beauty, the surf crashing against the rocks and sand, the churning turquoise water almost glowing with sunlight. Beautiful it is, but often not safe enough for swimming. Unless surf on the whole south shore is flat, you may find the waves crashing with enough force to knock you down, and currents powerful enough to make even local people wary.

Maha'ulepu is a lovely beach for walking and exploring. On the eastern end, a lovely half-moon of golden sand nestles at the base of a rocky cliff. A long walk to the west takes you past a rocky reef which at low tide juts out of the sand in fascinating formations. As you reach the end of the curve, the tip turns out to be a point, and on the other side, you'll find another, even longer stretch of beach. Here the water ripples in toward shore, protected by an offshore reef where the waves roll in long, even swells. You might see a fisherman casting his line or even a swimmer snorkeling among the rocks if the sea is calm. When the

Maha'ulepu

Solitude at Mahaʻulepu

tradewinds are strong, windsurfers splash color on the sparkling sea. At the westernmost end, at Gillin's Beach, you will find a new house built on the spot where plantation manager Gillin once lived. Sunwarmed tidal pools are shallow and still, and kids can catch tiny fish in nets.

At the far eastern end of Mahaʻulepu is a rocky bluff. After a moderate uphill climb, you will come to a promontory with spectacular views of the coastline. Rock formations are amazing, and a tiny beach set into the cliffside shelters interesting pools of tiny sea life.

Directions: Take Rt. 50 to Rt. 520 (the Koloa Road), and follow signs to Poipu. Take Poipu Road past the Hyatt Regency, continue on to the unpaved road, and pass the golf course and the quarry. When you come to a stop sign, turn right and head toward the water. This is sugar company land; at road's end, park or turn left to another lot. Map 3

Shipwreck Beach

Shipwreck Beach along Keoniloa Bay was never much of a beach—until the hurricane blasted the south shore of Kauai and created a new coastline. What was once a thin curve of sand is now a long, golden crescent divided by lava rocks. It's called Shipwreck Beach with good reason; the surf is powerful, breaking in long, shining arcs which crest slowly, one at a time, with deceptive smoothness, and then crash in thunderous explosions of spray not far from shore. Local people warn that beyond the break point are dangerous currents and large rocks. A better place for family swimming would be Poipu Beach Park, and novice surfers would be better off at Wailua Beach, where rocks and wind are not a problem and a lifeguard is on duty. Be particularly careful during summer months, when a south shore swell can bring big surf.

Instead of swimming, you can climb the cliff to explore strange caves

At Shipwreck Beach, you can walk along the rocky bluff and explore the rock formations.

and rock formations. The colors are breathtaking – the deep blue of the water and the gold of the cliffs dazzle the eye, and the view down is a dizzying spectacle of surf crashing against the rocks. Be careful, though. Avoid going close to the cliff's edge, as the footing is slippery with loose sand. It's great for photographers but not for children.

Directions: Take Poipu Road past the main entrance to the Hyatt Hotel. Turn toward the water on Ainako Road. Park in the lot. Public access restrooms and showers are by the parking lot. Shipwreck is 14 miles from Lihue; 24 miles from Kapa'a; 44 miles from Princeville. Map 3

Brennecke's Beach

Legendary for years as the best beach for body surfing in Hawaii, Brennecke's Beach is finally recovering from Hurricane Iniki, which smashed giant boulders into the seawall and washed away most of the sand. Today, as the sand is back, the waves are gradually returning to their old pattern, breaking far out for the big kids, and then again closer to shore for younger ones to catch a swift and exciting ride. After Hurricane Iwa caused a similar level of destruction in 1982, the return of the sandy bottom took ten years, and it's taken just about as long after Iniki. Wave riders must still be wary of rocks, and watch out for waves that head towards the sea wall. There is no lifeguard protection.

Directions: Adjacent to Poipu Beach Park, on the eastern side. Map 3

Poipu Beach Park

You could not imagine a more perfect beach for children than this lovely curve of soft golden sand sloping down to a gentle, friendly sea. The waves, with changing shades of turquoise sparkling with sunlight and dazzling white foam, break gently over a protective reef across the entrance to this small cove. For babies and toddlers, a ring of black lava rocks creates a sheltered pool where the water is shallow and still. For older children, waves beyond the pool roll to shore in graceful swells perfect for rafts or body boards. Children can explore the long rocky point at the far end of the beach and find tiny fish in the tidal pools. Bring nets and pails for the hunt! You'll find a lifeguard, as well as restrooms, outdoor showers, barbecues, picnic tables, and shaded pavilions.

Just around the rocky point, in front of the old Waiohai Hotel which is now a time-share resort operated by the Marriott, you can enjoy some of the best snorkeling on the island. Hundreds of fish in rainbow colors feed on the coral, so tame they almost swim into your hands. Carry snorkeling fish food in a plastic bag, or even a green leaf, and they'll swim right to

you. Stay inside the reef to avoid being caught in a strong current. Sometimes you may see a monk seal taking sun on the sand. It's resting, gathering strength to face another day in paradise!

Directions: In Poipu, take Ho'owilili Road to Ho'one Road. Park in lot. To park near the Kiahuna and Sheraton, turn off Ho'owilili Rd. at the Sheraton's sign, then turn left at Hoonani Rd. and continue to end. Enter the last driveways on the left and on the right to public parking.

Salt Pond Beach Park – great for families, and often a sunny spot when other parts of the island are cloudy.

Westside Beach Adventures

Favorite Beaches

  * **Salt Pond Beach Park** offers great swimming, protected by a reef, as well as usually sunny weather. Kids love the tidal pools (p. 71).

  * At **Kekaha**, you'll find firm sand and miles of beach perfect for beachwalking and running, as well as surf for body boards (p. 73).

  * Drive all the way to the end of the road to magnificent **Polihale Beach**, the westernmost part of the island, perfect for sunsets (p. 75).

  * On your trips west, stop off at *Wrangler's* in Waimea for great hamburgers and salads (p. 232), or Hanapepe's *Green Garden* for inexpensive island style food – and lilikoi chiffon pie (p. 229). *Hanapepe Café* serves vegetarian delights and espresso (p. 229), and *Grinds* in Ele'ele makes sandwiches on fresh homebaked bread. Enjoy a tasty lunch and check e-mail at Kauai's free wireless, *Waimea Plantation Cottages*.

Westside
Map 4

Miloli'i State Park

Nu'alolo Kai State Park

Kalalau Lookout

Pu'u o Kila Lookout

Koke'e Lodge & Museum

550

Pu'u Hinahina Lookout

Koke'e State Park

Waimea Canyon (1 mile wide and 3657 feet deep)

Waimea Canyon Lookout

Polihale State Park

Polihale Rd

Nohili Point

Barking Sands

Kao Rd

Mana

Waimea River

Old Mana Rd

Mana Point

50

Military Airfield

Koke'e Rd

550

Pacific Range Missile Center

Waimea Canyon Rd

Kokole Point

Kekaha

Kekaha Beach Park

Kikiaola Small Boat Harbor

Waimea

6 A

Lucy Wright Beach Park

5

Russian Fort Elizabeth

50

Drive Waimea Canyon 134 and hike at Koke'e 101

Na Pali Boat Tours depart from Port Allen 126

Pakala Beach ("Infinities")

Beaches
Salt Pond Beach Park 71
Pakala's Beach (Infinities) 72
Kekaha Beaches 73
Barking Sands 75
Polihale 75

Kaumuali'i Hwy

Olokele Rd

Hanapepe

4 3 2

Eleele

1

Port Allen

Lolokai

Lele

Salt Pond Beach Park

Hanapepe Bay

Port Allen Airport

Restaurants & Hotels
1   Toi's Thai Kitchen, Grinds 230
2   Green Garden 229
3   Hanapepe Cafe 229
4   Carving Stone
5   Wrangler's 232
6   Waimea Plantation Cottages 14
    & Brew Pub 231

Westside

Kauai

N

0   1   2
Miles

Great Days on the Westside

Day 1: Drive to Polihale Beach (p. 75) with a picnic lunch from Grind's, or drive Waimea Canyon Road to Koke'e (p. 137), and explore the forest preserve. Shave Ice at Jo Jo's on the way back. Dinner at Wrangler's (p. 232).

Day 2: Tour the Na Pali Coast by boat (p. 126), or Gay & Robinson Sugar Plantation (p. 133), or visit the quaint town of Hanapepe, test its swinging bridge, browse the art galleries and have lunch at Hanapepe Café or Green Garden (p. 229). Afternoon: Salt Pond Beach or Kekaha. Dinner at Toi's Thai Kitchen (p. 231).

Salt Pond Beach Park

What is most astonishing about Salt Pond Beach Park is the intensity of the colors—the brilliant blues of the water and sky, the bright gold of the sand, the vivid greens of fields extending in squares and rectangles up the slopes of nearby mountains—all bathed in sunshine that makes everything sparkle. The beach is a perfect semicircle, where the sand slopes downward with the lovely grace of a golden bowl to hold the sea. A reef near the mouth of this sheltered cove breaks the surf into slow, rolling swells that break again gently near the shore so that children can raft and swim safely inside this natural lagoon most of the year. At both ends of the beach, tidepools can be calm enough at low tide for babies and toddlers, and great fun for older ones when the incoming tide splashes over the rocks, making waterfalls. Kids can try their luck at catching tiny, swift fish in nets.

Walk along the beach and explore tidal pools and the ancient salt ponds where local people still harvest sea salt. The park is spectacular, especially when brightly colored windsurfers race out across the reef, and particularly favored in terms of weather. Even when clouds and rain prevail elsewhere, this little point of land seems to escape them, and in winter, the water seems a few degrees warmer and more friendly.

Showers, rest rooms, picnic tables, barbecues, and a lifeguard make Salt Pond a popular weekend spot for local families and increasingly for tourists, although the beach never seems crowded. Be careful in periods of high surf, however, as unpredictable currents can create hazardous swimming, and stay inside the lagoon. For lunch, stop at the Hanapepe Cafe or Green Garden (fabulous coconut cream or lilikoi chiffon pies).

Salt Pond Beach tidepool — perfect for kids!

Directions: Take Rt. 50 west to Hanapepe and pass through the town. Turn left at Lele St., and take the first right onto Lokokai Rd. Continue until you see the parking area. Salt Pond Beach Park is 18 miles from Lihue; 28 miles from Kapa'a; 58 miles from Princeville. Map 4

Pakala's Beach or 'Infinities'

On this lovely, curving beach, the sand and sea are deep gold, as if sprinkled with cinnamon, because the A'akukui stream carries red sugar cane soil to the sea. You can hear the crash of the waves as you walk across the pastureland, and by the time you pass through the trees which ring the sand, you'll feel like you're alone on a deserted island. It is a lovely spot. The waves rise gracefully in long, even lines crested with gold. Each wave breaks and rushes onto the sand in shining foam, and then it rolls back out again to meet the wave coming in, a fascinating ballet, sometimes meeting like dancers in perfect rhythm, sometimes colliding in bursts of spray. You could watch the waves for hours and never see two waves embrace in exactly the same way.

The bay is divided by a rocky point where local fishermen try for pompano. If you cross the stream and climb the rocky ledge, you come to a sandy beach dotted with shells, sea glass, and coral. Beyond the reef is a surfing spot famous for long, perfectly formed waves that surfers can ride on to 'infinity' (see p. 115). Paddling out over the shallow reef takes a long time, but the ride, according to our son Jeremy, is really special. Be careful at low tide, when shallow water over the reef can expose an unwary surfer to spiny sea urchins. To the right of the rocky point, the beach stretches a long way before disappearing around a bend. The firm golden sand is perfect for walking, and the waves can be quite gentle. This western spot is a good place to try when other parts of the island are in rain.

Directions: Drive west of Hanapepe on Rt. 50 past the mile 21 marker. Look for a low concrete bridge and a level area on the shoulder of the road for parking. Next to the bridge over the A'akukui Stream, an overgrown path leads through a pasture to the beach. Wear sturdy sandals and stay away from the thorny kiawe which grows near the beach. About 1 mile further on Rt. 50 you'll find public restrooms at the Russian Fort, and just across the Waimea River, public showers. Map 4

Kekaha Beaches

Stretching for miles along Kauai's western coast, the Kekaha beaches combine swimming, surfing, and walking with the predominantly dry weather of the island's leeward side. As Rt. 50 curves toward the sea at the small town of Kekaha, the beach is narrow, but a mile or two north, it widens and becomes more golden, with long, rolling waves breaking evenly in brilliant white crests. At times, the waves can break perfectly for surfing and body boarding, although, as everywhere on Kauai, surf and currents can be dangerous and unpredictable, and you may find high surf and rip currents. Watch where local people are swimming and follow their lead – especially if they are not going into the water!

Even if swimming is not advisable, the sand is firm and flat, one of the finest beaches on Kauai—or anywhere—for walking, running, or playing frisbee or football. We recommend driving the full length of this stretch of beach so that you can select the most favorable spot and then double back to park. Despite its clear, sunny weather, the western side of the island has not yet been developed as a tourist area, and so these beaches are frequented primarily by local residents and are not very crowded. You can walk for miles along the sand, with beautiful views of Ni'ihau, purple on the horizon. Or drive north towards Barking Sands and Polihale Beach, winding through sugar cane fields where silvery grasses wave in the breezes against the deep red-gold of cleared fields and the vivid blues of the sea and the enormous sky.

Miles of golden sand at Kekaha

Directions: Drive northwest of Waimea on Rt. 50 until the road curves towards the water near the mile 25 marker. Map 4

Barking Sands

The beach from Kekaha to Polihale extends about 15 miles. The section off the Pacific Missile Range Facility is open to the public only on weekends and federal holidays. Post September 11, access has tightened considerably. For a permit, you must first complete a "memorandum of agreement," then a background check at a local police station before signing in at the main gate. Contact thomas.h.clements@navy.mil for information, or to get the form by email, or call Security at 335-4821.

Like Polihale Beach, the surf here can be extremely strong, often too powerful for safe swimming. While the waves break magnificently for surfers, unpredictable currents and a sudden drop-off make swimming hazardous. You have to look carefully for channels through the coral reef fronting the beach to find sandy bottom. The wide, sandy beach is both hot and difficult to walk on, and shade is almost nonexistent. It is a spectacular place for a picnic, though, and you can see Niʻihau on the horizon, just past the golden, shining sand and glistening turquoise sea.

Directions: Main entry gate is northwest of Kekaha on Rt. 50. Map 4

Polihale Beach Park

From the time you leave paved road behind to jolt north through a maze of sugar cane fields, you know you're in for something special. Gradually, beyond the tall sugar cane rustling in the breeze, a dark ridge of jagged peaks appears on the right. As you get closer, these giant cliffs reveal splendid colors – trees and bush in vivid greens against the black rock slashed with the deep red of the volcanic soil. When you can drive no further, the beach at Polihale emerges from the base of the cliffs – an enormous stretch of brilliant white sand more immense, it seems, than the cliffs which tower above and the band of deep blue sea beyond. Only the sky seems the equal of this vast expanse of glaring sand, so wide that to walk from your car to the ocean on a sunny day will burn your feet, and so long that no single vantage point allows the eye to see its full extent. 'Beautiful' is too small a word for this awesome place. Polihale – home of spirits – is more appropriate, not only because the majestic cliffs and beach dwarf anything human to insignificance, but also because here man's access to the western coast really ends. Beyond lies the Na Pali wilderness, unreachable except by boat or helicopter, or by the handful of hikers who dare to climb the narrow and dangerous trails. Polihale is the threshold between the known and the unknown, the tamed and the untamed, the familiar and the wild.

Swimming is treacherous; the rolling, pounding surf even at its most gentle is only for strong, experienced swimmers. No reefs offer protection from the powerful ocean currents. Come instead for the spectacle, to picnic and walk, to gaze at the grandeur of cliffs above the endless sea and sand, to listen to the silence broken only by the crashing surf, to appreciate in solitude the splendor of nature's power. A feeling of awe lingers even after you return to paved road and a world of smaller proportions.

Directions: Just before Rt. 50 ends, a State Park sign will mark the left turn onto the dirt cane road. Follow signs for about 5 miles. Restrooms, showers, tables. Camping by permit only. However, be careful with your rental car. Don't get your wheels mired in muddy roads, or stuck in sandy dunes. Map 4

Westside shopping stops

HANAPEPE, Kauai's 'biggest little town,' has a cluster of specialty shops. *Kauai Fine Arts Gallery* offers a wonderful collection of antique maps and prints, with a particularly fine selection of nautical and Pacific themes. Next door, *Hanapepe Café* is a great place for lunch or a mid-afternoon coffee on a rainy day. *Dr. Ding* sells surf gear and surf fashions, including Lauren's favorite 'chicks who rip' shirts; *Arius Hopman* has beautiful photographs of Kauai's amazing scenery. (He'll be happy to discuss his latest experiments in digital technology, and help you solve your technical problems.) *Kama'aina Cabinets* offers carefully crafted wood furniture and ornaments, and also sells 'Aloha Angels' hand made on Kauai. Explore the famous swinging bridge, and visit the *Taro Ka* chips factory down the street and taste a sample (or two, or three...). Stop at *Kauai Kookie Factory* on Rt. 56 next to Mariko's (set back from road).

In **Waimea**, try *Liko's* for surf wear, and check out Liko's beautifully crafted surfboards. Hungry? Try Big Save's bakery, or shave ice from Jo Jo's.

Beach Safety

We describe the beaches in their summer mood, when the surf and currents can be at their most gentle. From mid-October to mid-April, however, swimmers must be particularly cautious on the windward beaches to the north and northeast where the surf and currents are more unpredictable and dangerous. On the south shore, surf is "up" in summer months, and the ocean more calm during winter. Plan your beach adventures according to surf conditions (Call 245-6001 for a report on the size of the swell, times of high and low tides).

A few simple suggestions: Don't swim alone or too far out at a beach where the currents are unfamiliar, and avoid swimming where a river flows into the sea. Never turn your back on the ocean; keep your eye on the waves. Before you swim, observe the water carefully. Look out for the fast moving water running laterally which indicates a strong current. Should you ever find yourself caught in a strong undertow or current, and if your efforts to free yourself are not successful, remember this: don't panic, conserve your energy and drift with the current until it weakens.

These currents usually weaken beyond the point where the waves break, and many are shaped like horseshoes, so that at some point you will probably be able to swim back in.

Be particularly careful when you are snorkeling, when you can easily get distracted by the fish and lose your sense of direction. Stay close enough to shore that you can swim in at any time, and remember that unfamiliar beaches will have unknown currents. You'll find the safest snorkeling in the rock-enclosed pool at Lydgate Park on the eastern shore, or at sheltered Poipu Beach to the south. Beware of walking or even standing close to the edge of cliffs or rocks to photograph the pounding surf, as waves vary in size and strength and a huge one may come up suddenly and wash your camera away – perhaps you along with it! These sudden large waves can be treacherous because they are unexpected as well as powerful, particularly on the northern and western beaches without reefs to protect against strong ocean currents. Avoid swimming in the murky water near where a stream flows into the sea.

When surfing, watch where the local surfers ride the waves. They know where to avoid strong currents, rocks, and dangerous wave breaks. They are also experienced, however, and seek a bigger thrill. Keep an eye out for that occasional oversize wave. Rather than trying to ride it (or worse, run from it), you may want to dive through or drop down under it. These big ones often come in threes, so be ready!

Portuguese 'men o' war,' tiny blue jellyfish, pack a walloping sting in their long, trailing tentacles. They sometimes dot the waterline after heavy surf. Don't step on them or pick them up. If you are stung while swimming, pull the jellyfish off carefully, trying not to touch the stinger any more than you have to, or use some sand to scrape the stinger off. Warm water helps or vinegar or meat tenderizer can be used as to help break down the poison. The best medicine, however, is prevention. If you see them on the sand, pack up and head out for another beach! An even smaller critter, the bacterium causing leptospirosis has been found in Kauai's rivers and streams, so avoid freshwater swimming far from the ocean's edge if you have open cuts or sores. Instead, swim in the ocean or the brackish water where a stream flows into the sea.

Your beachbag should contain some antibiotic ointment and bandaids for coral cuts, and, if possible, some vinegar in case you meet a man o' war. Keep a spare sun tan lotion in the glove compartment of the car.

On Kauai, as anywhere, follow normal rules of self-protection: Lock your car against theft as you would at home, store valuables in the trunk, and avoid walking alone at night in unlit, deserted areas – including those romantic beaches.

Beware the Hawaiian Sun

If you lie out in the sun between 11:30 am and 2:30 pm you will fry like a pancake, even in a half hour, because Hawaii lies close to the equator and the sun is exceedingly strong. You'll need a good sunscreen, even on cloudy days, for ultraviolet rays can cause a burn. Sunscreens which contain PABA may give some people a rash. 'PABA- free' sunscreens are available and are highly effective. Read the labels carefully. The best lotions protect against both UV and UA rays. Choose 'waterproof' rather than 'water-resistant' lotions, though don't put too much faith in manufacturer's claims. Even waterproof sunscreens wash off in salt water and should be reapplied periodically, as we do every two hours. We've had good luck with lotions forming a skin-like coating, like Sundown, and sticky gels like 'Bullfrog.'

Children need special care and effective lotions. Dermatologists currently recommend a lotion rated SPF 15 for kids (and everyone else). For spots which kids rub often, like right under the eyes, you can try sticky gels like 'Bullfrog' or a lotion in chapstick form. It's a good idea to make a rule that kids get 'greased up' in the room or parking lot before heading for the beach as they hate to stand still once the sand is in sight! Bring tee-shirts (the most reliable sun-protection) for after-swimming sandcastle projects. It's a good plan to schedule family beach visits for the early morning or late afternoon, and plan meals, naps, or drives for the noonday sun hours. Sunburns are often not visible until it is too late, but you can check your child's skin by pressing it with your finger. If it blanches dramatically, get the child a shirt or consider calling it a day. Keep a spare lotion in the car, for without lotion, beaches can be hazardous to your health!

Babies need a complete sunblock and a hat to protect the scalp; use lotion even on feet. Babies should stay in the shade as much as possible, so an umbrella (K-Mart, Wal-Mart, Longs) would be a wise purchase for the beach.

*Activities &
Discoveries*

Kahili onboard at Anini Beach

Artists & Artisans

For a listing of Kauai's artists and open studios, contact Kauai Society of Artists (PO Box 3344, Lihue HI 96766; www.kauaisocietyofartists.org; 822-9304). Visit galleries featuring more than 40 KSA members at *Kinipopo Fine Art Gallery* in Wailua (822-4356; www.kauai-art.com) or *Evolve-Love Art Gallery* in Hanalei (826-4755). In Coconut Plantation Marketplace, Wailua, find maritime art, maps, and antiques in *Ship Store Galleries*; and Hawaiian art at *Kahn Galleries* (also in Hanalei, Kilohana, Koloa and Wailua). *Wyland Gallery* in Wailua and Lihue has seascapes.

You'll find the largest selection of works by island artisans at the *Kauai Products Store* at Kukui Grove (246-6753). *Kauai Museum's* shop has quilts, native wood boxes, shell leis and jewelry (245-6931). For pottery, visit *Kilohana Clayworks* (246-2529). Explore *Life's Treasures* near the Wailua Safeway. In Kapa'a, don't miss *Kela's Glass Gallery* (822-4527; www.glass-art.com) for beautiful colors and shapes; try *William Zimmer* for furniture of koa and exotic hardwoods. The outdoor *Kauai Products's Fair* opposite Otsuka's has inexpensive bargains in jewelry and crafts. In Hanapepe's art colony, visit *Kama'aina Koa Wood Gallery,* and *Arius Hopman* (www.hopmanart.com; 335-0227) for beautiful watercolors. In Waimea, *Wranglers* has wonderful local crafts. Stay for lunch!

ATV

Tour Kauai's wilderness areas by ATV. Several companies offer tours. *Kipu Adventures* tours Kipu Ranch, 3,000 acres from the Hule'ia River to the top of Ha'upu mountain, on wide wheel-base Honda 350 all terrain vehicles ($99/3 hrs $145/4 hrs). 246-9288; www.kiputours.com. You maneuver up and down grades, cross valleys and forest areas, bounce into

streams, through pastures with cattle, and up the rocky road to the Ha'upu mountain pass – a spectacular lookout to gorgeous Kipu Kai beach. You may see Nene geese, wild pigs, pheasant, turkeys, amazing trees, as well as explore those famous locations of Raiders of the Lost Arc, Jurassic Park, Mighty Joe Young, and others. The guides are great. Wear old clothes, as anything you wear will soon become an original red dirt shirt! *Kauai ATV* takes you through streams and into all kinds of mud. The company provides head lights, which you will need when you go through an old cane tunnel (great fun!) leading up to a waterfall picnic. If you forgot your camera, the company provides a CD of digital images of your tour (see right), plus some of their stock photos. They rent mud-gear for a wet and wild 4 hour tour to 2 waterfalls, through a 'mud splash' and a sugar cane tunnel near Koloa ($145) or a 3 hour tour of south shore movie sites ($99). 742-2734 or 877-707-7088; kauaiatv.com.

Kauai Backcountry claims the "fastest paced" ATV tour on the island. Speeds average around 20 mph, with no "governors" to regulate speed. Guides set the pace by the slowest rider – in our case 35 mph. The terrain is roughly 1/4 mud and rocks, and 3/4 dirt and gravel trails. The tour includes a picnic lunch (sandwiches, chips, and cookies) and an optional swim in a secluded waterfall. It's great fun – and it's wise to rent the full ATV clothing package (long plants, water shoes for crossing a stream to the picnic area, long sleeved shirt, gloves, bandana to keep out dust, and helmet for $10. ($135/ 3.5 hours). www.kauaibackcountry.com; 888-270-0555 or 245-2506. The companies emphasize safety, and limit riders to those over 16 (some offer a larger vehicle 'mule' to carry the kids). Westside: *Gaye & Robinson* has an ATV tour of the Makaweli Ranch and uplands (335-2824).

Beachwalking & Running

Our favorite running beaches, with firm sand and just the right slope, are Hanalei Bay and Kalihiwai on the north shore, Kalapaki on the east, and Kekaha to the west. For long meandering walks, we like Moloaʻa and Larsen's Beach in the north, Mahaʻulepu in the south, and on the eastern shore, Anahola Beach or Lydgate Park along the Wailua Golf Course – beautiful at sunrise or sunset. For races, call *Hawaii Visitors Bureau* (800-262-1400). Remember the sun! Fluids, sunscreen, even a hat are a must!

Biking

Tours: Take a south shore bike tour from Kipu to hidden Mahaʻulepu Beach, along the cane roads and through an old tunnel carved into the mountain leading to Koloa sugar mill ($100/adult $75/junior). After a brief tour of the mill, it's on to Mahaʻulepu for a picnic, swim, and a short beach hike. It's 8 miles of great scenery, an easy grade, and family fun. *Aloha Kauai Tours* (245-6400/800-452-1113; www.alohakauaitours.com).

On a mountain bike, you can try a 'downhill tour'– 12 miles of winding road from Waimea Canyon, at an elevation of 3,500 feet, to the coast, with *Kauai Coasters* (639-2412; www.aloha.net/~coast) or *Outfitters Kauai* ($80) daily at dawn, for the beautiful early morning light, and 3 times a week for sunset (742 -9667; www.outfitterskauai.com). *Outfitters* also offers bike and kayak tours, and bike rentals.

Bike Rentals: On the north shore, tour Hanalei and Ha'ena. Call *Pedal & Paddle* (826-9069). Eastside, explore the coastline of Kapa'a town, on a mostly level bike trail with ocean views. Call *Kauai Cycle & Tour* in Kapa'a (821-2115; www.bikehawaii.com/kauaicycle). Southside, *Outfitters Kauai* (742-9667). Repairs? Call *Bicycle John* (245-7579). Rent a **Harley**? Call *Ray's* (822-HOGG) or *Hawaiian Riders* (www.hawaiianriders.com; 822-5409) which also rents mopeds & 'exotic vehicles.' For that rainy day alternative, try small motorbike racing at *Fifty/Fifty* (245-2222), with an observation deck overlooking the entire indoor track.

Camping

Camping is permitted at Anahola, Ha'ena, Anini, Salt Pond, and Polihale Beach Parks, as well as specified areas of the Na Pali region and other wilderness preserves. For state parks, the camping limit is 5 nights in a 30 day period per campground (less on some stopovers on the Kalalau Trail). For information, permits, and reservations contact *Department of Land and Natural Resources,* Division of State Parks, P.O. Box 1671, Lihue, HI 96766 (274-3444). Download permit forms at www.hawaii.gov/ dlnr. For Alakai Swamp or Waimea Canyon, contact *Division of Forestry* at the same address (274-3433). *Kauai County Parks* limit camping to 4 days per park, or 12 nights total. (241-6670). Allow 30 days to process permits.

YWCA Camp Sloggett is set in spectacular Koke'e State Park, with access to 45 miles of hiking trails leading to the Kalalau Lookout and its amazing views of the Waimea Canyon and Na Pali coastline. Group and hostel accommodations include tent camping and a bunkhouse with kitchenettes, shared bath facilities and hot showers (from $20/pp/night). Reserve at least two months in advance: YWCA of Kauai, 3094 Elua St., Lihue HI 96766 (245-5959; www.campingkauai.com).

For those who want to be close to nature – and to a shower and refrigerator at the same time, *Koke'e Lodge's* cabins might be just the answer. Cabins include stove, refrigerator, hot showers, cooking and eating utensils, linens, bedding, and wood burning stoves; prices start at $45/night (maximum stay of 5 nights during a 30 day period). Make reservations well in advance: *Koke'e Aloha Lodge*, Box 819, Waimea HI 96796. (808-335-6061). The Lodge serves breakfast and light lunch (9 am - 3:30 pm). Bring warm clothes for cold nights, and remember, on Kauai as elsewhere, to lock your gear in the trunk of your car before you head out. Map 4

Located between Lihue and Koloa, *Kahili Mountain Park* has reasonably priced, rustic cabins (from $55) in a serene meadow and mountain setting. Temporarily not available for rental. Call for an update: 742-7851. Map 3

Waioli Mission Church

Near road's end on the north shore, *YMCA Camp Naue* in spectacular Ha'ena offers beachfront camping in bunk houses (or your own tent). It's popular with local clubs and families, but individual tourists are also welcome to stay in the bunkhouse ($12/ night; children half-price), or if you bring your own tent, it's only $10. YMCA of Kauai, Box 1786, Lihue HI 96766 (246-9090 or 742-1200). Map 2

Rent camping equipment at *Pedal & Paddle* in Hanalei (826-9069 – ask about current trail conditions), *Kayak Kauai* in Hanalei (826-9844) and Kapa'a (822-9179), or *Outfitters Kauai* (742-9667) in Poipu. Buy camping equipment in *Long's Drug Store, K- Mart, Wal-Mart* in Lihue, as well as small variety stores like *Waipouli Variety* (Wailua), *Discount Variety* (Koloa), *Village Variety* (Hanalei), or *Ace Hardware* (Hanalei).

Churches & Temples

Churches on Kauai give 'aloha' a whole new resonance. Whatever your faith, you'll feel welcome at Sunday services. The Missionary Church in Kapa'a (822-5594) welcomes visitors with a shell lei and a warm greeting. Wai'oli Huia Church in Hanalei (826-6253) conducts services in Hawaiian and English, and the very friendly family atmosphere is evident in the announcement at the top of the Sunday Bulletin: "Our keikis are apt to wander during church. They do this because they feel at home in God's house. Please love them as we do." In Waimea, the 9 am service is conducted in Hawaiian at *Hawaiian Church*, circa 1820 (338-9962).

The Kadavul Hindu Temple in the Wailua valley draws thousands of

Hindu followers each year, as well as tourists fascinated by the botanical gardens and stone temple, and 300-kg crystal *Siva Lingum*. Visitors to the temple and monastery may be invited to join a *puja* (cleansing) ceremony. Just off Kuamo'o Rd. (open to public 9 am - 11:30 am); call 822-3012 for the 2 hour tour (www.saivasiddhanta.com/hawaii).

You'll pass many lovely old churches on Kauai, from back roads in Koloa to cane fields on the west side. Stop and visit!

Coffee

Kauai Coffee is grown near Kalaheo and Koloa, near the location of Hawaii's first coffee plantation (1836). Coffee grown today on this 4,000 acre estate is free of insecticides. At the visitor's center in Lawai, sample local coffees roasted daily (335-0813 or 800-545-8605; www.kauaicoffee.com). Try *Black Mountain Premium Hawaiian Coffee*, grown near Waimea. Espresso cafes are perking (p. 227), including the island's first Starbucks (Kukui Grove Center, next to Jamba Juice)! *Java kai* (javakai.com) sells fresh beans and bakery treats in Lihue, Hanalei, and Kapa'a and Koloa (866-JAVA-KAI). *Kalaheo Coffee Company (*www.kalaheo.com) sells fragrant beans along with tasty deli choices. Buy Lapperts beans, or the red-bag favorite, *Lion Coffee,* at Walmart or K-Mart or 800-338-8353; www.lioncoffee.com.

Family Beaches

Our favorite family beaches, with something for everyone, are *Kalihiwai* (p. 49) and *Anini Beach* (p. 51) on the north shore, and *Poipu Beach Park* (p. 68) and *Salt Pond Beach Park* (p. 72) on the south shore. On the eastern shore, the best family beaches are *Kalapaki Beach* (p. 30) and *Lydgate Park* (p. 32) where you can snorkel safely and see families of very tame, colorful fish living in Lydgate's unique, enormous man-made ocean pool enclosed by lava rocks. A smaller rock-rimmed pool is perfect for babies and toddlers, a favorite with local families. At Lydgate Park you'll also find the best playground on Kauai – *Kamalani Park* – 16,000 square feet of funland with mirror mazes, a suspension bridge, lava tubes and circular slide. Visit Kamalani's new section less than a half mile south, along the beach. Drive towards the water on Leho Road just south of Kaha Lani Condominium. A new paved walkway/bikeway along the ocean connects the two sections. Lydgate, Anahola, Poipu Beach, Salt Pond, Kealia, Wailua Bay, Hanalei Bay, Ke'e Beach have lifeguards.

With a plastic pail and an inexpensive net ($6 for an 8" net at Long's), children can have lots of fun trying to catch fish trapped in tidal pools. Net fishing is fun at the rivers behind the beaches at *Anahola, Kalihiwai*, and *Moloaʻa*, and at the tidal pools at *Salt Pond Beach Park* and *Poipu Beach Park*. Bring home sand, shells and driftwood for great kids' art projects.

Family Fun

Kids will love the free hula shows sponsored at the major shopping centers, some on a regular schedule, and others, like Coconut Plantation Marketplace (822-3641), only occasionally. At Poipu Shopping Village the show is 5 pm on Tues and Thurs. (742-2831). Kukui Grove offers a free 'Aloha Friday' entertainment (7-8 pm on Fridays) 245-7784. Kids can dress in their aloha finery for the free hula show, sometimes with local kids, at the Poipu Hyatt (6 pm, Seaview Terrace). 742-1234, free valet parking.

Children will love the *Children's Discovery Museum* in Wailua (www.kcdm.org; 823-8222) where learning adventures, hands-on activities, summer camps give kids a chance to meet new friends ($40/day or $3.50/ hr). For a family friendly fun, call Kelley at *Kauai Backcountry* and ask about the Tubing adventure (www.kauaibackcountry.com; 888-270-0555/ 245-2506), and Greg at *Watersports Kauai* for scuba lessons. Would-be young surfers can call Roni at *PlayDirty Kauai* (823-9133) or 'Uncle Ambrose' (822-7112). For windsurfing lessons, call Celeste Harvel (828-6838). Young artists will enjoy *Kilohana Clayworks*; Keith Tammarine helps them craft, glaze and fire their creations in his studio (246-2529).

For cribs and child equipment rentals, call *Ready Rentals* (823-8008 or 800-599-8008; www.readyrentals.com). $15 delivery.

Day camps are offered at the Children's Discovery Museum ($40/day). Hyatt, Marriott, Princeville Hotel, Kiahuna, and the Sheraton typically charge guests about $50 per day. The Sheraton Kauai Keiki Aloha Club in Poipu features lunch, kite and lei making, pole fishing, and Hawaiian legends ($45/day guests; $70/day non-guests). Kids golf free (after 1 pm) at Puakea Golf Course (245-8756).

Great children's books: *Hawaii is a Rainbow* (beautiful photographs), *Peter Panini and the Search for the Menehune, Pua Pua Lena Lena, Keiki's First Books* board books. Look for them at *Borders,* where kids can enjoy *Keiki Story Time* (246-0862).

Farmers' Markets

Farmers' Markets happen almost each day of the week – some are 'official,' some informal – and all are a great place to catch the flavor of the island, talk to local people, and enjoy a kaleidoscope of tastes and colors. Come early for the best selection! From truck beds, tiny stands, or the trunks of cars, local farmers will sell their fruits, vegetables, and flowers at prices more reasonable than the supermarkets. Manoa lettuce, as little as $2

Shoppers wait for starting time at the farmers' market. Bananas, pineapples, papayas cost only a dollar or two, flowers just a bit more.

for a half-dozen small heads, will be fresh from the garden and taste of Kauai's sunny skies and salt air. You'll never want iceberg again! You may find avocados at 2 for $1; fresh basil, oregano, chives or marjoram; a shiny dark purple eggplant with just the right sound when you thump it, and bananas of all kinds – Williams, Bluefield, and apple-bananas. Don't be put off by the short, fat, drab-skinned exterior, for inside the fruit looks like golden sand at sunset and tastes like bananas laced with apples.

The starting time is important to know. At the Koloa market, you'll see a rope tied across the parking lot which serves as a starting line, complete with a shrill whistle, to ensure an equal chance for buyers and sellers. It drops at noon on the nose, so don't be late! At some markets, official opening time doesn't deter buyers. They simply 'reserve' their selections, permitted as long as no money changes hands. Sellers write buyers' names on bags of fruit, or on pineapple leaves, or even give out numbered tokens, like a hat check. The actual buying can be accomplished in a matter of moments – but you have to remember where everything is stashed.

Sellers quickly become friends. One may offer you a slice of star fruit, or a section of honey sweet orange with deceptively green skin, or a slice of juicy pineapple topped with passion fruit. Papayas will be giants, the sunrise variety if you're lucky, for their red-orange center rivals the color of the sun. Try fresh lime juice, or Jeremy's favorite, the juice from a passion fruit, to spark the papaya's mellow sweet flavor with tartness. Even if you aren't cooking, you'll be tempted by stringbeans as long as shoelaces, squash with squeaky skins, tomatoes still warm and fragrant, all kinds of vegetables with odd shapes, even fresh coconuts. You may even find leis of pakalana or plumeria for $3 a strand. Take home tropical flowers by the bunches – bird of paradise, parrot colored heliconia blossoms, stalks of fragrant white or yellow ginger. Be ready to bargain if you are buying in quantity, and take their advice about venturing into new tastes. Most sellers price in $1 or $2 packages, so bring singles.

The largest markets are in Kapa'a, Koloa and Lihue, and they are a little tricky to find. On Fridays, the Lihue market is in the parking lot behind the Vidinha football stadium just south of the airport. Enter off Kapule Highway (Rt. 51) at the small street leading into the stadium at its

Farmers' Markets

Monday	noon	**Koloa**, Ball Park on Rt. 520 next to the fire house. Map 3
	3 pm	**Lihue**, Kukui Grove by Star Market
Tuesday	2 pm	**Hanalei,** west of town on Rt. 560. Map 2
	3:30	**Kalaheo** Neighborhood Center, Papalina at Rt. 50. Map 3
Wednesday	3:00	**Kapa'a** behind the armory. Map 1
Thursday	3:30	**Hanapepe**, Town Park. Map 4
	4:30	**Kilauea**, Kilauea Neighbor Ctr. Map 2
Friday	3:00	**Lihue**, Vidinha football stadium parking lot, near airport. Map 1
Saturday	9 am	**Kekaha** Neighborhood Center, Elepaio off Rt. 50. Map 4
	9 am	**Kilauea**, Christ Memorial Church. Map 2

northern corner, or turn off Rice St. at Holoko Road. The Wednesday Kapa'a market is opposite the armory; take Kukui Road off Rt. 56 and turn right at the end; then make the next right onto Kahau Road and park on your left. Or take the new bypass road from Wailua to Kapa'a; it comes out just at the end of Kahau Road. For the Koloa market, turn left off Koloa Road just before the baseball field. You'll see all the cars parked in the lot.

Just missed the market? You'll find roadside produce stands all over the island. Look for low acid, 'Sugar Loaf' pineapples from Kahili Farms, strawberry papayas, bananas of all kinds. Near Lihue, stop at *People's Market* on Rt. 56 in Puhi. Just outside Kilauea, stop in at *Moloa' a Fruit Stand* for a great selection of wonderful fruits, smoothies, and frosties.

Fitness & Athletic Clubs

Kauai Athletic Club next to Kukui Grove Shopping Center in Lihue offers daily, weekly, and monthly visitor rates, a variety of classes and machines, and squash courts (245-5381). Nearby is *Curves* for women only

(245-9790). In Poipu, *Hyatt Resort* offers classes, first-rate facilities, as well as massage and therapy (742-1234; www.anaraspa.com). A $115 massage allows you to use all spa facilities. You can make it an all day deal! Northshore, *Princeville Health Club*, in the Prince Golf Course clubhouse, has sweeping views of the fairways and ocean (www.princeville.com; 826-5030) and visitor rates for classes, personal training, massage, and yoga.

In Kapaʻa, a 'local' style gym at modest rates: *Kauai Gym* (823-8210). Hours are limited. *At Your PACE* (822-4111) features hydraulic resistance machines ($5/visit). Westside, *Iron Hut* (335-3383) and *Kauai Xtreme Fitness* (335-0049) in Port Allen. North shore: *Devaki* offers yoga and personal fitness training (826-9990), and *Pure Kauai* offers personalized fitness with a full range of activities, accommodations, and organic cuisine; it's not cheap ($400-$1000/day/pp) 866-457-7873; www.purekauai.com.

Fresh Island Fish

You can sometimes find locally-caught fresh fish at roadside stands or farmers' markets. Otherwise, try *Fish Express* in Lihue (245-9918) for filets of shibiko (baby yellow fin tuna), ono, ulua, and snappers of all hues – pink, grey, red. Prices vary with the weather, the season, the tides, even the moon, and are generally higher in winter, when fishing boats face rougher seas. The adventurous can try opihi (limpets) raw in the shell with seaweed, or smoked marlin. Your fresh fish can be vacuum sealed for shipping. Also try

G's Fish Market (246-4440) 4361 Rice St., Lihue. In Hanamaʻulu, stop in at *Ara's* for homemade ahi poki (raw fish, onions, Hawaiian salt and shoyu) and sushi platters. In Kapaʻa, try the inexpensive *Kuhio Market* and *Pono Market*, a local favorite for

Bouquets of heliconia and ginger for $3.50

poki. The fresh ahi in *Safeway* in Wailua is first rate, and nearby *Cost-U-Less* sells fresh fish in large packages for a family barbecue. On the north shore, try *Hanalei Dolphin*'s fish market.

Flowers

The exotic shapes and colors of heliconia – 'lobster claw,' 'sexy pink,' 'caribea' – the fragrance of pikaki and plumeria! At farmers' markets, you can buy armfuls of spectacular flowers for a few dollars. And for those friends back home taking care of your dog, what better way to say thank you than a bouquet? You can order a lovely assortment of flowers (about $48), boxed and shipped via Federal Express, arriving fresh and gorgeous in any mainland city – red and pink ginger, anthurium, heliconia. Some pieces last nearly two weeks. An internet search leads to a dozen small family farms selling flowers online: www.flowerskauai.com or www.a-tropical-flower.com. In Hanapepe, visit Mackie Orchids: www.mackieorchids.com. In Kilauea, try Kauai Orchids (828-0904; www.kauaiorchids.com). Learn about varieties; buy plants to take home. *Hawaii Tropical Flower & Foliage Associations* mails a free color brochure of Kauai's flowers (PO Box 1067, Lawai HI 96765).

Flower Leis

Lei in ti leaf wrap

The fragrance of pikake or white ginger; the cool, silky touch of petals; the delicate yet rich colors of orchids and plumeria – even in words, flower leis conjure up moonlit nights and ocean breezes. No vacation is complete without one, especially on your last night. Many stores (even Safeway, Longs, Wal-Mart) offer ready-made leis in a refrigerated case, but these strings of imported carnations cannot compare with a local lei which reflects the traditions of the island as well as the individual artistry of the lei maker. Order a day in advance, and pick your lei up on your way to dinner.

The *Mauna Loa lei* ($20), is a wide woven band of small purple orchids; very handsome, it is often given to boys at graduation. *White ginger* makes spectacular creation of white, or sometimes pink buds tightly threaded almost like feathers, and so fragrant that heads will turn as you walk by. Try the slender strand of fragrant green *pakalana* ($10/strand of 100 flowers), or the small, white *stephanotis,* similar in shape to a lilac blossom and even more fragrant ($10). *Pikake,* a tiny and delicate white flower the Hawaiian lei for weddings, has a wonderful, spicy scent ($10/ strand). *Plumeria* leis are the most common. Usually white or yellow and sometimes pink or deep red, the large blossoms have a lovely perfume.

At farmers' markets, you can sometimes find leis for $4 to $5. At *People's Market* in Puhi (245-2210), opposite Kauai Community College, you'll find leis made fresh each morning, usually plumeria and sometimes, pikake, pakalana, or ilima. In Anahola, you can buy plumeria leis in yellow or mixed colors from a roadside stand opposite Ono Char Burger, or at 3805 Makio (turn off Rt. 56 towards the ocean at the 'lei' sign just south of town, and follow the signs). For something really special, order a lei from one of the island's artists. Winnie Cummings in Anahola (821-1514) and Linda Pitman in Kilauea (828-1572) grow their own flowers and will create a lei just for you, with fragrant pakalana, ginger, or orchids, at reasonable prices ($10 to $15). Commercial florists include *Flowers & Joys* (822-4415); *NJB Flowers* in Kapaʻa (821-1569); and *Flowers Forever* (Lihue 245-4717). Check display cases in *Pono Market* (822-4581) and in Wailua at *JC's Minimart* (822-5961), where a plumeria lei can also be strung while you wait. Lei makers demonstrate techniques and designs at the Kauai County Fair each August. Order leis online at www.kauaiflowers.com.

Your lei will look wonderful for one wearing, but the fragrance lingers even when the petals turn brown. Store your lei in a plastic bag in the refrigerator overnight so you can wear it, even though wilted, at breakfast, then dry it for a Hawaiian potpourri. You can wear your lei onto the plane home, though the flowers quickly turn brown in air conditioning. Preserve it in a plastic bag so it stays fresh to cheer your morning coffee back home.

Fruits & Island Sweets

Fresh fruits can be bought all over the island, sometimes from a truck parked by the side of the road. In Kilauea, on the road to the lighthouse, the Martin Farm sells papayas on the honor system. Choose your fruits and leave your money in a box (closed Sundays). In Anahola, visit Aunty Audrey's small roadside stand on Holualele Road; turn towards the mountains just north of Ono Burger on Rt. 56 (closed Sundays). To taste Kauai's strawberry sunrise papayas back home on a cold winter morning, call Boy Akana Farms in Kalihiwai (800-572-7292), and they will ship 10 pounds by federal express (about $40) – a great 'care package' idea for exam week – and worth every penny on a dark, cold winter morning.

You'll love fruit 'frosties,' a tasty confection of frozen fruit whipped smooth like soft ice cream. Try combinations of mango, banana, papaya, pineapple – whatever is in season – at the *Moloa'a Sunrise Fruit Stand* on Rt 56 north of Anahola and *Banana Joe's* (Kilauea). Stock up on local fruits. Tropical fruit 'smoothies' are made at fruit stands like *Moloa'a Sunrise, Banana Joe's* and *Mango Mama's* (Kilauea), *Killer Juice Bar* and *Java Kai* (Kapa'a), *People's Market* (Puhi, opposite Kauai Community College) and of course *Jamba Juice,* now in Lihue.

Be sure to sample local sweets. *Pono Market* in Kapa'a is like a visit to the island's past, with ethnic favorites like coconut manju. Try the light, sweet pretzel cookies at *Hamura's Saimin.* Macadamia nut cookies taste like Kauai even if you're back home. Try the traditional island favorite, *Kauai Kookie Kompany,* sold in most supermarkets or at the factory store in Hanapepe. In the Waipouli Complex, *Po Po's* mixes macadamia nuts with chocolate chips or coconut. Try *Kauai Tropical Fudge* in wonderful island flavors, including banana, macadamia nut, Kona coffee, even pina colada! Look for it in the *Kauai Products Store* in Kukui Grove, Lihue.

Lilikoi chiffon pie is a Kauai tradition – a light confection of passion fruit. A local legend, *Omoide Bakery* (Rt. 50 in Hanapepe), has baked the island's best pies by secret family recipe since 1956. Pies are sold frozen

(order in advance 335-5291) and will keep for several hours in the car (best in a cooler). Sample pies at Hamura's Saimin in Lihue, Green Garden Restaurant in Hanapepe, Camp House Grill in Kalaheo, and pumpkin crunch pie at Oki Diner in Lihue. On your way to the airport, stop by at Hamura's and pick up a pie – it will be frozen – and if you put it into a carry-on plastic insulator pack (at Walmart for $10), it will arrive home safe and sound. Don't miss Anahola Granola, wonderful with apple bananas for breakfast! Papaya seed dressing, created in Kalaheo, gives salad a whole new dimension, and also look for Aunty Lilikoi's mustard, with perfect bite and sweetness. Huli Huli Sauce is a family favorite marinade for fish or chicken. Country Moon Rising makes terrific guacamole and mung bean salsa. Look for these treats in grocery stores, even Wal-Mart.

In Hanapepe, taro chips are still made in the *Taro Ka* factory. When taro is scarce, they make potato chips, including some flavored with Chinese spices. Ready for a new twist to your PBJs? Just east of Kalaheo, stop in at the *Kukui* factory for jams like guava-strawberry or passion fruit, or coconut syrup to try on pancakes. Make up gift boxes at factory-direct prices (.8 mile past the junction of Rt. 50 and Rt. 530).

Kauai Gifts

Look for special island-made gifts at the unique *Kauai Products Store* (246-6753) in Kukui Grove Center, as well as *Hilo Hattie's* in Lihue, *Kong Lung* in Kilauea, *Hula Moon* in Koloa. *Island Soap* in Kilauea and Koloa

Papaya tree – reach up for breakfast!

(handmade-soap.com) is fragrant with coconut, pikake or plumeria. For handmade clothes, stop at *Kapaia Stitchery* just north of Lihue on Rt. 56 (Don't take the bypass road, or you'll miss it) where island seamstresses still make quilts and dresses with the same care their own grandmothers did. Custom aloha shirts made by Julie's seamstresses fit better and cost less than most mass-produced shirts. *Kilohana Clothing* at Kilohana has beautiful women's and men's clothing designs in vintage cloth by Melody (246-6911). For colorful Hawaiian fabrics, visit *Discount Fabric Warehouse* (246-2739; gotfabric.com) in Lihue, and Vicky's in Kapaʻa (822-1746). Nearby is *Kauai Products Fair* for bargain prices. For fresh poi: 826-4764; hanaleipoi.com.

Kauai's Golf Magic *by Robert Trent Jones, Jr.*

I have played golf all over the world, and I keep coming back to Kauai! The island has unique courses, offering both challenges and enjoyment. With the north shore's spectacular landscape to work with, I laid out the original Princeville Resort course in three distinct nines to take advantage of the dramatic cliffs and breathtaking ocean views. The Ocean nine have great vistas and the sounds of the sea off the cliffs; the Woods thread through the trees, with a wonderful Zen-influenced bunker, an idea from my many trips to Japan.

Ranked first in Hawaii by *Golf Digest*, The Prince Course is more bold and dramatic, and I designed it to retain some of the wilderness character of its site. Carved out of heavy vegetation, it meanders through valleys, with panoramic views. It's a tough course (I'm told the beverage cart driver sells more golf balls than drinks) but from the proper set of tees, I guarantee you'll enjoy this golf nature trek!

On the south shore, the Kiahuna Plantation Course is a fun, yet memorable test with rolling fairways, sweeping bunkers, and small, traditional greens. Our newest creation, Poipu Bay Resort adjacent to the Hyatt Regency, is the site of the PGA's Annual Grand Slam of Golf. The back nine border the ocean, where the almost constant yet variable wind is the challenge. You have to make precise shots, judging both distance and the wind, or it will blow the ball off the green. Many holes hug the cliffs, and special attention has been given to ancient Hawaiian sacred grounds.

On the east side, the Wailua Golf Course is one of the best public courses in the country. Many holes flank the ocean and are protected by palm trees. This course is a must! I am also a fan of the Kiele Course. The finishing holes really get your attention, particularly the par-three 15th, requiring skill and a brave heart to tame.

No matter which course you choose, you really can't go wrong on Kauai. The people are friendly, temperatures comfortable, the pace slow – and a nice surprise around each corner! There's something magical about Kauai that brings people back. I know. I'm one of them!

Golf Courses

The *Princeville Makai Course* in Hanalei, designed by Robert Trent Jones, Jr., is a 27 hole, world-class championship course with 3 challenging nines: Lake, Woods, and Ocean, famous for spectacular views and the dramatic 141-yard seventh hole, where the ocean, foaming like a cauldron, separates tee and green. Ranked 6th in the state, and one of *Golf Digest's* top 25 resort courses for 20 years. Fees, including carts, are $125 ($105/ Princeville Hotel guests; $110/Princeville Resort guests); $85 after 1:30 pm. Tee times: 826-5070 or 800-826-1105; www.princeville.com (virtual views). Same day tee times: 826-3580. Enter Princeville main gate. Map 2

The Prince Course is Hawaii's number-one rated course, according to *Golf Digest.* The 18 hole, 6521-yard course, designed by Robert Trent Jones, Jr., is spectacular, set in 390 acres of pastureland, with rolling hills, deep ravines, tropical jungle with streams and waterfalls. Fees, including carts, are $175 ($130/Princeville Hotel guests; $150/Princeville resort guests). After 12 noon, $120. Call 826-2727 or 800-826-4400 for tee times, or visit princeville.com (check out the virtual views). For same day tee times call 826-5001. Located just east of Princeville on Rt. 56. Map 2

Kiahuna Golf Club, Poipu, designed by Robert Trent Jones, Jr., is an 18 hole, par 70, links-style course, predominantly flat, with smooth, fast greens and tradewind challenges. At 6,353 yards from the tips, this course is geared for the recreational golfer. Fees: $45/9 holes or $65 after 11 am ($45 after

2:30 pm/weekdays), including shared cart. Ask about weekly pass ($265). 742-9595; www.kiahunagolf.com. Map 3.

Poipu Bay Resort Golf Course, Poipu, designed by Robert Trent Jones, Jr. has been the home of the Grand Slam of Golf since 1994. Par 72 Scottish links-style course, 6845 yards from the blue tees, set in 210 acres of sugar plantation land along the ocean. Views are spectacular! With cart, $125. Discount times: $95 after noon; $45 after 3 pm. Inquire about discounts for guests at some hotels. 742-8711 or 800-858-6300; www.gvhawaii.com/ poipubay/poipubay.htm Adjacent to the Hyatt Regency Resort. Map 3.

Wailua Municipal Golf Course, Rt. 56 in Wailua. *Golf Digest* ranked it in top 25 U.S. municipal courses. Popular 18 hole, 6658 yard, par 72 course is built along the ocean on rolling terrain amid ironwood trees and coconut palms. Fairways are narrow, greens smallish, grass on the tough side, but unbeatable fees: $44/weekends (it gets crowded!) $32/ weekdays. Half price after 2 pm. $14/cart/18 holes. 241-6666; www.gvhawaii.com/wailua/ wailua.htm. Map 1.

Kukuiolono Golf Course, Kalaheo. 9 holes, par 35 with spectacular views over 178 acres and a lovely Japanese garden. Located on a bluff with challenging tradewinds. Greens fee: $7; carts available. A local favorite, a secret most don't want to share! Turn south off Rt. 50 in Kalaheo at Papalina Rd. (the stoplight) and drive .8 mile. Enter gate on right. 332-9151; www.gvhawaii.com/kukio/kukio.htm. Map 3.

Kauai Lagoons Golf & Racquet Club, in the Kauai Lagoons Resort, Lihue, overlooks beautiful Kalapaki Bay. Designed by Jack Nicklaus, the 262 acre *Kiele Course* is geared for golfers with a 20-handicap or better, and was named one of the Top 100 courses in America by *Golf Digest*. The front nine are long and rugged with many mounds and swales. The back nine run out to the ocean, with spectacular views of waves crashing against the rocks, and prevailing tradewinds of up to 15 m.p.h. on the southeast corner. Fees, including cart, are $170 ($135/$140 outside resort; $125/ Marriott guests). After noon, $110/$115. An extra-long course (7070 yards) with 4 tees, the *Mokihana Course* (previously called *Kauai Lagoons Course*) ranked by *Golf Magazine* in the top ten of "America's most playable courses," is a shotmaker's course with many bunkers and undulating greens. 6,942 yards from the tips. Fees, including cart, are $120 ($85/ outside resort; $75/Marriott guests) $65 after 11am. 241-6000 or 800-634-6400; www.kauailagoonsgolf.com. Ask about the *'Kauai Golf Challenge'* rate ($346 for Kiele, Princeville, and Poipu Bay courses). Map 1

Grove Farm 'Puakea' Course near Kukui Grove Center, Lihue, designed by Robin Nelson, winds through 200 acres of former sugar plantation land–sheer ravines, freshwater streams and views of Mount

Hau'upu, the Hule'ia Stream, and the ocean. Recently expanded from 10 holes, the 18 hole course offers varying wind and weather conditions, with a local-style friendliness. Managed by Billy Caspar Golf. 6,954 yards. $125/ before 1 pm and $65/after 1 pm; 9 holes/$65. 245-8756. A great website for photos, online bookings, and an e-newsletter: www.puakeagolf.com. Map 1

Many hotels/condos have contracts with the pro shops, so ask about a 'resort discount.' An *'Ohana Card'* ($21.95) earns a 'visitor discount' at some island courses. 383-5500; www.gvhawaii.com.

Hiking

Hiking can be a spectacular way to see Kauai, for more than half of the island's 551,000 square miles is forestland, and many of its most beautiful regions are inaccessible by car. However, hiking Kauai is not without risks. Many trails can become dangerous from washouts and mudslides, and in the

The Kalalau Trail into the Na Pali wilderness begins where paved road ends, at Ke'e Beach on the north shore.

Reward: The view after climbing the first quarter – mile.

Na Pali coastal region, where trails are often etched into the sides of sheer cliffs, hikers must be wary of waves crashing over the rocks without warning, as well as vegetation which masks the edge of a sheer drop. A friend, for example, broke his ankle one summer when plants gave way under his feet near the edge of a ravine.

Careful planning is a must. Before your trip, get maps. Order a recreational map of hiking trails in the forest preserves from *Na Ala Hele*, a non-profit group helping with trail improvement, by sending $6 (cashier's check or money order only) to *Division of Forestry*, Kauai District (3060 Eiwa St., Room 306, Lihue HI 96766), or save $1 and pick it up at the office. The *Na Ala Hele* trail specialist for Kauai is Craig Koga, *Dept. of Land and Natural Resources*, 3060 Eiwa Street, Lihue, Hawaii 96766 (808 274-3433). For an overview, check the *Na Ala Hele* website (www.hawaiitrails.org), and the DLNR site (www.hawaii.gov/dlnr). For information on the Na Pali region, contact Wayne Souza (808-274-3444).

Some private companies offer excellent information. For an overview, visit www.teok.com for maps of Kauai's geological, archeological and topographical profiles. For downloadable maps and some trail descriptions, try www.hawaii-guide.net. Look at Bob Smith's *Hiking Kauai,* the original guidebook to hikes on Kauai; Kathy Morey's *Kauai Trails;* or Jerry and Janine Sprout's *Kauai Trailblazer.* Request a catalog of books and maps for hiking and camping on Kauai from *Hawaii Geographic Society,* PO Box 1698, Honolulu HI 96806. When you arrive, you can call the *Division of Forestry* in Lihue (274-3433) for current trail conditions.

The most famous trail, the *Kalalau trail,* is a spectacular but strenuous 11 mile hike through the Na Pali cliff region, though even recreational hikers can enjoy the first few miles. This subsection, the *Hanakapiʻai trail,* has breathtaking views of the coast along switchbacks which take you into forest and back out to the ocean. About a quarter-mile of uphill walking brings you to a magnificent view of Keʻe Beach and the Haʻena reefs. Two more miles of rigorous up and down hiking will bring you to Hanakapiʻai Beach, nestled like a brilliant jewel in a picturesque, terraced valley. Unfortunately, this beach has currents far too dangerous for swimming, and the rip currents can be so powerful that more than one unwary hiker standing in the surf at knee level has been caught up in a sudden, large wave, pulled out to sea and drowned. On a recent hike, we helped some folks who were stranded on the sand bar by high surf; fortunately we had a rope and a tall, strong friend! Beyond the beach, you can take the trail to Hanakapiʻai Falls. It's very strenuous; the path crosses the river in several places and at times you may have to hold onto trees to keep your balance on the rocky and wet footing. Allow 6 hours for the round trip from Keʻe

The Kalalau trail from Keʻe Beach to Hanakapiʻai winds along the rugged Na Pali coastline, through dense vegetation, along switchbacks and over rocks, sometimes only inches away from a sheer drop. Views are incredible! Mud from the frequent rain showers can create slippery conditions, so good footgear is a must.

Beach to Hanakapia'i Falls, with a rest stop for a picnic. Carry plenty of water and fill up at Ke'e Beach, the last source of safe drinking water.

Important safety information: When it rains, this narrow trail gets muddy – and dangerously slippery, a fact we appreciated first hand when we saw a woman slip over the steep edge and disappear down into the slick vegetation. Fortunately, her quick-thinking companion had managed to grab her hand so that we could pull her back up. In many places, the trail is actually a stream bed, and fills with water after heavy rains. Essential items: shoes with good traction for slippery rocks and mud (instead of jogging shoes or flip flops), sunscreen, strong insect repellent, a hat, perhaps a nylon poncho, and even a walking stick. (Consider a telescoping stick that can double as a monopod for your camera; a great one by Cascade can be found at www.rei.com). Carry drinking water because the bacterium causing leptospirosis is found in almost all of Kauai's rivers and streams. For an update on trail conditions in Na Pali, call *Pedal & Paddle* (826-9069) in Hanalei, the *Division of State Parks* (274-3444), or *Kayak Kauai Outfitters* (826-9844), which offers guided hikes of the Kalalau Trail. *Kauai Visitor's Bureau* (245-3971) can help arrange local guides.

In Wailua, we like to hike *Mount Nounou Trail*, on Sleeping Giant Mountain. This semi-strenuous 1.75-mile hike takes you to the Ali'i Vista Hale picnic shelter on the 'chest' of the Sleeping Giant. From this vantage point, you can see the inland mountains to Mount Wai'ale'ale and the Wailua River winding to the sea. The trail head is on Halelilo Road in

Hanakapi'ai Beach

Wailua. From Kuhio Highway (Route 56), take Halelilo Road for 2 miles and park on the right near telephone pole #38. After a moderate ascent over switchbacks, about an hour or less, with some climbing over boulders, through dense guava and eucalyptus, you'll come to a junction marked by multiple-rooted hala trees. The trail to the left leads to another fork, and either of these paths will lead to the shelter. Explore for the best view, though avoid trails leading south towards the giant's 'head' as they can be hazardous. Coastal views are exhilarating!

The *Koke'e Forest* region has a different kind of beauty. Within this 4,345 acre wilderness preserve are 45 miles of trails, from pleasant walks to rugged hikes, as well as fresh water fishing streams, and the 20 square mile highland bog known as Alaka'i Swamp. From the Koke'e Lodge, day hikers can choose from three trails which explore the plateau and Waimea Canyon rim, ranging from the half-mile 'Black Pipe Trail' to the 1.5 mile 'Canyon Trail' along the north rim of Waimea Canyon, past upper Wa'ipo'o Falls to the Kumuwela Overlook. From this perch you can see the canyon's 3,600-foot depth and 10 mile stretch to the sea. Download maps, detailed trail information, helpful hiking tips at www.aloha.net/~inazoo/kokee.htm. For guides, contact *Koke'e Museum* 335-9975 (www.aloha.net/~kokee), make reservations for guided summer Sunday walks, and sign up for an e-newsletter. For hunting and fishing licenses: *Koke'e Lodge* (335-6061).

The *Sierra Club* sponsors hikes on Kauai each month. Popular destinations: in Na Pali, the Kalalau Trail to Hanakapi'ai; Sleeping Giant Mountain trails on the eastern shore; Shipwreck Beach to Maha'ulepu on the south shore; on the west, the first few miles along the coast beyond Polihale. Send a stamped, addressed envelope to PO Box 3412, Lihue HI 96766 (www.hi.sierraclub.org/Kauai/kauai.html .

Princeville Ranch Hike & Kayak offers a terrific hike (45 min) combined with kayaking along a secluded stream (1/2 hour), picnic lunch at a hidden waterfall, before the return trip (4 hrs total/$94). Great views, peaceful quiet, and healthful lunch (www.kauai-hiking.com; 826-7669 or 888-955-7669). You can hike to spectacular *Kipu Falls* with *Outfitters Kauai* ($119), explore a hidden but previously inaccessible gem on private land (742-9667; www.outfitterskauai.com). Guides are knowledgeable, and the group (up to 20) proceeds at a leisurely pace on foot and by kayak to the falls, a tour for recreational hikers and kayakers (those who like to push ahead may feel constrained) amid wonderful scenery. *Kauai Nature Tours* (742-8305 or 888-233-8365; www.teok.com) features naturalist guides with impressive knowledge, and hikes at all skill levels. *Aloha Kauai Tours* takes you into the back country by 4x4 to hike into the 'blue hole' at the base of Mt. Wai'ale'ale: www.alohakauaitours.com. 245-1113/ 800-452-1113.

Horseback Riding

Guided trail rides are a unique way to explore Kauai. NORTH SHORE: *Princeville Ranch Stables* (formerly Po'oku Ranch) offers rides across the ranch lands and towards the mountains for views (from $65), or a four–hour ride ($120) with a hike to a waterfall for a picnic lunch and swim (www.princevilleranch.com; 826-6777). Groups of 6-8 are taught horse-manship, a unique feature. A morning ride avoids the heat of the day. Take sunglasses and a hat which won't blow off. (Once you're on board, it's hard to climb down and chase it). Closed Sundays. *Silver Falls Ranch* in Kilauea escorts groups along the beautiful Kalihiwai Ridge ($80-$110 for 2 to 3 hrs) with lunch and swim at a waterfall (828-6718; www.silverfallsranch.com).

SOUTH SHORE: *CJM Stables* offers one or two-hour tours near Maha'ulepu Beach for $75-$95 (Poipu, 742-6096; www.cjmstables.com). Tour guides are very friendly and provide historical information, as well as photo-opportunities (you can trot). Closed Sundays. *Red Dirt Trails* takes you through Koloa town to the fields beyond. (652-4045). Map 3.

EASTSIDE: call *Esprit de Corps* in Kapa'a for lessons (from $36) and trail rides (you can canter on the advanced ride!) in the lush Sleeping Giant Mountain area. From $111, including a ride to a spiritual meditation overlooking Mt.Waile'ale (822-4688; www.kauaihorses.com). Try a wedding on horseback! Owner Dale Rosenfeld enjoys children (she has ponies), and visitors with disabilities. Map 1. WESTSIDE, near Waimea, *Garden Island Ranch* offers tours of the ranch land along the ocean and lower western rim of the Waimea Canyon (limit 2 riders). 338-0052. Map 4

Ice Cream & Shave Ice

Kauai has its own ice cream factory, founded by Walter Lappert who wanted to retire in paradise – and ended up in business. Demand exploded for his creamy island flavors like 'Kauai pie,' and now tourists in far away Silicon Valley enjoy *Lappert's* cones. Coldstone Creamery has made its way to Kauai, in Lihue's Kukui Grove Center and next to Safeway in Wailua. Hawaiian made *Meadow Gold* ice cream, available in Foodland and Big Save Markets, makes our favorite version of Macadamia Nut. The more calorie conscious can try TCBY in Wailua (white chocolate macadamia nut) and Kukui Grove Center and *Zack's* in the Coconut Marketplace.

Shave Ice is a special island treat. Stop in at the *Wishing Well* in Hanalei (the silver trailer by Kayak Kauai) for some of the best flavors and textures. Also try the Shave Ice stand next to *Hamura's Saimin* on Kress St., Lihue. On main street, Waimea (Rt. 560), try all 60 flavors at *Jo Jo's*.

Internet

Local dial-up: AOL: 245-4284 and Earthlink: 855-0020. Arrange local dial-up with Hawaiian.net for $10/2 weeks (no set-up charge). 800-536-5162 /808-245-4598 or accounts@hawaiian.net. At last, high speed has come to Kauai! The Hyatt charges $20/day for it; Waimea Cottages offers it free (and wireless), and you can also try the island's internet cafés (p. 233).

Jewelry

Goldsmith's Kauai in the Kinipopo Shopping Village, Wailua is a must stop! You'll find original designs crafted of gold, silver, precious gems, or lustrous pearls. Dana Romsdal and her award-winning designers create beautiful pieces. Check photographs of their designs, or let them create something special. Seashell designs in gold are lovely, gem settings are exquisite, yet prices are very reasonable. We worked with Dana to create a pearl birthday pendant, watching the design develop on its own page at www.goldsmiths-kauai.com (822-4653). In Kapa'a, *Jim Saylor* works with fine gems. While you watch, he can sketch a special setting for a loose gemstone, or help you select from his portfolio (822-3591). Ni'ihua Shell leis can be found at *Kauai Gold* in Wailua's Coconut Marketplace, and at the *Kauai Museum Shop*, with certificates of authenticity and a guarantee of workmanship. Without the certificates, prices are less.

Luaus

For centuries, Hawaiians have celebrated birthdays, weddings, anniversaries, and festive occasions, with a luau feast, featuring a whole pig roasted in an imu or underground oven and served with a colorful array of dishes, including sweet potatoes, poi, fresh island fish, chicken cooked in coconut and taro, tropical fruits and salads. The Hyatt, Sheraton, Marriott, and Coconut Coast Resort all offer luau extravaganzas. At the *Princeville Hotel* on the north shore, dancers perform by the oceanside pool; kids will love the view from the bridge! (826-9644). The show at the *Hyatt* features more contemporary music and choreography along with the traditional (742-1234). *Marriott Courtyard* in Wailua (822-3455) has a new Hawaiian extravaganza by Tihati (www.tihati.com) ($55/pp/ one child free with adult). *Smith's Tropical Paradise* (821-6895 in Wailua) offers Asian/ Polynesian dances, and you can buy a ticket to the show, presented in a natural amphitheater, without also paying for the buffet. Go early to see the gardens, though the bar does not open until 6:30 pm, even for soft drinks. *Kilohana Plantation* tells the story of Kauai as well as Tahitian, Maori, Polynesian dances. The buffet includes vegetarian items (245-9593; www.gaylordskauai.com). $50/adult; $20/child.

Some excellent local shows are free. Call *Coconut Plantation Marketplace* in Wailua 822-3641 about occasional shows. At Kukui Grove in Lihue, Aloha Friday entertainment changes weekly (245-7784). Southshore: showtime at *Poipu Shopping Village* is T & Th at 5 pm (to check, call 742-2831). *Hyatt Regency* has a free show, great for kids, 6 pm nightly, at *Seaview Terrace* (742-1234). Northshore, at *Princeville Hotel*, Mauliola Cook enchants audiences with Hawaiian stories & legends in dance and chants (*Living Room* Th, Sun at 6:30 pm). Stay on to hear Ken Emerson and Michaelle Edwards sing and play slack and steel guitar. In Hanalei, Sandy and Doug McMaster serenade sunset with free slack key concerts each night at Hanalei Pavilion Beach Park, sharing their love for music and Kauai (826-1469) p. 106.

Massage, Kauai Style

For something truly special, try a truly unforgettable, Hawaiian lomi lomi massage at *Mu'olaulani* in Anahola. This special massage experience, developed by Auntie Angeline Locey, takes place in a wood steam room, and begins with a 'salt scrub' with sea salt to cleanse your skin in preparation for the amazingly soothing lomi lomi performed by a team of two. Auntie Angeline, her family and staff consider lomi lomi sacred to the Hawaiian tradition of healing. This extraordinary, incredibly relaxing two-hour experience costs a reasonable $125. Since the steamer is shared, specify if you prefer being with your own gender (though steam makes a nice curtain!) or if you'd like a massage without steam. The newest massage combines fragrant oils with smooth, heated rocks gathered on Kauai. Amazing! Reservations 822-3235. Mornings only. Closed weekends.

At *Tri Health Ayurveda Center* in Kilauea, try Samvahana, a healing oil massage. Following centuries old Kerela Ayurveda tradition, two therapists massage warm oils fragrant with herbs into your skin, one therapist working on the right, the other on your left body, in synchronized, rhythmic patterns, as Indian Music plays. Then, you rest in a specially designed steam chamber, to allow the healing oils to penetrate, followed by a refreshing cool shower enhanced with aromatic bathing powder. Those seeking a blend of the physical with the metaphysical will love it, as will those looking for an exceptional bodily delight (from $130/pp). Reservations 828-2104; 800 455-0770. Take home wonderfully fragrant oils (www.oilbath.com).

Day Spas are becoming a feature on Kauai. *Makaiwa Spa* in the Kauai Coast Resort, *Wailua* (821-2626) offers massage, wraps, facials, manicures, including a 'Hot Stone Raindrop Therapy': warm essential oils drip gently onto your back and are then massaged into the skin with smooth, hot rocks. A wonderfully soothing experience. *Aloha Day Spa* in Lihue (246-2414) offers a full range of treatments, close to the Marriott. At *Hyatt's Anara Spa* a massage ($115) or pedicure ($70) allows you to use spa facilities, including lap pool, steam room, sauna, weight room. (742-1234; anaraspa.com).

Hawaiian Music

Hawaiian music has a more contemporary sound, thanks to Keali'i Reichel and others who compose in Hawaiian language. Keali'i's first album, *Kawaipunahele*, exploded onto the music scene in 1994 and has become *the* bestselling album of Hawaiian music. His next albums, *Lei Hali'a, E O Mai,* and *Melelana*, should be in your car's CD changer to soothe those traffic blues! Keali'i's newest album *Ke'alaokamaile* ('The Scent of Maile') is a beautiful tribute to family, especially his grandmother. Find the English and/or Hawaiian lyrics of many of his wonderful songs at www.interpac.net/~nahenahe/kealii/songbook/.

The classics include the Brothers Cazimero (*Hawaiian Paradise* and *The Best*), The Makaha Sons of Ni'ihau, whose newest release, *Na Pua o Hawai'i*, also features some of Hawaii's singing greats like Robert Cazimero, Cyril Pahinui, and Dennis Pavao. Also listen to Israel Kamakawiwo'ole's albums *E Ale E*, and *Facing Forward*, and Hapa's *Namahana* and *Collection*. Slack key guitar music brings you haunting melodies. Listen to Keola Beamer's wonderful new album, *Island Born*, featuring some of his original music and lyrics. Don't miss Makana, an up and coming slack key star, and *Hahani Mai* by female vocalist and songwriter, Kekuhi Kanehele.

Keali'i Reichel
Ke'alaokamaile

Find links to musicians' homepages on www.mele.com and www.hawaii-music.com; listen to Hawaiian music radio while you surf.

Musicians on Kauai

Meet some of Kauai's talented composers and musicians and listen to them play. Guitarist and vocalist

Norman Ka'awa Solomon plays his beautiful original music as well as island favorites on his albums *I Like Go Back* and *Aloha Ke Kahi*, including one of our favorite 'Kauai' songs, his unforgettable "Kalapaki." Norman plays at Happy Talk Lounge and also helps plan weddings (for details and to order CDs: www.geocities.com/kaawakauai). Don't miss Ken Emerson and vocalist Michaelle Edwards playing original slack and steel guitar compositions (order CDs *Swingin' in Paradise* and *Slack and Steel* at www.kenemerson.com) at Princeville Hotel (Th, Sun at 7 pm) and Happy Talk Lounge, where you can also hear singer/songwriter/guitarist Malani Bilyeu. His album of beautiful songs, *Islands*, includes some with a Christian emphasis.

For more than twenty years, Doug & Sandy McMaster have delighted audiences with traditional slack key guitar music. Every evening they can be found serenading sunset at the Hanalei Pavilion Beach Park. They also perform weekly benefit concerts ($10) at Hanalei Community Center (Fridays at 4 pm; Sundays at 3 pm). Call 826-1469 for ticket details. On cold winter evenings, their hauntingly beautiful music will call you right back to Hanalei. Don't miss their CDs *Hanalei Sunset, Kauai Homecoming,* and their newest *In A Land Called Hanalei* with a slack key "Puff the Magic Dragon." A resource for Hawaiian music and slack key, Doug and Sandy's web site (alohaplentyhawaii.com) features slide shows of Hanalei sunsets.

NaPali's *Pacific Tunings* is a great collection of original slack key and steel guitar. Kauai's own Jhawaiian group, The Shakers, records terrific original music as well as reggae classics on *Good Days Ahead*, or *Strictly Pleasure*, featuring Ronnie Rhoades, one of Hawaii's few female reggae singers (www.aloha.net/~shakers). Blond Boys play can't-sit-still 1960's rock classics on *Then is Now. Hal Kinnaman* plays Hawaiian, contemporary or classical guitar (335-0322) on his CD of wedding music.

For night life on Kauai, check out these local nite spots. Call for performance schedules: Eastside : Rob's Good Times Grill (246-0311), Tradewinds (822-1621). North shore: Amelia's (826-9561), Princeville Hotel (826-6522), Happy Talk Lounge (826-6522), Hanalei Gourmet (826-2524), Sushi and Blues (826-9701). Southshore: Keoki's (742-7534), The Point (Sheraton, 742-1661), Seaview Terrace (Hyatt, 731-1234), Joe's on the Green (742-9696).

Find CDs at Borders (listen before you buy), Paradise Music (www.hawaiianparadisemusic.com) at Coconut Marketplace, Koloa Big Save, and Princeville Ctr. Talk story with the friendly folks at Hanalei Video & Music (www.hanaleivideoandmusic.com). On Kauai, KKCR (96.9), north shore public radio, plays Hawaiian music (listen at home on www.hawaii-music.com). KSRF (95.9) features local musician DJs.

Photographing Kauai

***Shoot in early morning or late afternoon.** Strong sunlight can wash out colors and shadow your subjects' faces. Mornings (before 10:00) or late afternoons (after 4:00) have better light. Light is best coming from the side rather than over the photographer's shoulder.

* **Vary your composition.** For a 3-D effect, combine something in the foreground, like a palm tree, with the middle-ground and background. Try vertical shots, great for people and flowers; a vertical composition of sky, ocean, surf and sand can look like a "slice of Kauai."

* **Watch out for horizons.** They should be level, not tilting. The sea might look like it is "dumping water" to the right or left, if it's not straight. Placing the horizon across the middle of the picture cuts it in half. A higher horizon emphasizes the foreground; a lower one is a better "sky shot" for great sunsets or cloud scenes.

* **Use ISO 200 film.** Faster films will allow you faster shutter speeds and sharper images. For action shots, ISO 400 film. A polarizing filter can enhance color and improve the appearance of clouds, the ocean, and the surf break. A cap or lens filter, a zipper case, will protect against sand and salt.

* **Download images/burn CDs**: See cyber cafés, p. 233.

* **Move in close for people pictures.** Fill the frame with your subject. If you are trying to show your companion as well as the location, place the person to one side, the location to the other. Watch out for the palm tree that may appear to be growing out of the subject's head.

* **Great spots for great shots:** Sunsets & rainbows from Princeville Hotel's terrace, Na Pali cliffs from Ke'e Beach (or first mile of Kalalau trail), windsurfers at Anini or Maha'ulepu, Allerton Gardens, Kukuiolono Park plumeria grove, farmers markets, sunrise at Lydgate Park, sunset overlooking Menehune Fish Pond from the road.

Scuba & Snuba

You can dive Kauai's reefs and play with sea turtles on the south shore near Poipu or, weather permitting, on the north shore near the Ha'ena reefs. More than a dozen companies offer introductory and refresher lessons, 3-5 day PADI certification, shore and boat dives, full or half-day charters, as well as free introductory pool lessons.

Want to learn to dive? Contact *Watersports Adventures* for professional yet friendly scuba instruction, PADI certification, even refresher classes for 'rusty' divers. It has a perfect safety record, and reserved parking at Tunnels Beach! The company specializes in educational 'naturalist' dives, and night dives (even night snorkeling) when the sea lights up in vivid colors, the coral comes alive, and you can see glowing fish and eels, turtles hunting for a place to rest (821-1599).

If you have never tried diving, *Watersports Adventures* will make it special. In a free introductory lesson, you learn about diving equipment and safety and have a chance to practice with the gear in a swimming pool. Your first real dive ($106) will probably be at sheltered Koloa Landing (winter) or Tunnels (summer). Greg Winston is terrific with beginners. If you feel nervous, he may ask you to swim next to him and hold onto his arm. Greg is a very strong swimmer, so when you swim next to him, holding on to his arm, you actually cover a lot of territory. You are soon absorbed in the amazing sights – magnificent arrays of red and green coral, schools of silver or brilliant yellow fish swimming in geometric precision. You may see a ray gliding along in the shimmering water, possibly an eel hiding in the rocks, maybe even an octopus. Before you know it, you are swimming along quietly and comfortably, relaxed on your adventure! Gregg makes sure you have a good time and develop confidence. It's so great you want to head out again! Certified divers will appreciate Greg's extensive knowledge, careful planning, and well-maintained equipment.

Among the other companies, the longest established on Kauai, *Ocean Odyssey* (Lihue: 245-8681), offers a full range of lessons, shore and boat dives, certification classes, as does *Seasport Divers* (Poipu: 742-9303/800-685-5889; www.kauaiscubadiving.com) which also offers children's

programs and rental equipment, and *Dive Kauai* (822-0452/800-828-3483 www.divekauai.com).

Eastside*: Wet-n-wonderful* (Kapa'a: 822-0211), *SeaFun Kauai* (Lihue: 245-6400), *Nitrox Tropical Dives* (800-NX5-DIVE). North shore: *North Shore Divers* (828-1223) or *Hanalei Water Sports* (Princeville Hotel: 826-7509). South shore: *Fathom Five Divers* (Poipu: 742-6991 or 800-

972-3078) offers classes, certification, and dives for every level of experience, including night dives. Want to see fish but avoid carrying scuba gear? *Snuba of Kauai* offers tours with your air source on an attached flotation raft. 823-8912; www.snubakauai.com.

The best diving in all of the Hawaiian islands can be found off **Niʻihau**, the privately owned, largely undeveloped island which has been preserved by the Robinson family as a place for Hawaiian people and culture. It's a unique opportunity to explore untouched reefs, though surf is too rough in winter months. *Seasport Divers* does an all-day boat dive to Niʻihau for experienced divers ($275/3 tanks). *Blue Dolphin Charters* offers boat dives on Tuesdays and Fridays for experienced divers, as well as "fun dives" (no experience required, accompanied by an instructor) $145/one tank. 335-5553 or 877-511-131; www.kauaiboats.com. *Bubbles Below*: 332-7333.

Snorkeling

On the south shore, *Poipu Beach Park* offers excellent and relatively safe snorkeling most of the year. Just west of the rocky point dividing the park from the new Marriott (old Waiohai), you can find yellow tang, striped manini fish, butterflyfish, parrot fish, and silvery needle fish feeding on the coral. More than once, we have met a spotted box fish (Lauren has nicknamed him 'Fred') who seems curious enough to swim right up to our masks. When surf is strong, watch out for the current at the edge of the reef. Our family also enjoys '*Tunnels*,' on the north shore, so named (in part) for the intricate 'tunnels' along the edge of the reef where the water seems to plunge to unfathomable depths. In summer, we also like *Keʻe Beach*, where we find *humu humu nuku nuku apuaʻa*, Hawaii's state fish, and at any season, *Lydgate Park*, where fish swim in friendly families along the sandy bottom of a huge rock-rimmed pool.

Plan snorkeling with an eye to the tides, the weather, and the season. North shore is best in summer, when the ocean is relatively calm and you can even find it pancake flat. In winter, when surf is up on the north, Poipu Beach Park and Lydgate Park will probably have calmer water. If you snorkel where others are snorkeling, you can get help if you need it – so

Fred

avoid snorkeling at deserted beaches. Try not to lose track of where you are while you admire all the fish, and avoid snorkeling if the surf looks too rough, or a rippling wave pattern indicates strong current.

Feeding the fish can be lots of fun. If you use commercial snorkel fish food, however, you may have a problem when the plastic film casing begins to disintegrate in the water, bringing lots of fish, perhaps too many fish, for your taste! This plastic is biodegradable, not like the tougher plastics which are dangerous to sea life. We carry fish food in a plastic zip-lock bag for more control. It really doesn't matter what you put inside the bag as long as it stimulates the fish's curiosity. (Just don't use frozen peas, which are hard for the fish to digest.) Try a green leaf or piece of seaweed inside the plastic bag – it attracts the curious, rather than the ravenous, fish. Tuck your plastic bag securely into your suit, then once you are in the ocean, let the water fill it and float your 'visual display' around. Swirl the bag gently and you'll be amazed at how much interest it creates! Be sure to take your bag out of the water with you.

Both Blue Dolphin and *Holo Holo Charters* have all-day snorkeling tours to Na Pali and Ni'ihau, whose age and remoteness create unique opportunities to explore sea life. Learn about the island from experienced guides. Blue Dolphin: 335-5553; www.kauaiboats.com. Holo Holo: 335-0815; www.kauaisnorkeling.com. For other companies which tour Na Pali and offer a snorkeling stop, see Boat Tours (p. 126).

Coral cuts can be dreadful. Keep bandaids and antibiotic ointment in your beach bag and avoid touching the coral with any body part. Don't walk on it or try to pick it up. Fins won't completely protect your feet.

A well-fitting mask is important. To test the fit, place the mask on your face (without using the straps) and breathe in; a well-fitting mask will stay on by itself. Pack your own if you can. A dilute solution of detergent and water – even spit – coats the lens to avoid fogging. Greg Winston's tip: find a Naupaka leaf, crush it and rub it into the mask, then rinse. The effect is amazing!

Jeffrey Barrett snorkels with Greg Winston, Watersports Kauai, during his parents' scuba lesson

Renting gear: About $3-$5/day or $15/week for a good quality mask, fins, snorkel; about $5-$8/day for a body board.
Lihue: *Kalapaki Beach Boys* at the Kauai Marriott 246-9661.
Wailua: *PlayDirty Kauai* 823-9113. *Kauai Water Ski & Surf* 822-3574. *Kayak Kauai*, Coconut Plantation Marketplace 822-9179.
Hanalei: *Pedal & Paddle* 826-9096. *Snorkel Depot* 826-9983 has first-rate equipment, including optical snorkel masks, body boards, and surf boards ($15-$25/day).
Poipu: *Nukomoi Surf Co.* 742-7019. *Snorkel Bob's* 742-8322.
Snorkel tours: *SeaFun Kauai* 245-1113 or 800-452-1113; www.alohakauaitours.com. *Kauai Snorkel Tours* 742-7576; www.kauaisnorkeltours.com. See also Boat Tours. p. 126.

Sport Fishing

Kauai's warm tropical waters offer great fishing for big and medium to light tackle game fish. No fishing license is required, and you can depart from ports all over the island, depending on surf and season. The north shore is beautiful though too rough during winter months. From Port Allen on the west side, you have the advantage of being close to the spectacular Na Pali coastline and its amazing cliffs – fishing with a view! Most companies equip their boats with sonar, and help to pair you up with other anglers to share the cost. Expect to pay upwards of $100 for a half-day shared rate, or as much as $875 for the all-day exclusive.

EASTSIDE: Kapaʻa: *Hawaiian Style Fishing*, owned by a seasoned commercial fisherman, takes only 4 passengers on a 25 foot Kauai-built Radon, emphasizing reasonable prices and personal attention. People have a great time, and the catch is shared, not sold to restaurants. $182/8hrs or $104/4 hours as well as charters (635-7335). *Hana Paʻa Sport Fishing Charters* offers a larger craft, a 38 ft. Bertram with fly bridge, full tuna tower, main cabin, 2 bunk rooms and full head. Fish are filleted and shared. $190/6 hrs or $140/4hrs. (800-PRO-FISH; 823-6031; www.fishkauai.com). Nawiliwili: *True Blue Charters* operates the 55-ft Delta 'Konane Star' for fishing and snorkeling charters, or touring Na Pali or Kipu Kai (245-9662; www.kauaifun.com).

WESTSIDE: *Kauai Fun Tours* represents 5 small companies (335-5555; www.kauaifuntours.com). *Sport Fishing Kauai* (639-0013; www.fishing-kauai-hawaii.com) operates 3 Bertram Sport Fishers: 38-ft 'Kauai Kai,' 33-

ft 'Marlin,' & 28-ft 'Vida Del Mar,' for a maximum of 6 fishermen, cruising up to 5 miles offshore. The specialty: a 10 hour private charter to Ni'ihau ($1075). *Hoku Au Charters* operates a 30-ft Force Sport Fisher (822-5010). Also call *Open Sea Charter* (332-8213). NORTH SHORE: *Anini Charters* (828-1285; www.kauaifishing.com) departs from Anini Beach; Captain 'Honeybear' Bob shares the catch. *North Shore Charters* operates the 30-ft 'Ho'omaika'i,' for 6 passengers, departing from Anini Channel. Contact the McReynolds (828-1379; aloha.net/~themcrs). Also try *Blue Ocean Adventures* (828-1114) or *Kai Bear Sportfishing* (826-7269).

Fish for Kauai's large mouth bass on the largest freshwater reservoir in the state of Hawaii. Contact *Fishing in Paradise* (245-7358, or book online through www.trykauai.com; 821-1000).

Sunset Watching

Watch spectacular sunsets from the 'Living Room' at the Princeville Hotel, and enjoy cocktails and music, or at the Beach House on the south shore. Or go right to the beach! Bring a blanket (and possibly beach chairs, CD player with headphones, a Keali'i Reichel CD, a good book, a small ice chest with drinks and snacks). On the north shore, visit Tunnels or Ke'e, or closer to the eastern shore, Anini Beach. On the south shore, try Poipu Beach Park (you won't see the sun actually 'set' but a gorgeous 'glow'), or if you are really ambitious, drive west to Kekaha or even Polihale Beach.

Sunset Drive to Hanalei

If your accommodations are on the eastern shore, consider dinner in Hanalei, for the drive north as the sun begins to set is an experience not to be missed in summer! Check the paper for the exact time of sunset, which may be earlier than you expect because Hawaii never changes to daylight savings time. Allow an extra ten minutes to park and ready your camera.

As you begin the drive, hundreds of clouds, already tinged with peach and gold, float in an azure sky above a shimmering sea. Rt. 56 winds through the countryside and along the coast, with fields of sugar cane turning silver, and the colors of land and sky changing almost mile by mile as the declining sun deepens the greens and blues and touches everything with shades of pink and gold. At Kilauea, where the road curves to the west, a line of tall, graceful Norfolk pines stands starkly silhouetted against the blazing sky. Even the grasses, their feathery tops waving gently in evening breezes, are touched with pink, and the cattle grazing in the field seem positioned by an artist's hand. Near Princeville, the clouds, luminous with reflected golds and pinks, seem enormous, dwarfing the cliffs, whose great jagged peaks have turned an astonishing purple.

We never tire of this drive, as each sunset is different. The gleaming expanse of ocean, the sharply angled mountains, the masses of clouds are blended each night by the sun's magic into a composition of colors that will never occur again in exactly the same way. One night the sun's descent may be screened by great masses of clouds rimmed with gold and glowing tangerine against the deep purple mountains and the shimmering blue grey sea. Another time, the sun may almost blind you with its blazing, fiery gold, suffusing nearby clouds with impossible shades of orange and pink and brushing distant clouds with peach. Or, one evening, the clouds may be so thick that the setting sun is apparent only in delicate touches of apricot on the clouds hovering over the sea, muted purples on the mountains, and a silver sheen on the surface of the sea. As seasons change, so does the angle of the sun, gilding the landscape with new patterns of light and color.

A sunset in the rain is the most amazing of all. Mountains are shrouded with grey, yet above the sea, the sky is brilliant with color, with sunny clouds stretching along the horizon, rimmed with pink light from the setting sun. As dark showers move across the horizon like 'legs of the rain,' blurring the line between ocean and sky, the sun descends into stormy clouds moving slowly toward it, and, as the last light fades, dark clouds

sunset in the rain near Bali Hai Restaurant

hovering above the cliffs slowly creep across the mountains, and the world turns slowly still and dark.

If the clouds are not too thick, you can enjoy the sunset from several places in Hanalei. Less than a mile past the entrance to Princeville, you can park at a scenic overlook on Rt. 56 and see most of Hanalei's western side. But you have to contend with the distractions of traffic and car radios as well as conversations of other sunset seekers ("Ralph! I *told* you we were going to miss it!"). For a more panoramic view with greater privacy, enter Princeville and follow the signs to Pali Ke Kua, park in the lot, and enjoy the view discreetly from the lawn between the buildings.

The drive home after dinner is another sensuous experience of cool evening breezes you can almost taste as well as feel. As you drive south, you can hear wonderful sounds – the chirping of crickets, the leaves rustling in the breeze – and see the different shades of darkness in the landscape, lit by the moon against an enormous star-filled sky and the shimmering waves of the wide ocean beyond.

Surfing & Body Boarding

Surfing, like everything on Kauai, depends on the tides, the winds, and the season. In summer, the surf is 'up' on the south and west; in winter, the swell is mostly on the north. Experienced surfers will like north shore beaches like Kalihiwai, Hanalei, and Kilauea in winter, when surf is big, and in summer prefer Shipwrecks, Pakala's (or 'Infinities'), or Kekaha. To surf at Pacific Missile Range Facility at Barking Sands requires obtaining a pass, a 3-step process (see p. 75). Eastside, Wailua Bay is a local favorite, though currents near the river mouth can be dangerous. Lifeguards are on duty at Hanalei and Wailua. At any season, and no matter your skill level, be careful: the wave pattern varies along the beach – some spots are safer than others – so surf where local folks are surfing. Avoid going out alone, and observe the protocol of surfers waiting their turn out on the waves.

Channel 15 on local cable TV recycles National Weather Service buoy readings on water, surf and wind conditions. Check www.hanaleisurf.com or www.kauaistyle.com for current surf information and links. For a personalized surf forecast, call Bruce Pleas (hisurf@aloha.net or leave message at 337-9509). He reviews a myriad of data each day, and can tell you where to go, what to expect ($5/day). He also repairs surfboards, same-day if possible, with a loaner if necessary.

Want to learn to surf? On the south shore, several surf schools operate next to the Sheraton Resort in Poipu, where surf conditions are usually relatively safe – waves less than four feet and winds moderate. With *Aloha*

sharing the wave at Kalihiwai

Surf Lessons, run by Kauai-born surfing pro Chava Greenle and his father Danny, his first teacher, you can have a first-rate lesson combining one hour of personalized instruction followed by one hour of surfing on your own. One instructor works with up to six students. Skilled and supportive, Chava and Danny make sure everyone gets "up," and they really love making that happen! ($50/pp; also private lessons (639-8614). Also in Poipu, 7- time world surfing champion *Margo Ober*g has a surf school for all skill levels (742-8019). $50 for 1.5 hours. 7 students/instructor (742-8019).

Surfing pro Charlie Smith offers individualized lessons island-wide. He will drive you to wherever he thinks he'll find the island's best surf, and his unique personalized 2-hour lessons ($50/pp) can extend to include family picnics and snorkeling. For experienced surfers, it's a great way to learn the island; he knows the best breaks, has high performance boards. (634-6979; www.blueseassurfingschool.com). On the east side, *Play Dirty Kauai* offers rentals and lessons; the instructor is also lifeguard certified. They can even film the family lesson and burn a DVD. Their equipment is new, and the people friendly (823-9113). Also on the eastside, call one of Kauai's most experienced teachers, Ambrose (822-7112), who also does repairs. *Kayak Kauai* (822-9179) and *Learn to Surf* (826-7612) are other options.

Northshore: call Celeste Harvel (828-6838) or Brando Wattson *Aloha Surf & Kite School* (821-1000). Skilled surfers can arrange a lesson with elite coach Russell Lewis (828-0339). Brando also teaches **kitesurfing** ($175/2.5 hour group lesson or $250/private) with advanced equipment.

Surfboard rentals (about $25/day): Poipu: *Nukomoi* (742-8019), *SeaSport Divers* (742-9303) and *Progressive Expressions*, which also offers lessons (Koloa 742-6041). Hanalei: *Hanalei Surf Co.* (826-9000), *Kayak Kauai* (826-9844), and *Kai Kane* (826-5594). Lihue: *Kalapaki Beach Boys* (245-9662 kauaifun.com). Wailua: *Tamba Surf Shop* (823-6942).

Body Boards: When they were small, our kids loved to take their boogie boards to Poipu Beach Park. Then they grew up and craved the bigger waves. Family favorites for body boards are Kalihiwai on the north shore and Kealia on the east, also Hanalei and Kalapaki, according to surf conditions. As the sand returns to Brennecke's Beach (washed away by Hurricane Iniki) the famous wave pattern is forming once again, and you can see dozens of kids riding the first break, and younger ones catching the wave as it re-forms closer to shore. Be careful of the rocks by the seawall.

When surf is too flat (or too rough) for body boards, kids can use skimboards to catch long, exciting rides across the shallows at Kalihiwai, where the stream flows into the ocean, Hanalei, Anahola, and Kalapaki.

Tubing

As the island's economy shifts from sugar cultivation to tourism, the vast sugar lands are finding new uses. Tubing along Kauai's sugar plantation irrigation system doesn't require washboard abs and can include the whole family. You meet in Hanama'ulu, drive upcountry to a launch dock where, encircled by your big innertube, you wade into the canal, then float with the gentle current towards the sea, along the route carved out of dirt and rock by Chinese immigrant workers in the 1870's. Make it a bumper car ride if you like, kicking off rocks or the sides of the canal, or even off each other, spin the tubes, or just relax and float through hidden Kauai. You'll pass through amazing tunnels, wearing your headlamp through the first four, trying the last one in the dark! The ride goes over a mini waterfall, supervised by a staff member. At the end, there's a picnic lunch ($85). 888-270-0555 or 245-2506; www.kauaibackcountry.com. Map 1

Water Skiing

The Wailua River on the eastern shore is a great spot for water skiing, wake boarding, kneeboarding, slalom, and other water sports. For $85, you can get a driver, equipment, lessons, and the boat, and you can put the whole family onboard. *Kauai Water Ski & Surf Co.;* 822-3574 /800-344-7915. Map 1

Weddings on Kauai

There are no residency, citizenship, blood test, or waiting period requirements. Bride and groom must both be at least 18 years old to marry without parental consent, and both must apply in person for a license, valid for 30 days (pay in cash: $60). For a free "Getting Married" pamphlet, contact the *State Department of Health,* Marriage License Office, 1250 Punchbowl St., Honolulu HI 96813 (808-586-4544; www.hawaii.gov/doh/records). For a Kauai company list, check www.bestplaceshawaii.com for a registry with links to company sites like www.kauaialohawed.com, *Kauai Aloha Weddings*, operated by Huanani Rossi, a native Hawaiian who emphasizes the warm touches of Hawaiian traditions (822-1477).

You can make some important arrangements yourself. Contact the *Division of State Parks* for a list of scenic wedding sites (274-3444). *Na'Aina Kai Gardens* in Kilauea has a great beachfront site, unique garden areas, including a maze (828-0525; www.naainakai.com). For a reception, reserve a private tea room at *Hanama'ulu Tea House* (call Sally at 245-2511), or the small private room at *Kintaro* (822-3341). Restaurants with elegant private dining rooms: *Plantation Gardens* (742-2116), *Gaylord's* (245-9593; www.gaylordskauai.com), *Hukilau Lanai* which also has a dance floor (822-3441). For stand-out catering, call *Aromas*. Order traditional leis from *Irmalee Pomroy* (822-3231), an artist in flowers, or from *People's Market* in Puhi. Kauai has many talented musicians who can make your wedding sound really special. *Hal Kinnaman* plays Hawaiian, contemporary or classical guitar (335-0322). Musician/composer/vocalist *Norman Ka'awa Solomon* (p. 107) plays his unforgettable Hawaiian music & also does wedding planning (823-6281; www.geocities.com/kaawakauai).

Windsurfing

Sheltered Anini Beach is ideal for windsurfing. An offshore reef creates a peaceful lagoon in most winds, and on most days, you can see brightly colored sails and students from two windsurf companies. At *Windsurf Kauai,* Celeste Harvel (828-6838) can teach the basics as well as a complete certification course. A gifted teacher, she has special size boards for kids, and a special dog, Kahili who actually may hop aboard and go for a ride. *Anini Beach Windsurfing* (826-9463) also uses the latest in equipment and teaches surfers at all levels. Both companies offer small group lessons ($60/pp for a 3-hour session, morning or afternoon). Drop-ins are welcome; you can rent equipment ($15/hr). Stop in at *Hanalei Surf Company* for advice. EASTSIDE: *Kalapaki Beach Boys* (246-9661) for rentals and lessons.

Yoga

EASTSIDE: Studio programs: *Bikram Yoga Studio* in Kapa'a (822-5053) $15/ 90 minute 'gentle' or regular sessions. Or call private teacher *Elandra* (823-8501). SOUTH SHORE. *Anara Spa* at the Hyatt (www.anaraspa.com; 742-1234). *Joy's Oceanfront Yoga* (639-9294; www.aloha-yoga.com) offers free morning hatha yoga on Poipu Beach ($10/donation); Joy also offers private lessons, guides hikes, and does complete yoga/wellness vacation planning. NORTH SHORE. *Prince Clubhouse* (826-5030) has classes; instructor *Nutan Brownstein* also does private sessions for a spiritually-oriented yoga (826-4093). In Hanalei, *Yoga Hanalei* (826-9642) offers Ashtanga, Bikram, and other disciplines, or you can schedule private sessions with *Devaki*, who combines yoga with massage and fitness training (826-9990). With *Michaelle Edwards*, practice yoga in a serene rural setting (826-9230; manayoga.com).

Zipline

Adventurers can now have a bird's eye view of Kauai's beautiful terrain on a zipline tour ($110/per person). *Kauai Backcountry* offers a 3.5 hour tour through 7 ziplines, the longest aproximately 950 feet. At the start of the course, guides describe the tour and the safety measures, then each adventurer zips off down the cable while a second guide waits at the other end, either to reel in those who don't quite make it to the landing pad, or act like a brake for those who come barreling in. The tour starts with a 'bunny slope,' a slow, easy descent, then takes you on increasingly exciting rides, ending with a picnic (sandwiches, kauai cookies, chips).

Ziplining is empowering – even the most timid can learn to love it. There is nothing quite like leaping off a platform (sometimes you are told to get a running start) and sailing over trees and jungle, surveying beautiful streams and waterfalls below before touching down hundreds of feet later. The only downside: with up to 11 people on the tour, you can end up waiting around to be hooked in, which slows things down. Long pants are required (rental $5) as are closed toed shoes (rental $2). $110/pp. You must be 15 years old and weigh at least 100 pounds. Maximum weight is 280 pounds. 888-270-0555 /245-2506; www.kauaibackcountry.com. Map 1

Adventures

Helicoptering Kauai

Many of the most beautiful places on Kauai are inaccessible by car. For this reason, a helicopter tour is an unforgettable way to see this spectacular island. Kauai is breathtakingly beautiful from the air, almost like an America in miniature, with rolling hills and valleys on the eastern shore and majestic mountains on the west. The island has a flat, dry southland as well as a forested wilderness to the north, and, on the west coast, wide sandy beaches where the setting sun paints the sky with gold before slipping silently into the enormous sea. There is even a 'Grand Canyon' on a small scale, where pink and purple cliffs, etched by centuries of wind and rain into giant towers, seem like remnants of a lost civilization. So much variety is amazing on an island only 30 miles in diameter!

And what you'll see is beyond your fantasies – a mountain goat poised for an instant in a ravine, a white bird gliding against the dark green cliffs, a sudden rainbow in the mist, incredible, tower-like mountains of pink and brown in the Waimea "Grand Canyon," a glistening waterfall hanging like a slender silver ribbon through trees and rocks, a curve of pure white sand at the base of the purple and gold Na Pali cliffs, a spray of shining white foam bursting upon the rocky coast. Then, like the unveiling of the island's final mystery, the entrance into the very center of Mt. Wai'ale'ale's crater, where in the dimly lit mists of the rainiest place on the earth, waterfalls are born from ever falling showers. You have journeyed to the very heart of the

island, the place of its own birth from the volcano's eruption centuries ago. From your hotel room, you would never have believed that all this splendor existed, and your only regret will be that you didn't take more film.

It's so special, you yearn to go up again. Even the second time, the tour is exhilarating. In fact, with a better sense of the island's geography, you are more sensitive to details too easily missed when you are overcome by the majesty of the scene for the first time. You may see some of the amazing irrigation canals and tunnels carved into the mountains a century ago to bring water to the sugar cane fields below. Or, on some remote and

www.explorekauai.com

sheer escarpment along the Na Pali coast, a terrace where taro was once cultivated by the ancient Hawaiians. Gilded by the sun, these knife-like green ridges look like the 'skirts of Pele,' goddess of the volcano's fire.

Because of the expense of helicopter tours, we worried about picking the "perfect day." We began on what seemed in Lihue to be only a partly sunny day, but once in the air, we realized that the clouds would be above us rather than in our way and even enhanced the island's beauty with changing patterns of light.

The helicopter touring industry was started by an extraordinary pilot, Jack Harter, who had the vision more than 30 years ago of showing visitors the island's hidden beauty by air. Jack became a legend for his extraordinary flying skill, mechanical savvy, and intimate knowledge and love of Kauai. People lucky enough to fly with Jack saw and learned more in their 90 minute flight than they could have imagined possible, and carried away memories of spectacular scenery and a flight as smooth as a dandelion seed even in unexpected winds. The more observant will remember how his hand rested just outside the open window, feeling the air currents, and more than one soggy utility worker working on an isolated mountain top will recall a mysterious 'drop' of warm pot roast, mashed potatoes, and beer falling into camp seemingly out of nowhere. In all his years of flying air tours on Kauai, Jack had a perfect safety record, and accomplished rescues in weather other pilots would not–or could not–dare to fly. As the sign at the tour desk at the Old Kauai Surf Hotel used to say, Jack Harter was 'imitated by many, equaled by none.'

Times change, and in many ways our book is about these passages. Following Jack, younger pilots like Will Squyres and Curt Lofsted started

companies on Kauai, piloting all the flights personally, and then, as more tourists discovered the island, their companies added aircraft and brought in and trained even younger pilots to fly them. The 'owner piloted' company became economically unworkable as a business model, and the Bell Jet Rangers, which accommodated 4 paying passengers, were gradually replaced by the larger '6 -pac' ASTARs now flown by

A rare clear view of the top of Mt. Waiʻaleʻale, highest elevation on Kauai & the wettest place on the earth! The rain gauge measures the almost constant rainfall.

The beautiful eastern shore and Sleeping Giant Mountain

Jack Harter Helicopters, Will Squyres Helicopters, Island Helicopters, and most other companies.

Jack retired several years ago to his farm on the north shore, but you can still fly with Will Squyres, another extraordinary pilot who has earned wide respect over the years for his good judgment and meticulous maintenance. Will has scouted locations for such memorable movies as 'Jurassic Park' and 'The Lost World,' and his company's hour-long tour coordinates pilot commentary with dramatic stereo music on a truly amazing sound system as you fly over the island's most spectacular scenery.

Looking at our slides and videos back home almost brings back the magic of that hour, when we seemed suspended in a horizon so vast as to seem limitless, and any effort to confine it within camera range was impossible. It is always the best day of the trip.

Helicopter Tours & Safety

Helicopter tours are big business, with intense competition for tourist dollars. Many people on Kauai feel that there is a wide variation in quality and safety, however. We have heard disquieting reports: some companies

speed up tours in order to cut costs and squeeze as many tours into the day as possible. Some companies are plagued with high turnover in pilots who may have sufficient flying hours to be licensed but limited experience over Kauai's unique wilderness terrain. With pilots from a dozen companies crowding the skies, safety is becoming increasingly important. In 1994, two accidents involving fatalities occurred on Kauai involving Papillon Hawaiian Helicopters and Inter-Island Helicopters. In 1998, an accident involving Ohana Helicopters claimed six lives, and in 2003, five people died in an accident involving Jack Harter Helicopters.

These accidents have focused more attention on safety. On Kauai, weather conditions can change very quickly, and the 1998 accident occurred when an Ohana Helicopters aircraft crashed into a mountain side shrouded in low hanging clouds. The accident involving Jack Harter Helicopters, which occurred in clear weather, is still under investigation by NTSB. The pilot was experienced and respected, and the NTSB preliminary report shows no evident mechanical problems with the aircraft. When the final report is issued, we will make the conclusions available on our web site and in the next edition.

These are some key questions to ask when you are interviewing companies. First, find out whether the company is operating under a certificate issued by the FAA under Part 135 of Federal Aviation Regulations. In order to maintain a certificate of this type, the company must follow a more rigorous (thus more expensive) maintenance program, and its pilots must pass annual flight tests not required of companies operating under Part 91 of Federal Aviation Regulations. This certificate must be displayed in the company's office. Ask to see it. To verify or ask questions, call the FAA in Honolulu at (808) 836-0615. The distinction between Part 91 and Part 135 operators can tell you about the standards a company operates under, although it is no guarantee of performance.

2003	Jack Harter Helicopters	5 fatalities
1998	Ohana Helicopters	6 fatalities
1994	Interisland Helicopters	1 fatality
1994	Papillon Hawaiian Helicopters	3 fatalities

You also have a right to know whether the company, or *your* pilot has been involved in any accidents during the past three years. (You can check with NTSB at www.ntsb.gov). Beware of companies which are reluctant to answer, or say they "can't be sure" who will be piloting your flight. You should also ask if the company's FAA certificate has ever been revoked or suspended, and whether it is currently under FAA investigation for accidents or maintenance deficiencies, as opposed to record-keeping violations. Since each helicopter must display its individual 'certificate of airworthiness,' look for it or ask to see it.

Another important question to ask is the exact length of the tour. Actual in-flight time for the around-the-island tour should be no less than 60 minutes, or Kauai will appear to whiz past your window, limiting your opportunities to explore the more remote terrain inside the island's perimeter, or to take satisfying photographs. Ask for the daily flight schedule, subtract 5 minutes for landing and changing passengers, and draw your own conclusions. In this area, in our opinion, economy is not always the best policy. Given the high operating cost of the air tour business, cheaper tours will almost certainly be short, possibly too short, and the extra dollars you spend for a longer tour will be well worthwhile.

Na Pali's rugged coastline

Also consider the type of aircraft you will be flying. We prefer the Bell Jet-Ranger, with windows that open, seating one passenger in front and three in back. The Hughes 500-D helicopter seats two passengers in the rear and two in front next to the pilot. The 6-passenger ASTAR helicopter, seats 2 passengers next to the pilot in front and 4 passengers in the rear. The ASTAR is air-conditioned, but for passengers in the center rear seats, the view can be obstructed by the passengers seated next to the windows as well as those in front. The newest ASTARs have oversized windows, so check the window configuration. Ask about the cancellation policy in case of bad weather. Even in a rainstorm, we often see choppers flying! You will want a refund if you're not very comfortable – or if you can't see very much – once you're in the air (*Jack Harter Helicopters* will try to reschedule your flight if visibility is below par).

    We consider helicopter tours a unique and special way to see Kauai. We wouldn't go ourselves, or let our children fly, if we thought they were unsafe. But we make careful decisions about the pilots we fly with. We think you should do your homework carefully and have all pertinent information when making your choices as well.

Boat Tours

    The spectacular cliffs of the Na Pali coast are off limits to most visitors – unless they dare to hike on narrow and slippery trails or explore these steep and jagged ridges from a helicopter. Coastal boat tours have provided an affordable way to see these amazing cliffs up close, and enjoy a some-times rough and ready adventure at the same time. You can explore caves etched into the cliffs, watch waterfalls sparkle in sunshine, and marvel at how tenaciously plants can cling to inhospitable rock. You'll see an enormous change in the landscape, from the dark, rich green of Ke'e Beach, where rainfall measures nearly 125 inches a year, to the reds and browns of Polihale on the west side, which it measures only 20 inches.

    Spectacular, yes! But Na Pali coastal tours have been controversial. Some feared the constant boat traffic would destroy the fragile ecosystem at

Beautiful Na Pali coast, a spectacular tour by boat.

the mouth of the Hanalei River where most tours once originated, pointing out the congestion, lack of parking, and unclear jurisdic-tion to regulate the competing companies, some operating without permits. Antago-nism escalated until the Governor banned motorized tour boats from operating out of Hanalei Bay waters in 1998. The courts, however, determined that the State did not have the power to impose such a ban. Despite the ruling, only a few companies operate out of Hanalei Bay, and most have shifted operations to the south and westside, traveling north to tour Na Pali.

Enjoying your boat tour depends on several factors: the season (winter seas are rougher, limiting the number of boats that will brave the high surf); the size of the boat (only smaller boats can enter the sea caves, and only those carrying fewer than 18 passengers are allowed to anchor off protected Nu'alolo Kai for some of the island's best snorkeling); the amenities onboard (restroom and shade); length of the tour (determining how far along the coast you can feasibly go before turning around to come back); and activities (snorkeling, scuba, lunch).

We like the small power catamarans which offer a comfortable ride along with the agility you need to go into the sea caves along Na Pali. From Port Allen, (7 am or 1 pm) *Makana's Tours* takes only 12 passengers on a 32-ft power catamaran with bathroom. Owner/captain Mike de Silva, whose family has lived on Kauai for generations, makes sure everyone gets a bird's eye view of the amazing scenery. You may frolic with a pod of dolphins, even play in a waterfall, and see amazing fish while snorkeling at protected Nu'alolo Kai. Small details make a big difference: flotation devices for snorkelers, excellent equipment, a terrific buffet lunch with fresh-baked bread, even a fresh water rinse after snorkeling ($109/5 hrs). Mike's knowledgeable and very accommodating crew shares a lot of

Power Catamaran Tours			
Makana Tours	822-9187	Liko Kauai Cruises	338-0333
Kaulana Kai	337-9309	Holo Holo Charters	335-0815
Hanalei Sport Fishing	826-6114	Kauai Sea Tours	826-7254
Sailing Yacht Tours			
Catamaran Kahanu	335-3577	Blue Dolphin	742-6731
Rainbow Runner	245-9662	Holo Holo Charters	335-0815
Kauai Sea Tours	826-7254	Captain Andy's	335-6833
Kayak Tours			
Outfitters Kauai	742-9667	Princeville Ranch	826-7669
Kayak Kauai Outbound	826-9844		

history, natural history, local lore and stories (822-9187).

From Waimea, Liko Kauai Cruises owned by Liko and his Hawaiian family offers an excellent 4 hour morning or afternoon snorkeling and sightseeing tour which goes into some of the caves, as well as fishing cruises on his 49-ft power catamaran, 'Na Pali Kai III' ($75-$110/pp) with all forward seating, shade, plus bathroom (338-0333 /888-SEA-LIKO; www.liko-kauai.com). *Catamaran Kahanu,* owned and operated by native Hawaiians, tours Na Pali on a 36-foot power catamaran, 18 feet wide with a 'flying bridge,' a great perch for watching spinning porpoises and humpback whales ($75-$105/pp). The crew demonstrates Hawaiian crafts (335-3577; www.catamarankahanu.com).

If you crave the bigger thrill, consider the *zodiacs,* whose 'rough and ready' ride often takes you up and over waves and head on into the surf. *Kauai Sea Tours* takes 15 passengers on a rigid hull ocean zodiac to NaPali; full day tours include a guided hike ($139/pp or $109/half day) 826-7254 or 800-733-7997; www.kauaiseatours.com. The ride can be very bumpy, so ask right away for gloves to hold onto the rope, especially if you want to sit towards the front. A waterproof camera is a good idea for when the boat goes under waterfalls and through the spray. Snorkeling depends on weather and surf, but bring anti-fog and your own mask if possible. On the ride home, the boat may feel as if it is driving against the waves at top speed, and so less adventurous passengers might like to sit towards the back on what is called the 'cadillac seat.' *Na Pali Riders,* leaving from Kekaha, has the advantage of touring the entire Na Pali coast all the way to Tunnels Beach on the northwest shore. It's a long tour, and you see everything (www.napaliriders.com; 808-742-6331). *Captain Zodiac,* now operated by

Captain Andy's, operates a 24-ft motorized rigid hull craft. The 5 hr Na Pali snorkeling adventure includes (weather permitting) landing at Nu'alolo Kai for lunch ($129). 826-9371 or 800-888-0000; www.capt-andys.com. *Na Pali Explorer* operates a 35

passenger, rigid hull zodiac complete with restroom and shelter for higher speeds in rough ocean conditions, as well as the 26-ft, 16-passenger 'Hurricane' Zodiac along Na Pali, or 3 hour south shore whale watching tours ($79-$118/pp). 335-9909 or 338-9899; www.napali-explorer.com. *Holo Holo* cruises Na Pali on a 42-ft aluminum power monohull.

For those who tend to get seasick, larger craft can offer a smoother ride. Several companies offer sailing tours, though often use power to ensure an 'on time' schedule. *Blue Dolphin Charters* tours Na Pali on the 'Blue Dolphin,' a 63-ft sailing catamaran, and the 'Blue Dolphin II,' a 65-ft catmaran ($120/5hrs). It begins, as most of the tours do, with a continental breakfast and safety briefing, and it offers both a one-tank dive for beginners and certified divers ($25) as well as snorkeling at the designated anchor spot. The crew is exceptionally friendly and professional. Blue Dolphin also offers shorter sunset cruises ($85-$64/3hrs). 335-5553 or 877-511-1311; www.kauaiboats.com. *Captain Sundown* takes 15 passengers in his 40-ft sailing catamaran, 'Ku'uipo,' out along the Na Pali coast, ($138/6hrs) and is one of the few companies leaving from Hanalei (826-5585; www.captainsundown.com). On its 60-ft sailing catamaran, 'Lucky Lady,' *Kauai Sea Tours* has an excellent Na Pali tour $139/6 hrs with snorkeling, as well as a sunset cruise ($89). The crew is very friendly, knowledgeable and courteous. A scuba option offers dives led by a divemaster from *Seasport Divers* for both beginners and certified divers (800-733-7997 or 826-PALI; www.kauaiseatours.com). Check for internet discounts.

Captain Andy's 55-ft sailing catamaran, 'Spirit of Kauai,' sails from Port Allen to Na Pali ($110/pp 6 hrs), and also offers shorter snorkel or sunset cruises (335-6833; www.capt-andys.com). Also from Port Allen, *Holo Holo Tours* goes along Na Pali on 'Leila,' a 48-ft sailing catamaran, as well as a 65-ft motor driven catamaran, very comfortable with little side to side rolling motion (335-0815 or 800-848-6130; www.holoholocharters.com).

During winter months (November till March), when seas off Na Pali are too rough and currents too strong, many tour operators cruise along Kauai's south shore looking for the humpback whales which frequent Hawaii's warm waters from December to April. Some, like *Kauai Sea Tours* even provides special hydrophones to listen to whale song. *Kauai Sea Tours* also offers excursions in ocean rafts, departing from Nawiliwili harbor near Lihue and touring the south shore to Kipu Kai, with a stop for lunch and snorkeling. *Rainbow Runner Sailing* (246-6333; www.kauaifun.com) sails a 40-ft trimaran out of Nawiliwili Harbor near Lihue year round, with 1 hour to a 3 hour picnic/ snorkel tours to Kipu Kai. Check for internet discounts.

If you have the time, consider a tour to **Ni'ihau**, the 'forbidden' island off limits to tourism, except by boats which can come close enough to snorkel and dive but not to land. Several companies offer all-day tours to Niʻihau, with snorkeling, or a scuba option. On Tuesdays and Fridays, Blue Dolphin Charters takes a comfortable 65-ft sailing catamaran ($159) to Niʻihau with snorkeling and an introductory scuba option or a certified dive ($25/one tank). Diving off Niʻihau in brilliantly clear water is an amazing experience, and Blue Dolphin's crew is both professional and helpful. Seasport Divers offers an all-day 3-tank dive trip with a knowledgeable and friendly crew. Holo Holo Charters offers only snorkeling on its Niʻihau tour ($156), and the craft can feel a bit cramped on the rough channel crossing.

When booking a tour, be sure to inquire about cancellation policies for weather and surf conditions, and check the weather report yourself (245-6001). Companies will claim they never go out in rough seas, but that depends on the definition! Rocking, rolling swells are fun for some, not so much fun for others, especially if there's no shelter from wind and spray, so think twice if your tour is ready to head out in marginal weather. Ask about the number of passengers usually on board, keeping in mind that the more crowded the boat, the less comfortable you may be. Only small boats can snorkel at Nuʻalolo Kai and go into the sea caves. Inquire about your captain's experience; although every captain has to be coast guard licensed, some have more experience than others. Bring sunscreen, especially if your craft doesn't offer shade, perhaps a hat and sunglasses for glare, a towel, a long sleeved shirt for early morning check ins, and if possible, your own snorkel mask (and anti-fog) that fits properly. Protect your camera and film in a heavy duty zip lock plastic bag, and bring a dry shirt for the long ride home when you may be soaked with spray and dreaming of a hot shower.

Kayaking Kauai's Rivers

Exploring Kauai's rivers by kayak can be fun, but increasingly controversial as the rivers become more crowded. The problem is most acute at the **Wailua River**, which as Kauai's only navigable river, offers a variety of

other water sports. On a summer day, you may see powerboats zipping along towing water-skiers, dodging the wide tour barges lumbering along in the center on their way to the Fern Grotto, while clusters of kayaks hug the banks trying to avoid the wakes! Now there is even a 'kayak lane' on the north side of the river (though motorcraft have the 'right of way'). *Rainbow Kayaks* has an excellent trip upriver to the waterfall, (about a mile) in two person kayaks. Knowledge-

Alakoko 'Menehune' Fish Pond & Hule'ia River

able guides describe local wildlife, history, and legends). After hiking another mile, you reach the waterfall for a swim and excellent picnic lunch. Since the trail can get muddy, shoes with some sort of sole are recommended (not slippers). Tour guides will take family photos (826-9983). *Outfitters Kauai* also offers a Wailua River tour ($94 with lunch) and waterfall hike. Or rent your own kayak (about $30/day/single; $45/day/double) from *Outfitters Kauai* or *Kauai Water Ski & Surf Co.* (822-3574).

For river tours of the **Hule'ia River**, where Indiana Jones was filmed, contact *Island Adventures* (245-9662; www.kauaifun.com). A one-way guided paddle ($89) follows the river through the Hule'ia National Wildlife Refuge and the State of Hawaii Conservation District, to the ancient Alakoko 'Menehune' Fish Pond, made, according to legend, by the 'Menehune,' Kauai's magical 'little people.' After a short hike, where you can observe many birds, waterfowl, and beautiful exotic plants, you reach Papakolea Falls for a swim, then a picnic nearby before a van takes you to your car. Hule'ia River tours ($75) are also offered by *Outfitters Kauai,* and can take you to **Kipu Falls**, a beautiful spot on private land ($129). This is the only safe and legal way to visit Kipu Falls. A group of up to 20 proceeds at a leisurely pace, a two-mile paddle upriver, then a hike along trails (often muddy). After a brief wagon tour of Kipu Ranch and lunch, you spend an hour at the rock pool and falls for swimming, and trying out the 25-ft rope swing. This tour is a great way for recreational hikers and kayakers to enjoy inaccessible places (not for those who like to push ahead), though a new 275-ft zipline ride across a waterfall is an adventure! www.outfitterskauai.com; 742-9667/888-742-9887.

On the north shore, *Princeville Ranch Hike & Kayak* offers a wonderful

after all the paddling, the watefall!

hike (45 min) combined with kayaking a secluded stream (1/2 hour), picnic lunch at a hidden waterfall before the return trip (4 hrs total). Great views, peaceful scenery, and healthful lunch (826-7669 or 888-955-7669; www.kauai-hiking.com). Explore the beautiful **Hanalei River** with *Luana of Hawaii* (826-9195), or rent a kayak from *Pedal & Paddle* and tour on your own. Go early for the best selection. *Kayak Kauai Outbound* (800-437-3507 or 826-9844; www.kayakkauai.com) offers tours and also rents 2-person and 1-person kayaks (2-hour minimum). From its convenient riverside location, you can travel upriver, or venture downriver to Hanalei Bay. In summer, when Hanalei Bay is calm, you may be able to paddle along the bay's edge and pull up on the Princeville Hotel's sandy beach. Everything in the kayak can get wet, so protect your camera in a waterproof bag. Bring drinks, snacks, perhaps snorkeling gear to explore the reef. A 2-hour trip may be all you need (and all your muscles can take). Or load the kayak onto your car and drive to the boat pier at Hanalei Bay, or to Anini beach or Kalihiwai Bay (about 10 minutes). When winter surf and currents are too strong, your best options will be Hanalei Kalihiwai Rivers.

Sea kayaking can be great fun, in the right surf conditions. *Kayak Kauai Outbound* (800-437-3507 or 808-826-9844; www.kayakkauai.com) offers a day-long kayak excursion between Ha'ena and Polihale State Beach on the westside. Views are spectacular, but be ready for a strenuous six hours of hard paddling. Occasional squalls and choppy water often punctu-ate the ride, but in your kayak you can explore sea caves, play with dol-phins, and visit with turtles ($175). When Na Pali waters become too rough (October till April), whale-watching tours go out along the south shore to Kipu Kai ($115). Poipu-based *Outfitters Kauai* (742-9667 or 888-742-9887; www.outfitterskauai.com) offers guided sea kayak tours along Na Pali ($165) and the south shore (winter), as well as bike and kayak rentals.

Be sure to clarify the tour cancellation policy carefully, or you may wind up being charged if you change your mind. If you are renting, check the kayak carefully for patches and leaks. And remember the sun! A hat, sunscreen, and drinking water are a must. Bring a towel and spare shirt. If you paddle up river, don't drink the river water, and if you have an open cut, be particularly cautious. The bacterium causing *leptospirosis* found in all of Kauai's rivers can cause serious, even fatal, flu-like symptoms.

Museums & Historical Tours

The story of Kauai is in many ways the story of the sugar plantations which shaped the island's multi-ethnic culture as much as its agriculture and economy. For this reason, a visit to the *Grove Farm Homestead* in Lihue offers a fascinating glimpse into the island's past. One of the earliest Hawaiian sugar plantations, Grove Farm was founded in 1864 by George Wilcox, the son of Protestant missionary teachers at Waioli Mission in Hanalei. Planting and harvesting Grove Farm's sugar crop, which grew from 80 acres to more than 1,000, ultimately involved a workforce of several hundred Hawaiians, Chinese, Koreans, Germans, Portuguese, and Filipino laborers, who brought to Kauai a rich heritage of ethnic cultures. A two-hour tour takes you through Grove Farm's cluster of buildings nestled amid tropical gardens, orchards, and rolling lawns, but be warned: the tour is extremely popular and you'll need to reserve a place at least a week in advance. You'll see the gracious old Wilcox home, the large rooms cooled by breezes from shaded verandas, and elegantly furnished with oriental carpets, magnificent koa wood floors and wainscotting, and hand crafted furniture of native woods. You will also tour the 'board and batten' cottage of the plantation house-keeper, who came to Kauai, like many Japanese women, as a 'picture bride' for a laborer too poor to travel home to select his wife in person. All buildings are covered by traditional 'beach sand paint' (literally sand thrown against wet paint) to protect them against both heat and damp for as long as 20 years. The leisurely, friendly tour includes a stop in the kitchen for cookies and mint ice tea. For students and scholars, the library's extensive collection of Hawaiiana and plantation records is available by appointment. Grove Farm Tours are conducted Monday, Wednesday, and Thursday at 10 am and 1 pm. Reservations required: 808- 245-3202 or PO Box 1631, Lihue HI 96766.

Man in gourd mask by John Weber, artist with Captain Cook

Like other Hawaiian sugar plantations, Grove Farm was established at a significant point in the economic history of the islands. In the 1850's, the monarchy first began to sell land, and Hawaii entered the age of private property. Before this time, land was not sold but given in trust to subjects in pie-shaped slices, from the interior mountains to the sea, so that each landhold would include precious fresh water as well as coastline.

The Wilcox family, particularly two Wilcox women, made significant contributions to the development of Kauai. Elsie Wilcox, a Kauai School Commissioner, was the first woman in the territory to be elected to the State Senate; Mabel Wilcox, a public health nurse, was decorated by both France and Belgium for outstanding service in World War I. Elsie and Mabel restored *Waioli Mission House* in Hanalei (open T, Th, and Sat 9 am-3 pm), and Mabel planned *Grove Farm Homestead* in 1971 at age 89.

If the Grove Farm tour doesn't fit into your schedule, you can visit the *Kauai Museum* on Rice St. in downtown Lihue, Monday-Friday 9:30 am to 4:30 pm. The Rice Building exhibits the *Story of Kauai* – the volcanic eruptions which shaped the land; the Polynesians who voyaged to the island in canoes and left behind marvelous petroglyphs, or rock pictures; the missionaries who altered its culture; and the sugar planters who, like George Wilcox, defined much of its agricultural destiny. Monthly exhibits in the adjacent Wilcox building display the work of local artists as well as rotating exhibits featuring the contributions of Kauai's ethnic cultures, like an exhibit of Japanese, Chinese, Hawaiian, and Filipino wedding dress and traditions. The museum shop sells books, maps and local crafts. $3/ adults (If you don't finish touring by the end of the day, you can get a free pass for the next). Gift shop is free. Call about exhibits and lectures: 245-6931.

The last family owned sugar plantation in Hawaii (one of only 3 left statewide), the *Gay and Robinson Sugar Plantation* in Makaweli offers a unique 2 hour tour of sugar production. Visit the fields to learn about growing and harvesting the cane, and then the processing plant, with hard hats & safety glasses, to see every phase from unloading the cane to spinning it into granular raw sugar. Sample sugar in three stages of processing, from simple syrup, into a molasses like stage, to raw sugar form. Tours ($30/pp) go twice daily M-F (808-335-2824; www.gandrtours-kauai.com).

History buffs will enjoy the 90 minute walking tour of Kapa'a Town's historic buildings (T, Th, Sat $15). Call 245-3373 for reservations. Online, find the history of Kapa'a (www.kauaihistoricalsociety.org). Armchair travelers can request a catalog of books on Hawaiiana as well as hard-to-find Hawaiian authors: Petroglyph Press 888-666-8644.

Movie Tours

A 5-hour guided narrated tour of Kauai's movie locations takes you in an air-conditioned van to locations of Kauai's most famous movies (*South Pacific, Raiders of the Lost Ark, Honeymoon in Vegas,* etc.) and at the same time shows the actual scenes on a TV monitor in surround sound ($100/pp). Some love the tinsel and the comic commentary, others are not so enthusiastic, but the real advantage may be seeing a good chunk of the island in a comfortable touring van (822-1192 / 800-628-8432; hawaiimovietour.com). Their 'offroad' tour (by 4x4 van) takes you to south shore Kipu Ranch, where you can scout dramatic forest and river locations of *Raiders of the Lost Arc, Outbreak, Six Days & Seven Nights, Mighty Joe Young, Hook, Jurassic Park,* and other box office hits. The more adventurous can tour these sites by ATV with *Kipu Adventures* (www.kiputours.com; 808-246-9288). You roll through the streams, into the forest, over the rocks, following the Hule'ia River where Indiana Jones took off in his seaplane.

Natural History Tours

Halfway between Kapa'a and Princeville, the *Kilauea Lighthouse*, built in 1913, once warned mariners away from Kauai's rugged north coast until technology replaced light flashes with radio transmissions. Come for spectacular views of the coastline and Mukuae'ae island, and if you're lucky, a glimpse of Spinner Dolphins or Humpback Whales on summer vacation in the waves. This is the northernmost point of Kauai, indeed of all the Hawaiian islands, and changes in weather are often first detected by the weather station here. Best of all, you will see a tiny part of the *Hawaiian Island National Wildlife Refuge,* which shelters more than 10 million seabirds in a chain of islands scattered over 1200 miles of ocean – like the Red-footed Booby. You will hear the amazing story of how seamen carried

4 tons of French prisms up a sheer cliff for the giant clam shaped light. Open 10 am - 4 pm daily except federal holidays; 828-1413.

Above the lighthouse, *Crater Hill* offers a panoramic view of the north shore, a great spot for a picnic. Sometimes the new road (You'll see the security gate on the right as you drive along Kilauea Rd. towards the lighthouse) is locked; at other times, open. For reservations for a 2.5 hour morning hiking tour of Crater Hill, call 828-0168.

More of Kauai's rare birds and plants can be seen at the *Koke'e Natural History Museum* in Koke'e State Park, open daily 10 am - 4 pm. 808-335-9975; www.aloha.net/~kokee. Donations welcome. Interested in birds? Go to www.kauaibirds.com for photos and facts. Arrange tours in the Koke'e area with *Kauai Nature Tours*. 742-8305 / 888-233-8365; www.teok.com.

Tropical Botanical Tours

The guided tour of *National Tropical Botanical Gardens* in Lawai is a unique opportunity to explore a 186 acre preserve of tropical fruits, spices, trees, rare plants, and flowers of astonishing variety and beauty – 50 varieties of banana and 500 species of palm. Instead of a formal garden, the plant collections are part of the natural landscape of the Lawai Valley. Park and join your group at Spouting Horn and climb aboard a vintage 1941 Dodge touring bus which takes you into Lawai Kai, the Allerton family's spectacular private gardens, a rustic paradise irrigated by an ingenious water system of fountains, streams, waterways, and rocky pools. Stroll at a leisurely pace among the shaded pathways, under spreading, giant trees, to pavilions where a statue reflects a graceful image in a pool speckled with fallen leaves. The 'cutting garden' has brilliantly colored heliconia. Reserve well in advance for the 2-hour, 2-mile walking tour Tues - Sat at 9 am, 10 am, 1 pm, and 2 pm ($25/pp). Bring your camera. Map 3. 332-7324; www.ntbg.org. NTBG, PO Box 340, Lawai HI 96765.

On the north shore in Ha'ena, a walking tour of NTBG's *Limahuli Gardens* will lead you uphill through 17 acres of lush rain forest and gardens filled with native plants to an ocean lookout. You'll love the ancient terrace constructed for growing taro nearly a thousand years ago by the earliest Hawaiians. Formal tours ($15/pp) and self-guided strolls ($10/pp) over the 3/4 mile loop trail. Tues-Fri and Sundays 9:30 am-4 pm. Reservations: 808-826-1053. Rt. 560, 1/2 mile past mile 9 marker.

> Many people ask about tipping: It's a really nice gesture to tip your tour and adventure guides if you think they give you exceptional service. About $ 5- $10 can show your apreciation.

Allerton Gardens NTBG in Lawai

At *Na'Aina Kai* in Kilauea, explore an amazing variety of plants in lovely gardens and groves. You'll find a shrubbery maze, 40,000 hardwood trees, a carnivorous plant habitat, and a gazebo overlooking the spectacular north shore coastline. A 3-hour tour proceeds on foot and by tram through gardens, waterways, and groves (T-Th $35/adults only) or you can take a shorter tour on foot. (808-828-0525; www.naainakai.com). Bring your camera. Nearby, *Guava Kai Plantation* teaches you about the propagation of this wonderful fruit. Map 2. On the south shore in Kalaheo, flower photographers will love *Kukuiolono Golf Course*'s plumeria grove – a rainbow of colors in summer! Turn south on Papalina (at the traffic light); after .8 miles, turn into the entrance on the right. Map 3

Above Wailua, the *Keahua Arboretum,* a 30-acre preserve of grassy meadows, trees, streams, is great for a quiet picnic. From Rt. 56, take Kuamo'o Rd. (Rt. 580) up Sleeping Giant Mountain, about 7 miles. Follow signs. Don't get discouraged when the road gets bumpy. You'll cross a stream and come to a grassy spot for a picnic surrounded by trees. You can hike on trails beneath the ancient trees. From the Arboretum, *Aloha Kauai Tours* can take you by 4x4 van though Kauai's wilderness to the 'Blue Hole' at the base of Mt. Wai'ale'ale, where spectacular waterfalls converge into a river (245-6400). Map 1

Waimea Canyon & Koke'e State Park

The drive to the top of Waimea Canyon, the 'Grand Canyon of the Pacific,' makes a great day trip. The drive along the Koke'e Road (Rt. 550) from Rt. 50 to the end of the winding road will take about 45 minutes. As you travel along the canyon's rim, ten miles long and 3,600 feet deep, pull over to enjoy spectacular scenic overlooks.

At *Koke'e Lodge*, stop for lunch – excellent soups and sandwiches, and visit the *Koke'e Museum* (donation) for exhibits and trail maps. If possible, plan some time for exploring this wilderness preserve. Even a short hike shows you great views. Bring a jacket; at nearly 4,000 feet, temperatures can be very cool. Some hikes are suitable for families and take only a couple of hours, like the trail to Waipo'o Falls which descends through wild ginger and orchids to a beautiful two-tiered waterfall. Mosquito spray, sun screen, canteen, camera (wildflowers are beautiful!) and a hat are musts.

Even if you don't hike, the drive takes you to a spectacular lookout, the Kalalau Lookout, with a vista of the island's west side. (Parents be careful: the railing won't keep small children safe.) Rental car companies will advise you to go easy on the brakes and transmission, and use low gear as you negotiate the curving road, even more important on the way down. The road is hard on cars, as we learned when our 1984 red Suburban made it to the top, then coughed and sputtered to a halt in front of Koke'e Lodge. Your rental car will probably do just fine, but we'll never forget the trip back down, with 'Red Rover' riding in style atop the gleaming flatbed, whimsically named 'A Tow in Paradise.' Only on Kauai would the driver park his enormous rig a half dozen times to share his favorite photo-stops!

Don't trust that rental car? Although commercial tours of Koke'e are no longer allowed, you can see some of the ecosystem, as well as Waimea Canyon with *Aloha Kauai Tours* in 4x4 vans (245-1113 or 800-452-1113; www.alohakauaitours.com). *Kauai Nature Tours* offers unique naturalist guided tours with an emphasis on Kauai's natural and cultural history. 742-8305 or 888-233-8365; www.teok.com.

At the end of the Waimea Canyon Road, a spectacular lookout.

Café Hanalei, Princeville Hotel

Eastern Shore Restaurants

Lihue

			page		meals
Aromas	245-9192	Eclectic	145	$$	BLD
Barbecue Inn	245-2921	Oriental	147	$$	BLD
Café Portofino	245-2121	Italian	151	$$$	LD
Dani's	245-4991	Island-style	153	$	BL
Duke's Canoe Club	246-9599	Seafood/steak	154	$$$	D
Duke's Barefoot Bar	246-9599	Burgers/sand	155	$$	LD
Garden Island BBQ	245-8868	Chinese/BBQ	156	$$	LD
Gaylord's	245-9593	Continental	156	$$$$	LD
Hamura's Saimin	245-3271	Saimin	158	$	D
JJ's Broiler	246-4422	Steak/seafood	162	$$$	D
Kalapaki Beach Hut	246-6330	Burgers/sand	163	$	BLD
Kauai Chop Suey	245-8790	Chinese	163	$$	LD
Kiibo	245-2650	Japanese	164	$$	LD
La Bamba	245-5972	Mexican	168	$	LD
Ma's Family Inc.	245-3142	Island-style	170	$	BL
Okazu Hale	245-6554	Island-style	174	$	LD
Oki Diner	245-5899	Island-style	174	$	21 hrs
Paradise Seafood	246-4700	Fresh fish	178	$$$	LD
Tip Top Café	245-2333	Amer/oriental	180	$	BL
Tokyo Lobby	245-8989	Japanese	180	$$	LD
Whaler's Brew Pub	245-2000	American	184	$$$	LD

Hanama'ulu

Tea House	245-2511	Chin/Japanese	159	$$	D

Wailua

A Pacific Café	822-0013	Pacific Rim	176	$$$$	D
Al & Don's	822-4221	American	145	$$	BLD
Ba Le	823-6060	Vietnamese	147	$$	BLD
Bull Shed	822-3791	Steak/PRibs	149	$$$	D
Caffe Coco	822-7990	Vegetarian	150	$$	BLD
Coconuts	823-8777	Pacific Rim	152	$$$$	D
Eggbert's	822-3787	American	155	$$	BL
Hong Kong Café	822-3288	Chinese	160	$	LD
Hukilau Lanai	822-3441	Pacific Rim	161	$$$	D
King & I	822-1642	Thai	165	$$	D

$ under $15 $$ under $20 $$$ under $30 $$$$ under $40 $$$$$ over $40

Kintaro	822-3341	Japanese	166	$$$	D
La Playita Azul	821-2323	Mexican	169	$	LD
Lemongrass	821-2888	Pacific Rim	170	$$$	D
Mema Thai Cuisine	823-0899	Thai/Chinese	171	$$	LD
Panda Garden	822-0092	Chinese	177	$$	D
Papaya's	823-0190	Vegetarian	178	$	BLD
Wailua Marina	822-4311	Everything	182	$$	LD
Waipouli Deli	822-9311	Island-style	183	$	BLD
Wahoo's	822-7833	Seafood	181	$$$	LD

Kapa'a

Blossoming Lotus	822-7678	Vegan	148	$$	LD
Kountry Kitchen	822-3511	American	168	$$	BL
Mermaids Café	821-2026	Vegetarian	172	$	LD
Norberto's El Café	822-3362	Mexican	173	$$	BD
Ono Family	822-1710	American	175	$$	BL
Sukothai	821-1224	Thai/etc.	179	$$	D
Wasabi's	822-2700	Japanese	181	$$	D

North Shore Restaurants

Kilauea

Farmers Market Deli	828-1512	sandwiches	187	$	L
Lighthouse Bistro	828-0480	Italian	198	$$$	LD
Pau Hana Pizza	828-2020	Pizza	195	$	LD

Princeville

Bali Hai	826-6522	Steak/seafood	189	$$$$	LD
Café Hanalei	826-9644	Pacific Rim	191	$$$$	BLD
C J's Steakhouse	826-6211	Steak/seafood	193	$$$	LD
La Cascata	826-9644	Italian	196	$$$$$	D
Princeville Restaurant	826-5050	American	201	$$	BL
Sabella's	826-6255	steaks/seafood	201	$$$	D

Hanalei

Bamboo Bamboo	826-1177	Pacific Rim	191	$$$	LD
Dolphin	826-6113	Seafood/steak	194	$$$	LD
Hanalei Gourmet	826-2524	Sandwiches	195	$$	BLD
Neidie's	826-1851	Brazilian	199	$$	LD
Postcards Café	826-1191	Seafood/vege	200	$$$	BD

Sushi & Blues	826-9701	Japanese	202	$$	D
Tahiti Nui	826-6277	luau	203	$$$	Bar
Zelo's Beach House	826-9700	American	203	$$	BLD

South Shore & Westside Restaurants

Koloa

Pizzetta	742-8881	Pizza/pasta	187	$$	BLD
Tomkats Grill	742-8887	American	227	$$	LD

Poipu

Beach House	742-1424	Pacific Rim	207	$$$$	D
Brennecke's	742-7588	Seafood/steak	208	$$$	LD
Casablanca	742-2929.	Italian	211	$$$	LD
Case di Amici	742-1555	Italian	212	$$$	D
Dondero's	742-6260	Italian	213	$$$$$	D
Keoki's Paradise	742-7534	Steak/seafood	216	$$$	D
Naniwa	742-1661	Japanese	218	$$$	D
Pattaya	742-8818	Thai/Chinese	218	$$	LD
Plantation Gardens	742-2216	Steak/seafood	219	$$$	D
Poipu Bay Clubhouse	742-1515	American	220	$$$	L
Poipu Beach Broiler	742-6433	American	221	$$$$	LD
Roy's Poipu Grill	742-5000	Pacific Rim	223	$$$$	D
Shells	742-1661	American	224	$$$$	BLD
Taqueria Nortenos	742-7222	Mexican	225	$	LD
Tidepools	742-6260	Seafood/steak	225	$$$$$	D

Kalaheo

Brick Oven Pizza	332-8561	Pizza	209	$$	LD
Camp House Grill	332-9755	Burgers/sand	210	$$	LD
Kalaheo Coffee Café	332-5858	Deli/coffee	215	$	BL
Kalaheo Steakhouse	332-9780	Steak/PRibs	215	$$$	D
Pomodoro	332-5945	Italian	221	$$$	D

Hanapepe, Ele'ele & Waimea

Green Garden	335-5422	Everything	229	$$	LD
Hanapepe Café	335-5011	Vegetarian	229	$$	LD
Toi's Thai Kitchen	335-3111	Thai	231	$$	LD
Waimea Brew Pub	338-9773	American	231	$$$	LD
Wrangler's Steakhouse	338-1218	Steaks/sandw	232	$$	LD

READERS' CHOICE . . .

FOR OCEAN VIEW
Eastern Shore
  Bull Shed 149
  Duke's Canoe Club 154
  Café Portofino 151
North Shore
  Bali Hai 189
  Café Hanalei 191
  La Cascata 196
South Shore
  Beach House 207
  Shell's 224

FOR PASTA
Eastern Shore
  Café Portofino 151
North Shore
  La Cascata 196
South Shore
  Casablanca 211
  Casa di Amici 212
  Plantation Gardens 219
  Pomodoro 221

FOR FRESH ISLAND FISH
Eastern Shore
  A Pacific Café 176
  Duke's Canoe Club 154
  Bull Shed 149
  Hukilau Lanai 161
North Shore
  Café Hanalei 191
  Hanalei Dolphin 194
  Postcards Café 200
South Shore
  Beach House 207
  Brennecke's 208
  Plantation Gardens 219
  Roy's Poipu Grill 223
  Tidepools 225

FOR FAMILY FRIENDLY DINING
Eastern Shore
  Ba Le 147
  Barbecue Inn 147
  Bull Shed 149
  Duke's Canoe Club 154
  Hanama'ulu Tea House 159
  Hong Kong Café 160
  Kountry Kitchen 168
  Norberto's El Café 173
  Ono Family 175
North Shore
  Café Hanalei 191
  Postcards Café 200
  Zelo's 203
South & Westside
  Brennecke's 208
  Brick Oven Pizza 209
  Camp House Grill 210
  Pomodoro 221
  Wranglers's 232

FOR STEAKS & PRIME RIB
Eastern Shore
  Duke's Canoe Club 154
  Bull Shed 149
South Shore
  Keoki's 215
  Kalaheo Steakhouse 215

FOR ORIENTAL FOOD
Eastern Shore
  Hanama'ulu Tea House 159
  King & I 165
  Ba Le 147
  Kintaro 166
  Mema Thai Cuisine 171
South & Westside
  Toi's Thai Kitchen 231

Eastern Shore Restaurants

'favor...eats'

The eastern shore's potpourri of dining reflects Kauai's rich multicultural heritage. The **Hanama'ulu Restaurant and Tea House** combines reasonable prices and friendly service with excellent Japanese and Chinese cuisine. In LIHUE, **Barbecue Inn's** bargain-priced lunches and dinners include soup, a beverage, fresh-baked bread, entrée, even dessert. In this family-friendly restaurant, you'll find some of the tastiest food and best values on the island. Looking for local saimin? Try **Hamura's Saimin** or **Okazu Hale** for great noodles.

Gaylord's at Kilohana provides a romantic garden setting for lunch and dinner in an elegantly restored sugar plantation estate house. At the Kauai Marriott, **Duke's Canoe Club** offers a beautiful beachfront setting, as well as excellent food, reasonable prices, and the most sumptuous salad bar on the island. **Duke's Barefoot Bar** downstairs has well-priced burgers and sandwiches, while across the hotel's lagoon, **Whaler's Brew Pub** features a spectacular ocean view, as well as reasonably priced lunches and dinners. **Café Portofino** serves excellent Italian cuisine at affordable prices in its new oceanfront setting next to the Marriott. Nearby, newcomer **Aromas** offers a distinctive cuisine with flair and imagination. **Kauai Chop Suey** has reasonably priced Oriental food. At **Kalapaki Beach Hut,** try a first-rate hamburger or fish sandwich.

Ten minutes north of Lihue, WAILUA is becoming the dining center of Kauai, with a wide range of cuisines and prices. **Mema Thai Cuisine** and

King & I offer truly memorable Thai food at a great price. **Kintaro** prepares the best Japanese dinners, sushi and sashimi on Kauai. For imaginative Pacific Rim cuisine, particularly fresh fish, Jean Marie Josselin's **A Pacific Café** has earned fame. **Coconuts** offers Pacific Rim cuisine at slightly lower price, though the no-reservations policy may lead to an irritating wait for a table. **Hukilau Lanai** serves wonderful fresh fish and local vegetables in inventive presentations. Don't miss the **Bull Shed** for the biggest, tastiest prime rib on the island as well as steaks, chicken, and excellent fresh fish – with an ocean view – at terrific prices. Vegetarian, or even vegan cravings? Try **Caffé Coco, Mermaids Café, Blossoming Lotus,** or **Papaya's.**

On a budget? Find tasty Vietnamese food at **Ba Le** near Wailua Safeway. At Coconut Marketplace, try **Aloha Kauai Pizza** and **Fish Hut.** For hearty breakfast it's **Kountry Kitchen** or **Ono Family Restaurant** in Kapa'a; for coffee, tea, and bakery treats, **Java Kai,** and for delicious vegetarian (or non-vegetarian) wraps, curries and salads, **Mermaids.**

Al & Don's

From roomy booths next to Al & Don's enormous windows, you can see the ocean, rimmed with ironwood trees, stretching to the horizon. The decor, though nondescript, is pleasant, and tables are large and comfortable. Waitresses bring coffee immediately; your order is prepared quickly and served cheerfully. Kids feel welcome. (If asked, Chef Bobby will serve them hard boiled eggs, complete with happy faces). Food is reasonably-priced, hearty in portion, and some visitors rave about the waffles. Check out the senior's menu and early-bird dinner specials for under $10.

Al & Don's is family friendly, with a view parents – and grandparents – will enjoy. The chief attraction is what you see out the window, so breakfast is best, when you can enjoy it in full daylight (but be sure to arrive before 9 am). For dinner, time your arrival before sunset.

Wailua, Kauai Sands Hotel. 822-4221. Open 7 am - 10 am, and 6 pm - 8:45 pm daily. Credit cards. Map 1

Aromas

Just opposite the Marriott in Lihue, tucked in the back of the upper level of Harbor Mall, you'll find a small restaurant with large dreams and great potential. Chef Robert Moler, whose hotel training spans New York and Palm Springs, creates an imaginative cuisine with surprises at every

turn. Take pear salad. Here you'll find the pear poached with star anise, garnished with purple sweet potato strings, pecans, and sauced with tahini and sweet onion vinaigrette. In some hands, these ingredients might turn a medley of flavors to mush, but not here. Each flavor is distinct, and the total effect distinctive. Or consider a crepe stuffed with roast chicken and vegetables, served with a sauce of melted cheese and spices, and tomato cubes. Sound heavy? It's light as a feather and very tasty. Summer rolls like mini towers stuffed with soba noodles, avocado, and greens are cool and refreshing with a delicately spicy sauce. And the soup, a true test of any kitchen, is outstanding; try carrot pureed with ginger and coconut–not creamy, but with genuine substance.

The hardest part of dining at Aromas may be deciding what to choose. It's tempting to make a meal of the appetizers, though the fish, meat or poultry, or pasta entreés are first rate. Vegetarians will love 'Aroma's Celestial Plate' ($17.50) in which scallion-seared tofu arrives with grilled vegetables, a generous plate of bok choy, onions, green peppers, zucchini, and eggplant, served with a honey soy sauce. Each component is perfectly cooked, and the mix flavorful without being sharp.

The wine list, though small, has excellent choices in the medium range, and even some fine choices at just a bit more, like a Grgich Hills chardonnay ($45). Italian and California wines join Chilean wines favored by the chef. The restaurant serves 3 full meals a day, 6 days a week. Breakfast features omelets with inventive fillings, and lunches include homemade soup ($5.50), panini style sandwiches and imaginative salads ($6-$9). A half bowl of soup and half-sandwich is a bargain $6.75.

The dining room is painted a cheerful yellow, with wood grain tables and comfortable rattan upholstered chairs. Colorful table settings and wall hangings suggest the South American heritage of the owner. Two dining areas as well as a small patio provide comfortable seating with well separated tables. It's fun to peek at the chef performing through the pass through to the kitchen. Portions are generous, and service friendly yet professional, if occasionally on the slow side, but that's because the chef cooks everything to order. The restaurant is smoothly run, and the word of mouth among local people keeps bringing more people in. Aromas is one to try for sure, especially if you are staying near the Marriott.

3501 Rice St., Harbor Mall, 2nd floor. 245-9192. T-Fri 7 am – 9: 30 pm; S & S 8 am – 9: 30 pm. Closed Mondays. Credit cards. Kid's menu. Take out/ catering. Map 1

Ba Le

Tucked away in Wailua's Safeway shopping center, Ba Le has a loyal following among local people for well-cooked meals at a fair price. Vietnamese specialities are terrific, including *pho*, a fragrant beef broth with noodles, prepared with a variety of additions, including chicken, pork, or beef, shrimp, tofu and vegetables for an amazingly reasonable price ($6.50-$9.50). Or try a big bowl of vermicilli, long rice noodles served without broth, accented with chicken ($8), beef ($9), shrimp ($9) with delicious curry, coconut, or lemongrass flavors. Stir fried noodles are served "almost no fat" and are very light and tasty. Fresh fruit smoothies ($3.75) are a great accompaniment. Don't like noodles? You can even taste these flavorful choices sandwich-style on home baked bread. Phone ahead and order a wonderful beach picnic lunch.

Dinner plates are generous, like tofu eggplant rice plate (fully half the portion is tofu and eggplant) ($7.95), and tofu and vegetables vermicilli, served at room temperature ($7.95). Each has a distinct flavor and delicious sauce, great for vegetarians. You'll love vegetables roll – two rice paper rolls with carrots, sprouts and delicious peanut sauce ($5.50).

For first rate food and friendly service at an amazingly reasonable price, don't miss Ba Le. Owner Leon Lam takes great pride in his storefront operation, and wants your dining experience to show it.

Wailua. 4-831 Kuhio Hwy, next to Longs. 823-6060. 10 am – 9 pm daily. Credit cards require minimum purchase. Map 1

Barbecue Inn

Where do local folks go for a lunch which includes soup, a beverage, fresh bread, an entrée like a teriyaki chicken sandwich, and dessert for only $7.95? In this family-owned restaurant, you'll find some of the tastiest food and one of the best food values on the island. A local favorite since 1940, Barbecue Inn is the rare kind of place with something special for everyone in the family. At dinner, more than 30 choices – fresh fish, seafood, steak, prime rib ($6.95–$18.95) – include soup or fresh fruit, a salad, bread, vegetable, dessert, even a beverage! At lunch, entrées cost even less, averaging $7.95 (but you don't get salad).

first rate prime rib, steak & fresh fish!

Kids will love the cheeseburger ($3.95), which arrives still sizzling on a toasted sesame bun, smothered with melted cheese and garnished with fresh, local manoa lettuce. For only $4.50, kids can order fried chicken, hamburger, spaghetti, or chow mein dinners, ten choices in all, including a beverage, or a grilled cheese sandwich made on home-baked bread toasted crisp and golden. Grown-ups will love teriyaki steak ($17.95), a tender rib-eye with homemade sauce, or teriyaki beef kabob and light, crispy shrimp tempura ($14).

You will be surprised at the high quality of the 'extras' which many restaurants pay scant attention to. Miso soup is superb. Bread is homemade – light, fragrant, and exceptionally tasty. The fruit cup appetizer is so fresh – pineapple, papaya, watermelon, honeydew, and mango – that you'll almost hope your kids will refuse to eat theirs because there are no canned peaches. The green salad would win no awards for imagination, but you'd be surprised at how much fun the kids have picking out the shredded cabbage and homemade croutons. And everyone will devour the homemade pies–coconut, chocolate, or chocolate cream – pies so light they are almost as amazing as the price: $1.25 a slice, almost the same price as a Coke. Buy a bag of BBQ Inn's cookies or crunchy 'cinnamon toast' to keep in the car.

You will see a lot of working people coming off the job, and the portions are so enormous you can understand why. Waitresses are unfailingly cheerful, even when small children decorate the floor with crumbs and ice cubes. All this makes Barbecue Inn a good dinner choice for hearty eaters and hungry families, for anyone who appreciates ordinary food cooked extremely well, as well as some very special treats.

Lihue. 2982 Kress St. off Rice St. 245-2921. Closed Sundays. Breakfast 7:30 am - 10:30 am. Lunch 10:30 am - 1:30 pm. Dinner 5 pm - 8:30 pm (4:30 - 8:45 pm F, S) Air-conditioned. Credit cards. Map 1

Blossoming Lotus

You'll find 'vegan world fusion cuisine' in this somewhat funky storefront restaurant in downtown Kapa'a, and even non-vegan diners can navigate the menu to find something new and interesting, like green papaya salad with vegetables and ginger ($5.99), summer rolls, sandwiches (from $6.99), and wraps, including an option to 'build' your own with your favorite ingredients. Our maki roll ($6.99) with brown rice, vegetables, pickled ginger was tasty though quite a bit spicier than described by our waitress. Purple potato salad ($3.99) made quite a splash for its vivid color and distinctive flavor. Hummus ($3.99) was on the garlicky side. Try grilled papaya 'tuna' spread out in a nori sheet, with wasabi and shoyu, or green papaya cutlet, with daily soup and salsa, a dressing, paté, and hummus with steamed vegetables. The menu also features "live" selections not heated above 116 degrees.

The dining room is very small, only 6 tables, and an outdoor eating patio with four more. The décor is minimalist, to put it more mildly than our maki roll – a few bonsai plants, a couple of murals, and a bubble lamp pretty much do it all. The fun is watching the parade of folks, big and little, coming in for pastries and cookies. Lunches and dinners (from $14.99) feature sampling options (3 items/$11.99 and 4 items/$14.99) including grains, salads, soups, a good idea because à la carte portions can cause your bill to mount up quickly.

Tea lovers can embark on a 'sniffing' adventure through the 25 varieties. The menu also features a 'daily quote' (of wisdom), a daily drink blend like Kauai Chai with soy, a 'beloved bean du jour,' even a daily cookie (mint chocolate chip) which was excellent. An expansion is planned, which might make dining feel more spacious.

Old Kapa'a town. 822-7678. Lunch: 11 - 3 pm; Dinner 6 - 9 pm daily. Credit cards. Map 1

The Bull Shed

Since 1973, The Bull Shed has been famous on Kauai for high quality meals at unbeatable prices. Bull Shed's prime rib is truly special – a thick slice of tender beef, perfectly cooked with a tasty bone (if you ask for it), delicious *au jus* and fresh horseradish sauce – at $22.95 the best deal for the best portion on Kauai! Fresh island fish is another winner, a huge portion filleted by manager Tom Liu himself, then perfectly grilled. At Bull Shed, 'surf and turf' sets the island standard.

A glance at the menu will tell you why the Bull Shed is so popular. Prices are amazingly reasonable, entrées come with rice and the salad bar, and half cost less than $15. Combination dinners are served with a 7.5 oz. tenderloin filet instead of the usual small sirloin. Lobster tail is enormous, a full 12 oz., and perfectly cooked. The wine list is also reasonable, with half the primarily California selections around $20.

first rate prime rib, steak & fresh fish!

The Bull Shed has become a favorite with each member of our family, in itself a small

A banana flower bearing fruit

miracle. Our 6:45 pm arrival time is early enough to beat the crowds, and all four of our children eat everything that is served to them–a rare achievement. Lauren's teriyaki chicken breast ($13.95 or $6.95 child's portion) is always perfectly soft and juicy. Mike loves the teriyaki sirloin ($14.95), and Jeremy orders fresh island ahi, a huge portion for only $16.95, one of the best we have tasted, or rack of lamb ($23.95), a large portion, both tender and tasty, with a delicious teriyaki marinade. Even better, all four put away huge and healthful salads, picking their pickiest best from the salad bar ($6.95 by itself).

The Bull Shed offers one of the best food values on Kauai, in a pleasant dining room with friendly, efficient service. It's popular, so try to arrive before 7 pm to avoid the traffic jam. Or invite some friends because 6 or more can have a reservation. If it's warm, request a table by a window that opens (not all do).

Bull Shed has not only great food and prices, but an ocean view. In fact, the restaurant is built as close to the ocean as modern technology can allow, and our favorite table, in a tiny room by itself just a few feet from the edge of a seawall, offers a spectacular view of the waves rolling towards the wall and crashing in torrents of spray. During a storm, the waves splash right against the glass, an awesome sight. Come on a night when the moon is full, and watch the waves send gleaming ripples through the darkness.

Wailua, in Mokihana Resort, Kuhio Hwy. 822-3791. Dinner 5:30 pm - 10 pm nightly. Smoking at bar. Credit Cards. Children's menu (under 13). Look for the sign (it's small) opposite McDonald's, north of Coconut Plantation Marketplace. Turn towards the water. Map 1

Caffé Coco

In almost any season, you'll find something blooming or bearing fruit at Caffé Coco. The dining room is actually a tropical grove of mango, avocado, pomolo (a grapefruit cousin), and papaya, with 'walls' of thick, tall sugar cane. The decor is a bower of bougainvillea, ferns, and orchids. Garden chairs surround a collection of tables beneath a honeysuckle-covered arbor. The cuisine emphasizes the natural – local vegetables, fruits, and herbs–and everything is fresh and organic.

Some dishes are outstanding, like local mahi mahi ($14.50) crusted with black sesame seeds and accompanied with rice and a tasty wasabi cream sauce. Or try fresh ono with cilantro pesto, served with 'silver noodle salad' of bean threads with a delicious homemade peanut ginger dressing. Green salads arrive with unusual dressings – creamy feta, for example – and vegetables are imaginative, like fresh corn and green beans with eggplant, or a tasty sweet potato dumpling. Lighter choices include an ahi nori wrap, with soup and salad ($13), as well as omelets and vegetable salads. At lunch we enjoyed homemade soup and an ahi sandwich on foccacia bread. A spicy fish burrito contains a generous portion of ono, as well as rice and black beans.

You'll have to bring your own wine, or try non-alcoholic beverages served in blue or yellow goblets, like ginger lemonade or pomolo fizz, made when the enormous pomolo tree bears its fruit. Desserts feature local fruits, like mango tart from the mango tree.

You place your order at the counter where a refrigerated case displays the day's fresh ingredients. The staff will describe their favorites, even identify what's on a plate headed for the dining room. Dine in the garden, or inside, in what is called with a grin, the 'Black Light Art Gallery.' The paintings glow – you will too, if you are wearing anything white.

As the lights from the kitchen cast a golden glow into the garden, this beautifully lush, tranquil setting can ease your spirit as well as your hunger. If you like organic foods, Caffé Coco could become your favorite place. If mosquitoes pick on you while ignoring your friends, bring some 'Off' and request a mosquito coil. Come for lunch, and enjoy the garden in its full sunlit glory, and browse afterwards in the adjacent antique shop, Bambuli. Just turn left under the mango tree.

Wailua, 4-369 Kuhio Hwy. (across from Kintaro). 822-7990. Open 11 am - 9 pm. FAX 822-0066. Closed Mondays. Credit cards. Map 1

Café Portofino

A favorite for Italian cuisine for many years, Café Portofino has a wonderful new oceanside location at the Marriott. From tables on the deck, you can watch the waves roll across Kalapaki Bay, and enjoy the

beachfront dining & great pasta

evening breezes. Guiseppi Avocadi, a one-man band of talent and energy, is committed to high food quality and professional service. The new dining room is spacious, with tables separated for privacy, covered in linen and set with shining crystal.

The menu offers fresh fish, homemade pastas, chicken, veal and fish. Portofino's Italian cuisine is light and healthful, the sauces based on vegetable flavors rather than heavy with cream. Flavorful minestrone is served in a generous portion for a modest price ($6), and kids will love mozzarella marinara ($8). Vegetable lasagne ($16) is as festive looking as a wrapped birthday present, and tastes just as wonderful, the flavors and textures of fresh zucchini and spinach brought together with a wonderful marinara sauce with tasty chunks of tomatoes. Fresh ono is tender and moist, served with a delicious mushroom sauce. Other good choices are 'scampi alla limone' ($20), zesty and attractive, served with perfectly cooked broccoli, and an excellent rack of lamb ($28). A dinner salad ($6) is nicely presented; goat cheese salad with fresh mixed greens is excellent. Tiramisu ($8) is a great way to complete the meal.

Service is professional yet friendly. Everyone seems to care about your dinner, and willing to fetch extra bread or answer questions. The wine list is well selected, and if prices are on the high side, there are also some bargains, like a respectable vintage of Pinot Grigio for around $30. At Café Portofino, you'll find an attractive setting, reasonable prices, distinctive cuisine, and friendly, professional service.

Lihue, across from Kauai Marriott. 245-2121. Credit cards. Dinner 5 - 10 pm nightly. Live music. Map 1

Coconuts

Described as an 'Island Style Grill and Wine Bar,' Coconuts has a kind of Maui style chic, the signature of owners who hail from island life in a faster lane than Rt. 56, Wailua. Inside an exterior decorated with rowboats and tiki torches, the hum of happy diners blends with lite rock music, and all the surfaces shine, down to wood tables lit with candles. There's a feeling of energy in the relatively small dining room, due in part to other diners waiting to get to their tables (waits can be more than a half hour) and the sense of high occupancy. The new outside dining area, decorated with tiki umbrellas, has alleviated some of the pressure.

Coconuts offers an extensive menu, ranging from an inexpensive hamburger ($10.50) to fresh island fish ($17-$22), so you can find something for every degree of hunger and expense. Salmon ($16.50) is flavored with teriyaki, while onaga tasted disappointingly bitter from the grill. Ahi wasabi was the best ($19.95). Menu prices are reasonable except for expensive nightly specials, which can add $5 or so to the dinner price, so be careful when you order. Most entrées are imaginatively prepared, like a very tasty fresh island mahi mahi with macadamia nut rice ($21.95), with portions occasionally on the small side. To add a salad or an appetizer will add $6 to $10 more. Lobster ravioli ($9.50) is tasty if somewhat dense, and coconut crusted shrimp ($10.50) is delicious though surprisingly expensive for the portion of only two shrimps. Dinner starts with fresh baked buns and homemade hummus, and ends with tasty desserts ($5.50) including a first rate crème brulée. The wine list includes many good choices in the $25-$35 range, including excellent wines by the glass, as well as wonderful tropical drinks. Service is polite if sometimes slow.

With prices a dollar or two below nearby rival Pacific Café, Coconuts has a loyal following for its island-style cuisine. Waiting is almost inevitable, so consider making friends with some folks on the beach and going in as a six – then you can have a reservation!

4-919 Kuhio Highway, Wailua. 823-8777 Full bar. Dinner 4 pm - 10 pm. Closed Sundays. Credit cards. Map 1

Dani's

At Dani's, you won't find an orchid on your plate, but you will find hot, tasty, and filling meals, including local-style Hawaiian foods. Kona coffee comes free with breakfast, and you can choose from eggs, omelettes, pancakes, and tasty Hawaiian dishes from $3.50. The ham and cheese omelette is very cheesy and stuffed with ham, though the hotcakes are on the heavy side. The lunch menu offers a wide variety of Hawaiian, American, and Japanese dishes, as well as sandwiches and hamburgers. Prices start at $5.40 and include soup or salad, roll, rice, and coffee or tea.

With prices this low, expect to sacrifice atmosphere. The color scheme is woodgrain formica accented by fluorescent lights, but on the other hand, the large dining room is bright, clean, and comfortably air-conditioned, and service swift and efficient.

Lihue, 4201 Rice St. 5 am - 1:30 pm (1 pm on Sat). Closed Sundays. Credit cards. Smoking section. 245-4991. Map 1

Duke's Canoe Club

One of the most popular restaurants on Kauai, Duke's offers a sumptuous salad bar, which can truly be a meal in itself, as well as high quality, reasonably-priced dinners. Duke's also offers the Polynesian glitz which has made its sister restaurants, Keoki's on Kauai, as well as Kimo's on Maui, so successful, with this additional bonus: Since Duke's is perched right on the edge of Kalapaki Bay, you can be in the real Hawaii as well as the Hollywood version.

A stone stairway carved into an indoor waterfall draped with ferns and trailing flowers takes you up to the dining room, a perfect spot to look out over Kalapaki bay and watch the changing light tint the clouds while listening to wonderful Hawaiian music. Friendly performers stroll from table to table, offering to play your favorite Kauai songs, like 'Beautiful Kauai' or 'Hanalei Moon'.

Duke's reasonable dinner prices (from $14.95 for chicken) include the wonderful salad bar, with freshly made Caesar salad as well as an array of fresh vegetables and lettuces, fruits, pasta salads, tofu, fresh-baked banana macadamia nut muffins, and even rice – great for vegetarians ($10.95 alone). Fresh fish entrées ($19-$22) include tasty teriyaki broiled fresh ahi. You might find some sauces, like the orange-ginger,

very strongly flavored, so it's wise to have sauce served on the side. Most fish filets (8 to 10 oz.) are pre-glazed, but can be clean grilled.

The prime rib ($24.95 or $17.95/smaller cut), however, stopped the flow of conversation. Nearly 22 ounces, it was so thick that you didn't know where to begin to tackle it. More like a family-size roast, it was a significant dining event, and tender as well as juicy, served underspiced rather than over-salted. Described on the menu as "while it lasts," this dinner may be sold out by the time you order, so you might reserve a portion when you arrive. The wine list offers several good choices in the mid-$20 range. And be sure to try the famous 'Hula pie.'

Everyone in the family will enjoy Duke's. Children's dinners include fries and the salad bar (about $6), and adults can order 'Lighter Fare' (pasta, pizza, or a cheeseburger) for under $10. What comes to your table will be well-prepared, efficiently served, in a setting where you can watch the ocean and listen to wonderful Hawaiian music. An unbeatable combination (that's why you see so many local families crowding the tables). Reservations help somewhat, though there's usually still a wait; one section is set aside for walk-ins. Think twice about going in the rain, however, for you'll miss the view when they close the shutters.

Duke's Barefoot Bar

Downstairs, right next to Kalapaki Beach, Duke's Barefoot Bar serves lunch, informal dinner, and munchies all day. Try excellent hamburgers ($6.95) and sandwiches ($6.95-$8.95), as well as salads and crisp, hot french fries. You'll love the fresh island fish daily dinner special (only $14.95) – one fin each night, perhaps teriyaki ahi, or grilled moon-fish. Vegetable plate is fresh and colorful ($6.95), and you can visit the salad bar upstairs for $10.95.

In Lihue, on Kalapaki Beach, access through the Kauai Marriott. Free valet parking. Reserve a day in advance (246-9599). Dinner 5 – 10 pm nightly. Credit Cards. *Duke's Barefoot Bar* downstairs: 11:30 am to 11:30 pm. The bar is a smoking area. www.dukeskauai.com. Map 1

Eggbert's

Once upon a time, when eggs were king, many an enormous omelette was whipped up at Eggbert's in Lihue. Iniki changed all that. Eggbert's closed, and the world moved into synch with a different diet. Now Eggbert's has re-opened in Wailua at a time of low cholesterol chic, when people are counting calories and looking for ways to avoid fat. When you've got 'egg' all over your name these days, you take a hearty risk!

For 23 years, Eggbert's has been known for eggs –150 types of omelettes (even eggbeater options), and eggs benedict in 5 styles and 2 sizes (from $7.45). You can also try tasty banana pancakes with coconut syrup or french toast ($5.95). Kid's breakfast special is $3.65. For lunch, you'll find tasty burgers, salads, and sandwiches ($6-$8), and dinner choices from $6.50 (less for children and seniors "65 & Better").

The location in the Coconut Plantation Marketplace is great for families–a bright, white dining space with windows on all sides to encourage breezes. Plastic chairs provide adequate comfort, and blue formica tables have rounded corners, safe at eye level for short persons who like to explore underneath. Service can be a bit on the slow side, but there's cappuccino and espresso while you wait.

At Eggbert's, you'll find things largely sunny side up – a reasonable meal for a reasonable price.

Coconut Plantation Marketplace, Wailua 822-3787. Daily 7 am - 9 pm. Smoking on lanai outside. Credit cards. Map 1

Garden Island Barbecue & Chinese

Garden Island Barbecue in downtown Lihue serves big portions for small prices. At lunch or dinner, the rather spartan dining room will probably be full of local folks, and a glance around will show you why. Platters are mounded with colorful heaps of noodles and vegetables, and the four page menu has prices around $5.95-$6.95.

Food quality won't win any awards for inventiveness, but what the chef cooks is tasty and hot. Saimin steams in the bowl; wontons feature shrimps as well as ground meat, and vegetables are still crunchy. Lunch or dinner entrées include two scoops of rice and macaroni salad. Barbecue plate ($6.25) with rice includes a generous teriyaki chicken breast and beef thinly sliced and delicious. Shrimp with locally grown choi sun, a green vegetable somewhat like broccoli leaves and flowers, is very tasty.

The dining room is clean, cooled by fans, and seems friendly from the moment you walk in. Garden Island may not be fancy, but if you're on a budget, you'll appreciate the generous portions of inexpensive, tasty food.

Lihue, 4252A Rice St. 245-8868. 10:30 am - 9 pm. Closed Sundays. Cash only. Map 1

Gaylord's

Once the heart of a 1,700 acre sugar plantation, Kilohana is a special place. Rooms have the spacious beauty of large proportions and wide verandas, and you can easily imagine the gracious pace of life before airplanes and traffic lights. With the mountains behind and rolling lawns all around, you can glimpse, even if briefly, a way of life now forever lost.

Named for Gaylord Wilcox who built Kilohana, the restaurant's dining room and veranda look out over a manicured lawn and garden lush with leafy ferns and brilliant tropical flowers. In the evening, the flagstone terrace is lit with lanterns, and rattan chairs surround comfortable tables decked with white linen and pink napkins arranged like

fans. Gaylord's is one of the most romantic restaurants on Kauai, with the kind of setting you'd want to star in if your life were a black and white movie. Candles on the tables flicker in gentle breezes, and from your chair beneath the roof you can peek out at stars shining in the velvet sky. As you gaze out at the gardens lit by the moon and stars, you can feel soft tropical breezes which rustle the leaves. Waiters move discreetly, anticipating your every desire.

At Gaylord's you'll do best if you order simply, with sauces served on the side. Sautéed fresh island onaga ($26.95) and grilled ahi were both excellent, perfectly cooked, moist and flavorful, much better without the strongly flavored sauces. The special steamed vegetable entrée, cooked to order for our vegetarian, was outstandingly fresh, attractive, and flavorful. Prime rib ($18.95/10 oz. or $20.95/13 oz.) is a good bet, served with lots of *au jus*, as well as one of the least costly menu items. Entrées arrive with rice, potato, or pasta, as well as a vegetable, like still crunchy sugarpeas in the pod and sliced red peppers. Most cost more than $20 unless you come for 'light supper' (5 to 6:30 pm). Soup or salad raise the cost of dining quickly. While expensive, Gaylord's wine list has some good choices for less than $30.

The dining experience at Gaylord's can be wonderful. Waiters are polite, attentive, and professional, and in the quiet courtyard, you escape the usual noisy distractions of clattering trays and dishes. Small details get lots of attention: water is served in elegant iced glasses with tangy lemon slices, and coffee cups are watched carefully. If you like to linger after dinner, consider bringing a sweater, for winter temperatures can be chilly.

With such an elegant setting, Gaylord's is one of the island's special dining experiences, an image to haunt you when temperatures plunge back home. The food never quite seems to match the setting – though perhaps that's because of the setting! We have heard high praise of Gaylord's lunch, where excellent sandwiches, salads, vegetable platters, burgers and fresh seafood are reasonably-priced ($8-$11) and you can look out at the garden in the full splendor of sunshine.

Just west of Lihue, on Rt. 50. 245-9593. Credit cards. Lunch 11 am - 3 pm. Dinner 5 -10 pm daily. Sunday brunch (à la carte menu) 9:30 am -3 pm. Weekly luaus. Children's menu. Weddings. www.gaylordskauai.com

Hamura's Saimin

According to legend, Oahu businessmen have flown to Kauai just to have lunch at Hamura Saimin. To look at the weather-beaten exterior, you'd have your doubts. The tiny building encloses–just barely–three horse-shoe shaped counters with stools. Although a recent face-lift has made the room look cleaner and more like a luncheonette, you can still watch the cook stir and chop and make things sizzle. The inevitability of change, yes, though some traditions die hard. A sign still warns: "No Gum Under the Counter." Nowadays, sometimes someone peeks!

On this counter is served some of the finest saimin around, and you come to want to believe the legend about the Oahu businessmen and their expense account lunches. Airfare could certainly be offset with bargain food prices: for $5.95 you get the saimin special–tasty and fragrant soup with noodles, chock full of vegetables and meats. Perfectly flavored won ton soup or won ton min is only $4. To take the saimin out costs 25 cents for the container, but you can escape the cramped little room and head for the beach. Perfectly spiced barbecued beef or chicken sticks ($.75) are another find. Kids love homemade *manapu*, a sweet cousin of the pretzel ($1.50/bag). Don't miss lilikoi chiffon pie ($1.25) or one of the best buys on Kauai, $10 for the whole pie! (We take one home on the plane, frozen.)

When the waitress takes your order, she passes a bowl of the appro-priate size and color over the counter to the cook, who inserts the proper mix of ingredients, then covers all with ladles of steaming broth. If you visit often enough, you begin to appreciate technique, the consumer's as well as the cook's. The obviously experienced diners mix hot mustard and soy sauce in their spoons, dipping the mixture into the soup as necessary, and using chopsticks to pull the noodles through.

There's not much variety, but what the cook

no gum under counter!

cooks is very good indeed, and the visit is like a trip into the island's past, a time before tourism brought butcherblock tables and bentwood chairs, air-conditioning and gourmet teas – a time when sticking gum under the counter, though frowned upon, was still possible. So throw away your Bubble Yum before going inside, and try this taste of authentic Kauai!

Lihue, 2956 Kress St. Cash only. M-Sat 10 am - 9 pm. Open (and less crowded) Sundays for lunch. 245-3271. Map 1

Hanama'ulu Restaurant & Tea House

You could not select a better place to share a really special evening with friends than the Tea House, because this restaurant combines delicious food with the friendliest service on the island, and, as if that weren't enough, a Japanese garden setting to make everything seem just a bit magical. Here you can dine on soft mats at low tables next to the goldfish and water lilies. Children can wander around and count the carp (tell them to be careful; one of our two-year-olds tumbled in!). Local families have been coming here for more than sixty-five years. Today they still appreciate excellent cooking at reasonable prices, and it's a rare wedding, anniversary, welcome or farewell party that does not take place in one of the tea rooms by the garden.

The Miyake family cooks with subtlety and flair, and creates a genuinely special cuisine, with 35 Chinese and Japanese entrées at reasonable prices from $4.75-$14.75. We recommend the won ton soup ($6); garnished with scallions, pork, and slices of egg foo young, it's outstanding! Children will love crispy fried chicken with its delicate touch of ginger ($6); the boneless pieces are just the right size for little hands.

When our party is large enough, we ask the owner to order a several course dinner, and we are always delighted with the new dishes we discover. Fresh island tempura with fresh fish or shrimp is spectacular, served on an enormous platter, and the taste is just as wonderful ($9.75). Vegetarians will love the vegetable tempura ($6.50) or crispy tofu tempura ($4) served with teriyaki sauce and green onions. Sashimi of ahi and ono is fresh and elegantly arranged, and of the best quality. A specialty, mushrooms stuffed with crab ($5.75), is lighter than many versions of the dish, and very tasty. Chinese chicken salad has lots of chicken, lettuce, crispy noodles, and

Island style & family friendly

wonderful dressing. The sushi bar features excellent salmon skin handrolls with crispy grilled salmon.

Reserve at least three days in advance to choose where you dine. Avoid the rather non-descript front dining room, and try the teppan yaki room and sushi bar, where you will find excellent sushi and first rate sashimi. Our favorite, however, is the tea house by the gardens, where we can listen to crickets sing the songs of evening while stars light up the velvet sky. If mosquitoes like to pick on you while ignoring your friends, don't be bashful about asking for a mosquito coil. The incense smell is great, and it keeps the bugs away.

In more than twenty years of dining, this special restaurant has never let us down. The cooking is consistently excellent, the prices remarkably reasonable, the service exceptionally friendly, and children are treated with more than usual tolerance by waitresses like Sally and Arlene who genuinely love them. This is a restaurant where you should sample as many dishes as possible, and because it is such a special place, we save the Tea House for our last night, and ask any *kapunas* who might be listening to speed our return! You shouldn't miss the Tea House either.

Hanama'ulu, Rt. 56. Reserve a tea room in advance. 245-2511. Credit cards. Full bar. Closed Mondays. Lunch 9 am - 1 pm; Dinner 4:30 pm - 9 pm. Banquet facilities. Ask Sally about special wedding menus. Map 1

Hong Kong Café, Bar B Q & Noodles

Wailua's Hong Kong Café offers an excellent alternative to generic fast food. It looks like a luncheonette, with about nine green and black formica tables in an air-conditioned dining room, where the major visual point of interest is a poster of Hong Kong's Victoria Harbor. It's often full because the menu offers many choices – roast duck, crispy chicken, lo mein and chow mein, sweet and sour as well as vegetarian dishes –almost everything costs less than $8. The emphasis is on island fresh vegetables. Choose plate lunches from $4.50 to $6.75, bento lunches or vegetarian dishes, including a delicious eggplant with tofu ($6.75). We like saimin, of which there are nine varieties ($2.95 to $5.75), served in huge, steaming bowls of noodles, vegetables, and flavorful broth. Bring in your wine or beer. Hong Kong Café is not pretentious, and you can enjoy reasonable food at reasonable prices, and they will deliver nearby. Fax your order.

In Wailua Shopping Plaza, 4-361 Kuhio Hwy. 822-3288. Credit cards. Lunch: 10:30 am-2:30 pm. Dinner: 4:30-9:30 pm. Closed Tuesdays.

Hukilau Lanai

The restaurant in the Kauai Coast Resort (formerly the Beachboy) combines excellent dinners with a wonderful location looking out over the landscape to the sea. As darkness fall and evening breezes cool the open air patio and dining room, you can enjoy the night sky, spectacular when moonlight silvers the gardens and sparkles on the waves.

In the comfortable two-tiered dining room and dining lanai, every table has a view, enhanced by soft lighting, soft music, and performances by local musicians several nights a week. Dinner begins with homemade foccacia, which you can enjoy with a first-rate tropical cocktail, like a pineapple martini. The menu features flavors of the Pacific rim – fresh island fish, as well as poultry and meat. Entrées come with rice, potatoes, even risotto, and the kitchen will even prepare pasta you bring in yourself. Start with scallops with pineapple buerre blanc sauce, and if you are a seafood lover, try Hukilau seafood mixed grill ($24), a family favorite, with two good-sized pieces of fresh fish, like ahi and ono; be sure to ask for delicious homemade teriyaki sauce. Other fish choices include grilled ono, shiitake mushroom and panko crusted opah ($18.95), opakapaka dusted with herbs baked in a ti leaf with lop cheong, cilantro, green onion ($23.95). Meat lovers can try the grilled rib-eye steak with garlic mashed potatoes ($21.95).

When asked, the chef created a fresh steamed vegetable plate for Mirah, our vegetarian, a spectacular array of grilled eggplant, tomato, mush-rooms, vegetable ragout ($12.95). Beach Boy Burger is at the low end ($10.95). Don't miss desserts – tropical shortcake with lemon curd ($5.95) is a stand-out, and chocolate

The ne ne, Hawaii's state bird and an endangered species, is slowly increasing in numbers on Kauai

lovers will love the chocolate macadamia nut cheesecake.

Hukilau will satisfy the most exacting palates and diets. Switch what comes with the entreés? No problem. Bring your own pasta? A snap. Steam fish or vegetables in their own juices? Easy. And what's best, no extra charge for this personalized service. Children are welcomed with a special menu; an interesting idea, the wine list announces 20 wines costing less than $20. A banquet room is a great spot for a party.

Kapa'a, behind Coconut Plantation Marketplace in Kauai Coast Resort. Dinner from 5 pm Tuesday – Sunday. 822-3441 for reservations and entertainment schedule. Credit cards. Banquet room. Weddings. Map 1

JJ's Broiler

More than thirty years ago, Kauai's first steak house opened in an old plantation house on the main street of Lihue, then a sleepy town with a single traffic light. JJ's achieved local fame for its specialty, "Slavonic steak," a sliced London broil marinated in garlic sauce. When anyone in JJ's was served this dish, everyone else knew it! Then JJ's opened right on Kalapaki Bay, its garish, hot pink sign issuing a neon challenge to the hotel restaurants just down the beach. Just as the contest was getting interesting, Iniki struck and blew all the dining spots out of business.

Today, JJ's offers a reasonable meal at a reasonable price if you consider the salad bar which arrives at your table in a huge bowl of greens surrounded by vegetables and condiments in a lazy susan (at $9.95 by itself, it is one of the best inexpensive meals on Kauai). On one visit, the New York steak ($19.95 for 14 oz.) was tasteless and tough, while fresh opakapaka was well prepared, though served with a sauce so heavy that we were glad to have ordered it served on the side. Macadamia nut rack of lamb ($23.95) was excellent, both tender and moist, if a bit heavy on the mustard sauce. Bread is undistinguished, served without a plate to hold down the crumbs.

JJ's multi–level design affords each table privacy as well as an ocean view. Above the polished wood tables, in the enormous space of the open beam ceiling, hang actual sailboats. JJ's costs the same or even more than other steak houses like The Bull Shed in Wailua, or Duke's Canoe Club right down the beach, where, in our opinion, portions are larger and the food tastier.

Lihue, Anchor Cove Center. 246-4422 Lunch 11 am - 5 pm. Dinner 5 pm -10 pm, daily. Credit cards. Map 1

Kalapaki Beach Hut

In the green building right behind Kalapaki Beach, you will find one of our favorite sandwiches on Kauai – fresh ono, cleanly grilled, moist and tender, and wrapped in a soft roll with lettuce and juicy tomatoes. When fresh fish is scarce, it's made with frozen mahi mahi, but even that sandwich is tasty. You will also find some of the best hamburgers on Kauai – no surprise since the owner, Steve Gerald, originated 'Ono Burger' in Anahola more than twenty years ago. Since then, the term 'Ono Burger' has achieved near legendary status, a name spoken with reverence whenever fine hamburgers are discussed on Kauai.

Steve Gerald has flame-broiled many a burger, either beef or turkey, or even buffalo. Beef burgers are extra juicy, extra tasty, and meltingly delicious. The entry level burger costs $3.95 and comes with lettuce, tomato, and mayonnaise on a sesame bun. Buffalo burgers are about $2 more, but just think of the savings for your arteries! Teriyaki or barbecue style is forty cents more, or add cheese for sixty cents or a bacon and cheddar or mushroom melt for about $2. Kids' burgers include fries and soft drink for under $4. French fries are hot and tasty, with vinegar as well as catsup available. Vegetarians can try a veggie sandwich or a salad. Everything is cooked to order, so be patient, or phone the order in ahead.

It's open every day from 7 am (8 am Sundays) till 7 pm. Start your day with a 'breakfast sandwich' or omelette, and all the coffee you can hold. You can hardly spend your food money more wisely. Take it out, or dine in the upstairs porch with a view of the bay.

Lihue, on Kalapaki Bay, 3464 Rice St. 246-6330. Cash only. Map 1.

Kauai Chop Suey

Kauai Chop Suey combines unpretentious surroundings, excellent dinners, and unbeatable prices. The dining room, usually crowded with local families, is clean, bright, and cheerful, with well-spaced tables and fly fans to keep the air moving. The decor is a crisp combination of red and white, accented with red Chinese lanterns and green leafy plants.

The real attraction is the prices. A big tureen of minced beef with egg soup ($6.45) is sensational, subtly seasoned, with an egg-drop texture. Saimin ($2.75/$4.50) is excellent. Pineapple shrimp ($6.95) is a perfect balance of sweet and sour, and the shrimps, eight large ones, arrive crisp and exceedingly tender. Special fried rice (at $7.95) is indeed special – especially tasty, especially generous, and chock full of delicious roast pork, chicken, shrimp, black mushrooms and crunchy snow peas, as is Kauai Chow Mein ($8.15) with shrimp, chicken, char sieu, and broccoli.

Your level of satisfaction, we discovered, has a lot to do with the service, which has a lot to do with the work load in the kitchen. Even if you see empty tables, the owner may tell you to come back in 15 minutes, and in this way control the pace at which the chefs have to cook. Once you are seated, you may not see your waitress for a while. That's because, as we saw on our last visit, there was only one waitress, and she was taking orders from all the tables, while two other waitresses served and a couple of busboys cleared the plates. It's not a very efficient system, and it certainly lacks the personal touch, but the prices are amazing, and you can bring along your own wine or beer to make the waiting more pleasant. Think twice about bringing the kids – unless you feed them before you come! To bring food home in a box will cost you 21 cents (tax included). You pay and you pack! Be warned: your feet must cross the threshold by 9 pm or you will be told, with great politeness, the kitchen is closed.

Lihue, Pacific Ocean Plaza. No reservations. Cash only. Take-out 245-8790. Lunch 11 - 2 pm Tues. through Sat. & Dinner 4:30 - 9 pm Tues. through Sun. Closed Mondays. No beer or wine. Map 1

Kiibo Restaurant & Sushi Bar

Kiibo has a pleasant, though small dining room with a clean, though utilitarian decor. Comfortable upholstered chairs surround bamboo colored tables. At one end is a low table on rice mats for patrons wishing to remove their shoes. Everything is understated, even air-conditioning.

Order tempura à la carte and select from five different types of fresh fish, chicken, pork, beans, tofu, onion, sweet potato, carrots, even eggplant. On our most recent visit, however, what arrived at the table was more like breaded shrimp. Teriyaki chicken was a great success, sweet yet tangy, and both juicy and tender. Sukiyaki appears in a steaming iron caldron, rich and pungent with sauce and translucent noodles.

Priced from $5.50, entrées come with miso soup and rice attractively displayed on a square tray. Lunch is a better deal, however, with selections about a dollar less than the same choices on the dinner menu. Lunch is also the better meal; given the cautious size of the portions, dinner might leave you hungry. Spend a little more, and you might find a better quality dinner at Hanama'ulu Tea House or Kintaro.

Lihue, 2991 Umi St. 245-2650. Cash only. Lunch daily 11 am - 1:30 pm. Dinner daily 5:30 - 9 pm. Closed Sundays. Map 1

King & I

The King and I is one of those wonderful restaurants you always dream of discovering tucked away in a shopping center, like your child's favorite toy under the socks in the corner of his closet. The King and I is a dream come true, not only for the diner, but also for the owners, a family who fled Cambodia by boat, settled in Honolulu, and trained at the famous Keo's restaurant, waiting for the chance to open up on their own.

Comfortably air-conditioned, the dining room makes a compromise between attractiveness and utility. Orchids on the tables lend color to the white linen tablecloths topped with glass.

But the real attraction at The King and I is the food. For many people, each dish can be an adventure into unknown and exotic tastes. Don't be bashful. The menu is large enough to appeal to a variety of tastes. Spring rolls ($6.95/6) are crisp, light and wonderfully tasty, attractively arranged on manoa lettuce with mint leaf and cucumber, and served with delicious peanut vinegar dipping sauce,

Don't eat too many because it would be a mistake to miss lemon grass soup ($6.95) served piping hot, with wonderfully fragrant clouds of steam. Shrimps with peanut sauce are extremely tender, attractively arranged with shredded cabbage and tomato wedges. Or try the fried rice ($7.50) flavored with tomato, cucumber, and cilantro and garnished with sliced water chestnuts. Don't pass up the Siam Mee Kaob ($5.95), a small mountain of crispy rice noodles, bean sprouts, and scallions, served with a delicately sweet peanut sauce. Sa-teh ($7.95), served with spicy peanut sauce and cucumber dipping sauce, is delicious, whether beef, chicken or the truly amazing mahi mahi ($10.95), crisp and light.

You'll love ginger fish ($9.95) made with mahi mahi, fried crisp and served with a mild sauce flavored with ginger and scallions, or try one of the outstanding curries ($7.95-$9.95). Yellow curry is served with potatoes and onions; colored with saffron, it would be the easiest to identify as a "curry." Green curry takes its color–and flavor–from fresh basil, as well as coconut, lime leaves, and lemongrass. Red curry is the sweetest, flavored with coconut. Best of all, in our opinion, is a mild, sweet curry flavored with peanut and

mango–sunset wrapped in fruit

Island sunsets are especially lovely when reflected on eastern shores.

coconut and chock full of tender chicken. It's not on the menu, but you can ask for it as 'Evil Jungle Prince' ($9.25). Don't miss Siam eggplant ($7.95), pungent and wonderful. More than a dozen vegetarian specials range from $6.95, many flavored with basil and spices grown fresh in Kilauea. For dessert, try Thai tapioca pudding, which will be more soupy perhaps than the lumpy stuff you may remember from school lunches, and flavored with delicious apple-bananas and coconut. Most wines cost less than $20.

King and I is great choice for those times when you find it hard to look at another ahi or ono. The distinctive cuisine and friendly family atmosphere are great, and when you get your bill, your royal pocketbook will hardly notice.

Wailua, Waipouli Plaza, 4-901 Kuhio Highway. 822-1642. Dinner 4:30 - 9:30 pm daily. Reservations. Credit cards. Map 1

Restaurant Kintaro

There's almost always a line out the door of Kintaro's, and with good reason. For more than fifteen years, Kintaro has remained Kauai's best Japanese restaurant, a must if you are looking for delicious food in an attractive, comfortable setting. In fact, you will probably see the owner, Mr. Kim, hard at work running the smooth operation begun by his father. You'll also see a tasteful harmony of blues, whites, grays and tans in pleasing proportion. A fountain set in blue tiles and a sushi bar take up one long white wall. Nut-colored wood tables are set with chopsticks in blue and white wrappers, blue and tan tea bowls, and a striking single flower. Ceiling fans and air conditioning make Kintaro comfortably cool, and subdued Japanese music sets a relaxed mood.

Even with a reservation, you'll probably have to wait, and the new entry area makes waiting more pleasant than the old days, when there wasn't much room to stand in between the door and Rt 56. Cocktails and pu pus are served in a comfortable, attractive lounge, where you can sip a wonderful chi chi, sample elegant sashimi, or crispy fried won tons from the owner's factory next door.

In the main dining room, you can sit at the teppan yaki tables and watch talented chefs chop and flip and make things sizzle. As they will be happy to show you, the raw ingredients are fresh and of the best quality. Teriyaki New York steak ($18.95) or island chicken teriyaki ($14.95) are tender, tasty and juicy. If you prefer the reasonably-priced dinners on the regular menu, you might be seated in the smaller dining room next to the sushi bar, where, following delicious miso soup, dinner entrées are presented on traditional sectioned wooden platforms and include rice, zaru soba (chilled buckwheat noodles with a seasoned soy-based sauce) and pickled vegetables, along with tea served in a blue and tan pottery teapot. Crispy shrimp tempura with vegetables ($13.95) is light and delicious, particularly the green beans. Teriyaki beef with slices of NY steak is exceptionally tender ($16.95). Beef sukiyaki in a cast iron pot ($16.95) is dark and dusky with translucent noodles, meat, and vegetables. Teriyaki chicken is a family favorite with great sauce.

Sashimi is very fresh and generous. Ours arrived with six elegantly arranged selections: thin slices of ahi, translucent slivers of ono, dark strips of pungent smoked salmon, shrimps cooked so perfectly that they seemed to melt as you tasted them. According to our family expert Jeremy, Kintaro also makes the best sushi on Kauai. Spicy tuna rolls are great, as are California rolls ($4.50) which Kintaro makes with fresh crab meat, scallop rolls, hamachi or soft shell crab hand rolls, salmon skin hand rolls ($4.50), and a specialty seafood mix grilled in foil. Watching the sushi chef's lightning speed is great fun. Don't miss his Kilauea Roll or 'Bali Hai Bomb.'

Excellent Japanese cuisine & sushi

Children are welcome, as is appropriate for a restaurant named in honor of a legendary

Japanese boy hero, and service is polite and usually unrushed. As our children have grown up, Kintaro has become not just their favorite Japanese restaurant, but the favorite, period!

Wailua, Kuhio Hwy. (Rt. 56). Reservations necessary. 822-3341. Credit Cards. Dinner 5:30 - 9:30 pm. Closed Sundays. Map 1

Kountry Kitchen

For years, and despite changes in ownership, the best spot for breakfast on the island's east coast has been the Kountry Kitchen, which serves terrific food at equally terrific prices. The large menu offers delicious eggs, expertly cooked bacon and sausage, as well as omelette creations, including sour cream, or bacon and tomato, or 'vegetable garden.' You can also design your own omelette by ordering a combination of separately priced fillings. Kountry Kitchen's omelettes are unique –thin pancakes of egg rolled around fillings almost like a crepe – tender, moist, and delicious. Or try Eggs Margo, a version of Eggs Benedict with turkey instead of ham. Our children loved Cheesy Eggs – toasted English muffin with bacon and poached eggs, covered with golden cheese sauce, and our babies have all loved the honey and wheat pancake. All come with perfectly golden and crisp pancakes of shredded potatoes. For homestyle breakfasts, hot, tasty, and filling, you can't do much better!

Kapa'a, 1485 Kuhio Hwy. 822-3511 Open 6 am - 9 am; and 11 am - 2: 30 pm daily. Credit cards. Map 1

La Bamba

Located in Kukui Grove Shopping Center, La Bamba serves generous portions at reasonable prices in a dining room that gives less attention to decor than to orchestrating the best ingredients at the best price. The dream of a hardworking family, La Bamba's dining room is cheerful, with red and green painted chilis on the windows, Southwest scenes painted on the walls, Mexican hats above the booths lined up by windows that overlook K Mart. And it combines green vinyl tablecloths with genuine friendliness. The teen age daughter may take your order, while her father, the chef who hails from El Salvador, works in the kitchen and her mother looks on, managing and encouraging. You will be delighted with the fresh ingredients in generous portions. If you order a Mexican salad ($7.95), it fills the plate, stuffed with beans and chunks of chicken ($7.95). Entrées range from $7.50 - $11.95, including rice and beans, as well as and à la carte choices, like a delicious chicken enchilada ($3) with lots of tasty sauce.

If you're on a budget, La Bamba is a good choice for generous portions, reasonable prices, and the somewhat slow service that goes hand in hand with an informal, friendly family atmosphere. Try Mexican beer, wine, and margaritas.

Kukui Grove, Lihue 245-5972. 11 am - 10 pm daily. Credit cards. Map 1

La Playita Azul

Tucked under Safeway's wing in the Kauai Village Shopping Center, La Playita Azul is a tiny, very clean eatery with a half-dozen tables. The menu is Mexican with an emphasis on fresh ingredients, and portions of chicken, port, beef, vegetables, or seafood are generous and reasonably priced (between $8 and $10, with à la carte items at about $3). Fish burrito ($10.95) filled with fresh ahi, was tasty and tender. Seafood burrito ($12.95) adds scallops, shrimp and vegetables to the mix. Looking for fresh vegetables? Try Monica's Veggie Burrito ($8.95). All plates are served with homemade green or red sauce, rice, beans, many with avocado. Each is cooked individually, so service may be leisurely.

Sandy beaches rim the Eastern shore near Lydgate Park in Wailua.

La Playita Azul has no liquor license, but beer and wine are on ice at Safeway next door. Or try Aqua Fresco ($2) – a different fresh fruit each day (order without ice). You may not remember the spartan dining room after you leave (the decor is pretty much the sum of the cash register and drink cooler), but you will remember good food at reasonable prices.

Wailua, Kauai Village on Rt. 56, next to Safeway. 821-2323. Credit cards. Take out. Dinner 5:30 - 9:30 daily. Call about lunch. Map 1

Lemongrass Grill & Seafood & Sushi Bar

Lemongrass is actually an offspring of the popular Mema's, owned by the same hardworking Thai family. The restaurant has two stories, an elegant sushi bar, as well as an outdoor dining terrace lit with tiki torches and rimmed with wagon wheels. The menu offers flavors of the Pacific Rim, with a touch of Thai seasoning. Excellent fresh fish is served in arresting presentations, with local spices and vegetables, making each dish look special. Caesar salad ($7.50) arrives in a crisp oversize won ton skin, anchored to the plate with a dab of mashed potatoes, almost like a tostada filled with beautifully green lettuce and deftly flavored. Clam chowder ($3/$6) is thick with seafood , and fresh local spinach salad has dainty young leaves, tender enough to enjoy even without the delicious dressing that accompanies it. Herb muffins and fresh bread are meltingly soft and tasty.

Fresh island fish served on Thai spiced eggplant ($23) is flaky and very tasty. Scallop sauté ($20) is lightly spiced, with tender scallops. Garlic lovers will enjoy the shrimp sauté. Lamb ($21) is cooked perfectly, both juicy and tender. Don't miss banana cake with banana ice cream.

Lemongrass offers a welcome alternative to the pricey Pacific Rim cuisine restaurants nearby. Service is friendly and efficient, even though the staff spends a lot of time moving between the kitchen and multiple dining rooms. Everyone works hard to make the dining experience enjoyable.

Wailua, 4-885 Kuhio Hwy. 821-2888. Credit cards. Full bar. Dinner nitely.

Ma's Family, Inc.

Ma's tiny luncheonette is so far off the beaten path in Lihue that you'd probably never find it if you didn't stumble onto it by chance. For almost 30 years, Ma's has earned a reputation for well-priced and well-cooked breakfasts (about $5) and lunches, and you'll probably find the dozen tables filled with local people on their way to work in the morning or stopping off at lunch.

The few tourists who happen onto it will love Ma's expertly cooked eggs, delicious pancakes and waffles that one of our teenagers described as "about the best." The menu, which is posted on the wall over the pass-through to the kitchen, also lists some Hawaiian dishes, for example roast kalua pig that shreds perfectly for little fingers. Even toast is excellent, and fried min noodles with eggs and sausage may open your eyes to new possibilities for breakfast.

Thanks to Amy, Ma's daughter, service is fast and extremely friendly in the sunny, spartan dining room. If you don't like canned milk in your coffee, ask Amy for a small glass of the fresh stuff. When you leave, you'll be astonished to find how little your meal has cost you. When a hungry family can dine so inexpensively, you feel like popping into the kitchen to give Ma a big hug! And many of our readers do just that!

Lihue, 4277 Halenani St. Cash only. 245-3142. 5 am - 1 pm daily; till noon S, S, holidays (closed New Years Day). Coffee/tea free with breakfast!

Mema Thai & Chinese Cuisine

Can you believe it? Two excellent Thai restaurants within a half-mile in tiny Wailua! Mema's and The King & I are more like 'cousins,' operated by two branches of the same Thai family, though Mema features Chinese cuisine as well as Thai, and its Thai food is a tad spicier.

What comes to the table is both tasteful and pleasing. Spring rolls ($6.95) are crisp, attractively served with fresh leafy lettuce and peanut sauce, and can be ordered vegetarian style. On the Chinese menu, cashew chicken ($9.95) is chock full of nuts, and lemon chicken ($8.95) is excellent, very crispy and golden with a lightly flavored lemon sauce. Thai dishes can be very spicy, so ask your server for advice. Each dish can be prepared with vegetables or tofu ($8.95), with chicken, beef, or pork ($9.95) or with shrimp, fish, or calamari ($11.95). Green curry with coconut milk, lemon grass, kaffir lime leaves, eggplant, and fresh basil is not overly spicy. On the other hand, red curry looks deceptively placid, garnished with fresh basil and chopped cabbage,

but it's a scorcher! Mahi mahi sa-teh ($10.95) is delicious. Vegetarians have many choices on the menu, and the chef will also tailor dishes to specific tastes.

While experts may grumble that no authentic Thai peppers blister the dishes at Mema, the temperature is up a few degrees from The King & I. With reasonable prices, lots of variety on the menu, an attractive new dining room, and (mostly) friendly service, Mema's is a great choice for a pleasant, relaxing evening, and the Thai food is as good as you can find.

Wailua, 4-369 Kuhio Hwy. 823-0899. Credit cards. Lunch 11 am – 2 pm M-F; Dinner nightly 5 pm - 9:30

Mermaid's Café

At the tiny, walk-up window, you can order tasty and inventive dishes made with a healthful emphasis. Portions are generous, seasoning judicious, and prices amazingly reasonable. Choose wraps and burritos made with tofu, chicken, or fish ($7.95-$9.95), tempeh burgers, bakery treats, tea and espresso. Don't miss the ahi wrap: fresh grilled ahi and nori are stuffed into a delicious spinach tortilla. Or try an excellent chicken curry heaped with vegetables and rice, or organic salad ($7.95). Foccacia is crisp and fluffy, a treat all by itself. Have some hibiscus iced tea.

It's not fancy, and the only seating is outside: a couple of chairs in the sun or some stools along the side. So pack up and head for the beach – as lots of local folks do.

Kapa'a, Kuhio Hwy. 821-2026. Open daily 10 am - 10 pm. Cash only

Norberto's El Café

In the heart of Kapa'a, Norberto's has served first-rate Mexican food on Kauai since 1977. White stucco walls and woodgrain tables create a setting like a cantina, with hanging plants, sombreros, and gas lamps.

Over the years, prices have not changed much, and almost everything is very reasonable, including margaritas by the pitcher and à la carte entrées, as well as complete Mexican dinners with soup, vegetable, beans, chips and salsa for $18 or less. Be sure to ask for the homemade chips made with flour tortillas. Nachos are generously covered with cheese. When we finished our bean soup, we were asked if we wanted seconds!

The Burrito El Café deserves to be called a house specialty – a tortilla generously stuffed with flavorful beef, beans and cheese, baked enchilada style and topped with guacamole

Windsurfing lessons p. 117

and fresh red tomatoes and lettuce. The tostada is a huge colorful salad mounded over a crisp tortilla, and the chili relleno is dipped (not drowned) in egg and gently cooked. An El Café specialty, taro enchiladas are first rate, the taro leaves tasting a bit like spinach. Almost all dishes can be ordered vegetarian style. For the some who like it hot, plenty of home-made salsa is on the table.

Service is friendly, prices are reasonable, and children are treated with tolerance, even when cranky. When the salsa proved too hot for the short people, our fast-thinking waitress brought over a bowl of bean soup. Once kids started dipping chips, all you could hear was happy crunching!

Kapaʻa, 4-1373 Kuhio Hwy. 822-3362. 5:30-9:00 pm daily. Closed Sundays. Breakfast 6 am - 11 am except Monday. Credit cards. Map 1

Okazu Hale

Want to vote on who serves the best saimin on Kauai? Try Okazu Hale – we think it has the freshest noodles, the most fragrant, steaming broth, the best vegetables. Or try the Japanese style noodle soup, Miso Ramen, which has a richer flavor, and more spice. In this tiny eatery, inside a tiny shopping center across from Ace Hardware in Lihue, you'll find noodles, saimin, sushi, Japanese style 'local food', as well as chicken, fresh island fish, teriyaki and barbecue dishes, and even old-fashioned pot roast. Prices are inexpensive ($6-$9). The decor is spartan, to put it mildly. Fly

hidden saimin!

fans keep the air moving. It's jammed when the plate lunch crowd arrives, but the saimin is worth the crush. Try the saimin special ($5.95), which comes with shrimp tempura, chicken katsu and vegetables, or you might prefer the large plain version with a side of vegetables. This is local style Kauai – don't miss it!

Lihue, 4100 Rice Street. 245-6554. Cash only. Lunch: 11 - 2 pm. Dinner: 5 - 9 pm. M - Sat. Non-smokers, take your chances! Map 1

Oki Diner

Your body's still on east coast time and hungry in the middle of the night! Well, Oki Diner is open 21 hours a day, 7 days a week. For breakfast, you'll find a full range of eggs and pancakes. For other times, there are sandwiches, burgers, noodle dishes of all kinds, and 25 'local favorites' like stir fry or beef stew, Hawaiian style ribs and pork, complete with rice and salad ($5.95-$11.95). Saimin (from $3.50) is hot and tasty. Take it out to the beach, even though the container will cost fifty cents. Don't forget the pies. 'Pumpkin crunch' is a local legend, available by the slice (it's square!) The all-you-can-eat salad bar costs $8.95 with entrée.

Oki Diner may not win any awards for imaginative decor – it's formica utilitarian – or for inventive cuisine, but for straightforward meals at honest prices, and at any hour, it may just be what you need on Hawaiian time.

Lihue, 3125 Kuhio Hwy (next to McDonald's). 245-5899. Daily menu served 21 hours (closed 3 am – 6 am). Credit cards. Map 1

Ono Family Restaurant

Ono Family Restaurant has been a long-time local favorite for wholesome, inexpensive family fare, most recently winning a nod from the *New York Times.* Breakfasts and lunches are well-cooked, reasonably priced, and served in a cozy dining room, with polished wooden booths, some with a removable partition to accommodate large families.

At breakfast, you'll find more than 30 egg creations priced from $3.50, including 17 omelettes. For a new idea, try eggs with fresh ahi, a perfectly cooked filet, or tasty corned beef hash and scrambled eggs ($6.75). At lunch, you'll find a wide array of sandwiches, burgers, plate lunches, and salads from $6, as well as the famous Portuguese bean soup.

Service can be slow, but everyone is friendly and cooperative. Wait persons are helpful with things like crackers, straws, extra napkins and extra cups for tastes of grown-up coffee–those etceteras of family dining that don't seem essential until they're missing. People seem ready to help with each other's restless little ones. On one occasion, when we could not find our waitress to get a glass of water that had suddenly become a necessity, an adjacent Daddy passed over an extra. Just outside the door, two old timers shared their donuts with a wandering seven-year-old, patted his head as he chewed, and listened politely to his latest fish story.

4-1292 Kuhio Hwy, Kapa'a. 822-1710. Daily 7 am- 2 pm. Credit cards.

Ono Burger (Duane's)

For years, the shack next to the general store at Anahola was famous among local people for delicious hamburgers and fresh fruit smoothies. As tourists heard about the hamburgers, the shack, along with its reputation, expanded. Picnic tables appeared under the tree, and the menu grew. The business has changed hands, but the burgers are still delicious, if somewhat smaller than before. Quarter-pounders can be made with various cheeses (even blue cheese) or teriyaki style (from $3.90). Our favorites are the 'local girl' with teriyaki, Swiss cheese and fresh pineapple ($5.65), and the vegetarian sandwich ($4.95). Children can order 2.5 oz. hamburgers ($2.60) or deep fried chicken strips and fries ($3.40) that will make the rest of the party want to order the adult portion ($6.95). Add sizzling crisp french fries ($1.80 feeds two) and wash it down with

Waiting for the waves at Hanalei, near the pier

smoothies and ice cream shakes, floats and freezes ($2.95). Service can be slow, particularly at peak lunchtime. Be patient, pack up your sandwiches (each half will be separately wrapped) and head for beautiful Anahola Beach just a mile down Aliomanu Road. Phone your order in ahead.

Anahola, Rt. 56, next to Whalers Store. 822-9181. Open daily 10 am – 6 pm; Sunday 11 am – 6 pm. Credit cards. Map 1

A Pacific Café

A Pacific Café has achieved fame for blending the culinary traditions of Europe and the Pacific Rim, while emphasizing fresh ingredients from Kauai. When owner chef Jean Marie is in the kitchen, you'll find some of the best dishes prepared on Kauai. However, he is not always there, and if not, food quality and service suffer. So when you call for reservations, be sure to ask, and make your decision accordingly.

On a good night, you will be delighted with the ingenious, sometimes whimsical, artistry of each dish. Sashimi can be served tempura style ($10.50), the ahi wrapped in seaweed, then deep fried and sliced in elegant medallions, the fish cool in the center, the wrapping crisp outside. Even absolutely plain, sashimi of ahi and hamachi has a perfectly butter soft texture ($11.75). Soups are delicately flavored and vividly colored, like asparagus bisque or Thai coconut curry soup ($6.50). A dinner salad ($6.50) looks like kaleidoscope of greens. Familiar entrées appear in

Beautiful torch ginger

arresting fashion. Fresh fish can be almost magical– sizzling hot, meltingly tender, and enhanced with wonderful sauces. Try 'wok-charred' mahi mahi with garlic sesame crust and lime ginger sauce ($23.75), or delicate opah (moonfish). Ahi appears in a huge portion with stir fry vegetables, or try the fragrant and tender miso marinated sea bass ($23.50) served with a fabulous edamame purée. Jean Marie designs a tasting menu for vegetarians, with 'Buddhist dumplings' of couscous and poached tomato vinaigrette, an amazing 'forbidden black rice' ($32), a sesame cone stuffed with tofu, and other inventive treats. Another tasting menu has island fish.

Chocolate lovers will adore the hot chocolate tart, and sorbet aficionados will love fresh lichee. 'Toasted Hawaiian' remains a family favorite, as does crisp macadamia nut tart.

The dining room is attractive, with black lacquer chairs surrounding polished wood tables with bamboo placemats and shining crystal. Even plates are whimsical creations, and they frame the appetizers and entrées like culinary paintings. The only disadvantage in the air-conditioned room is noise. This café is best on a night when it's not busy. If you find chef-owner Jean Marie in the kitchen, you are in for a dining treat. If not, you may want to try another night.

Wailua, Kauai Village Shopping Center, Kuhio Hwy. 5:30 - 10 pm nightly. Reservations a day (or two) in advance: 822-0013. Credit cards. Map 1

Panda Garden

Next to the Safeway in the Kauai Village Shopping Center, Panda Garden looks clean and attractive. Tables with white cloths covered with shiny glass tops are set with blue and white china, in a white painted room both cheerful and bright. Local people like the place for its reasonable prices and friendly informality. Appetizers include hot, tasty won ton soup ($6.50) and crisp spring rolls ($4.95), and entrées, piquantly flavored lemon chicken ($7.50) and tasty moo shi vegetable ($7.95). Portions are generous, the food tasty, and service, though occasionally slow, is politely pleasant.

Wailua, Kauai Village Center, 822-0092. Lunch 10:30 am - 2 pm except Wednesdays; dinner 4 pm - 9 :30 pm daily. Credit cards. Map 1

Papaya's Garden Café

Papaya's is actually a full-service natural foods store. The deli offers a wide range of sandwiches and casseroles flavored in Mexican, Cuban, Indian, Szechwan, Thai, Greek and Italian styles, including tempeh, fish, or chicken burgers, as well as 'garden lasagne' and spanakopita ($4 to $8.95). Gilled tofu is excellent, as if the fresh ahi sandwich. You'll also find espresso, capuccino, lattes, mochas and teas. Dine outside at tables on the "patio," more accurately the walkway of the mall.

Wailua, Kauai Village Shopping Center, Kuhio Hwy. 823-0190. Open 9 am - 8 pm. Closed Sundays. Credit cards. Map 1

Paradise Seafood & Grill

Paradise Seafood serves the island's best fish and chips made with fresh local fish ($16.50 for 4 pieces). You'll also find complete fresh fish dinners, including salad or soup, and rice or baked potato, for $18.50. Non-fishy eaters can choose steak ($15.95 - $19.95), chicken ($14.95), even prime rib in two sizes ($16.95/12oz or $23.95/24 oz.), or pasta. Fish chowder is tasty and thick; fresh fish sandwich is tender on a soft bun.

The dining room looks clean and welcoming. Walls colored a soft grey are cheered by leafy green plants, and the concrete floor shines with white paint. Woodgrain tables with white wrought iron chairs are generously spaced, so you don't feel crowded. You can also dine outside on the porch, a popular spot.

On Rt. 50, Kipu. Open daily 11 am - 11 pm daily. 246-4884. Credit cards. Full bar. Map 1

Sukothai

Less than a mile away from the two local Thai favorites, King and I and Mema Thai Cuisine, Sukothai tries to find a market niche by offering a larger combination of cuisines: Thai-Chinese-Vietnamese, and, as if that weren't enough of a challenge for the kitchen, barbecue. A large store offering far eastern imports will please those who don't like to sit still while waiting for their food.

The small dining room is bright and welcoming, decorated in cheerful yellow, with a red carpet and red tablecloths woven with gold and covered with protective glass. Yellow orchids provide the tropical touch, while roomy rattan armchairs and air conditioning make dining pleasant and comfortable. Most dishes cost about $8. 'Tom Kar,' or coconut and lemon grass soup, is wonderful, presented in a lovely earthernware serving bowl ($7.95). Rice pancakes filled with minced chicken, cut in sections and deep

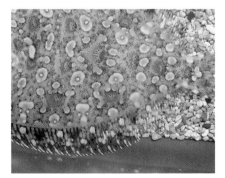

Political fish—blends in with current conditions!

fried, are also delicious ($7.50). Vegetable fried rice is colorful with vegetables ($6.95), and cashew chicken is very tasty. Pad Thai, made with rice noodles, is excellent ($8.25). We ran into trouble when we asked to alter a dish by eliminating or reducing one of its listed ingredients (garlic) or to modify the spiciness. Impossible, we were told, as sauces are prepared in advance.

Though in our opinion not as distinctive in cuisine as King & I or Mema, Sukothai offers a more varied menu at reasonable prices.

Kapa'a Shopping Center (near Big Save). 821-1224. Credit cards. Air-conditioned. 10:30 am - 3 pm and 5 pm - 9:30 pm daily. Map 1

Tip Top & Sushi Katsu

The name Tip Top conjures up certain 1950's - type expectations: a clean room for under $20, a square meal for $5. But you're not really sure that you should believe in this any more than you would in the tooth fairy! It is true, though. Since 1916, Tip Top has served fairly–priced, honest, unpretentious food, more popular with local people than the tourists who manage to find it on a side street of Lihue.

The dining room has comfortable, large booths, and on hot summer days, you'll appreciate the air-conditioning. The real attraction is the prices. Delicious pancakes with macadamia nuts, bananas, pineapples or raisins cost $4. French toast is only $3.25. Ham and cheese omelette or bacon and eggs, accompanied by a scoop of hash browns, are $6, with oxtail soup, the most expensive item on the menu, at $6.50. Meals are well-prepared if unexciting, but homemade pineapple and guava jam is special. Have it on toast, but that's à la carte.

At lunch, try hamburgers ($3.20) and plate lunches (from $5.50). Or visit Sushi Katsu, a small sushi bar (there are only 8 seats) inside Tip Top, and sample California roll ($4), or spicy ahi roll ($5). An enormous bowl of saimin is only $4.75. In the evenings, you can enjoy Sushi Katsu's full Japanese dinners at modest prices.

Tip Top is Kauai tradition. Breakfasts are hot, fast, and filling–perfect for those mornings when you're on the way to the airport and need every ounce of strength to get those bags through the agriculture inspection and security without misplacing anything–or anybody!

Lihue, 3173 Akahi St. Tip Top 245-2333. 6:30 am - 2 pm. Sushi Katsu 246-0176. Open 11 am - 2 pm; 5:30 - 9:30 Closed Mondays. Map 1

Tokyo Lobby

Tokyo Lobby's dining room is attractive in an informal way. Black lacquer chairs and grey tables are comfortable, and a jaunty red pagoda roof extends over the sushi bar.

The menu offers a wide variety of Japanese lunch choices from $3.95, and dinners from $9.95, which include an excellent miso soup, tsukemono and rice. Hibachi lemon chicken ($12.95) is tender, moist and tasty, served with a somewhat spicy salad with coconut dressing. BBQ salmon or fresh island fish ($13.95) is another good choice. Tempura ($10.95) is

light, crispy and filled with vegetables still crunchy and colorful as well as either fresh island fish or shrimp ($14.95). You can order tempura in the appetizer portion, which contains 5 pieces ($7.95), enough to sample and still have room to try some sushi, like California roll of crab and avocado wrapped in rice and nori ($4), or salmon skin hand rolls ($4). A special feature: the Tokyo Lobby Love Boat, a lavish display of sushi served for 2 in a wooden boat, with soup, salad and rice.

Service can be slow, particularly when it's full, but Tokyo Lobby is a good bet for well-prepared food in a comfortable, informal setting.

Lihue, Harbor Mall, 3501 Rice St. 245-8989. Lunch 11 am – 2 pm (M-F) Dinner 4:30 – 9:30 pm daily. Credit cards. Beer, wine, sake. Map 1

Wahoo's

With a new name and a new interior, Wahoo's Seafood Bar and Grill may have replaced its predecessor Fishbowls, but the menu has not changed as much as the dining room, where bamboo screens, bamboo wall coverings, and sheer drapes across the ceiling have replaced the faux aquarium look, to make the restaurant look more attractive. But the changes are largely cosmetic, since the menu remains basically the same.

The menu offers a range of seafood choices in imaginative, and sometimes elaborate preparations. Maui onion soup, for example, appears with lobster medallions ($9), and is as tasty as it is elegant in appearance. Seafood entreés (priced from $18 for scampi) all come with complex sauces, which we feel should be served on the side if you prefer the taste of the fish to the taste of the spice. Meateaters have several options, including baby back ribs ($16) as well as prime rib ($18), while those who steer a course between both fish and meat can choose pastas ($14-$17). Fresh ono, a generous portion of two large pieces, was well cooked but overwhelmed with a rather thick buerre blanc sauce. Dinners include a house salad or soup, except for fish specialties.

The best deal on the menu might be Wahoo's Garden Salad ($6) a huge plate of greens, shredded beats, shredded carrots, Japanese mushrooms, sprouts and mango. Ask for the dressing on the side as the house special guava basil is a thick-thousand island like dressing. Though not on the menu, the chef will make a vegetable plate ($14) with asparagus, carrots, roasted tomatoes, artichoke hearts and mushrooms. Carmel Custard ($6.50) is very light, served with delicious raspberry sauce.

Wahoos is struggling to find a niche between Pacific Café and Coconuts, both nearby. You'll find generous portions, but prices are on the high side, so choose carefully and have all sauces served on the side.

Wailua: 733 Kuhio Hwy. 822-7833. Credit cards. Lunch 11:30 – 3 pm ; dinner 5:30 daily. Call for entertainment schedule at Hana Pa'a Lounge.

Wailua Marina Restaurant

For more than 30 years, the Wailua Marina has been an island favorite for family dining. The large dining room features an enormous mural of an underwater vista complete with stuffed fish and a turtle shell. Weather permitting, ask to sit outside on the large covered porch decorated with plants and flowers. Cooled by delightful breezes, it looks out over the Wailua River, where boats rock gently in the docks. In the evening, candles light the tables with a golden glow, and the air is soft and fragrant.

A pleasant waitress will probably recommend the fresh fish, which is usually delicious. Fresh ahi stuffed with crab ($19) is well seasoned and flavorful. Fresh ono with marina sauce is also tasty, accompanied with small cups of both teriyaki sauce and drawn butter. Fried chicken ($14) may be more moist than teriyaki chicken, but kids love that teriyaki sauce for dipping, so order some on the side. Most entrées cost less than $18 and include rolls, rice or potato, a vegetable and salad bar. Hot, crispy french fries are considerably better than the somewhat oily fried rice, although even that's not too bad flavored with delicious teriyaki sauce.

To keep prices down, the Marina cuts a few corners, but they're the kind no one really misses if you catch the spirit of the place. The pleasantness of the setting more than compensates for paper napkins and placemats. The salad bar may lack imagination, but you can fill your plate with vegetables. Children can chose from ten dinners for about $3 less than adult prices. The dozen wines are not very exciting, but most cost less than $20. You'll love the homemade pies.

Prices are up, and the cost of the Marina's fresh island fish dinner is now almost even with the Bull Shed's. The Marina is still reasonable, however, and you'll come away with a pleasant memory of lights on the river twinkling as dusk deepens into night.

Wailua River State Park, just south of the bridge on Kuhio Hwy. 822-4311. Lunch: 10:30 am - 2 pm & Dinner: 5 pm - 9 pm. Early Bird Special 5 - 6 pm. Credit cards. Closed Mondays. Map 1

Waipouli Deli & Restaurant

Does this sound familiar? Your body clock is off. You're fully awake–and starving – 3 hours early. You'll never make it till lunch, but you want to spend the morning on the beach and not in some dark, air-conditioned restaurant with poky service!

Well, the Waipouli Deli is for you! Generous portions of tasty food coupled with speedy delivery and unbeatable prices have made the Waipouli Deli a favorite spot on the eastside for local families and increasing numbers of tourists. It looks like formica city, so don't go expecting orchids on the table. But though short on atmosphere, it's got a 'breakfast special' deserving of the name – an egg, two slices of bacon, and two pancakes – perfect for hungry children, not to mention adults. Eggs are expertly cooked, side meats not overly fatty, and pancakes light. On the lunch and dinner menus, you'll find bargains in American and Oriental food. Service is fast, efficient, and very friendly.

Wailua, in the Waipouli Town Center, behind McDonald's. 822-9311 for take-out. 7:30 am - 9:30 pm daily. Credit cards. Map 1

Wasabi's

The creation of a talented sushi chef from Hanama'ulu Tea House who wanted a restaurant of his own, Wasabi's is sushi 'cool.' You enter what looks like an under sea grotto, with a coral reef painted on the walls and fish all around you. And it's crowded with people. All four tables will probably be taken, as may be the nine stools by the small sushi bar. Wasabi's serves sushi, Japanese à la carte items, and dinners priced from $12.95, for example, for a yakitori chicken dinner with two sushi rolls, miso soup, salad and rice. Chef-owner Victor prides himself on his imaginative sushi creations, like his Lava Roll, which combines salmon, hamachi, crab, and shrimp, scallops and a delicious sauce ($12.50), or his tempura soft shell crab roll with lettuce, avocado and cucumber ($8.50).

Prices are reasonable, and everything is made fresh and individually, with organic vegetables and no MSG. Service may be slow, so order some delicious miso soup ($2.50) to tide you over. You can bring in beer or wine from the ABC store across the street.

With its tiny storefront in downtown Kapa'a (look carefully or you'll miss it), Wasabi's is unpretentious and fun – sushi local style.

Kapa'a, 1384 Kuhio Highway. 822-2700. Dinner 5:30 - 10:30 pm. Closed Mondays. Call for lunch schedule. Credit cards. No checks. Map 1

Whaler's Brew Pub

With its dramatic perch on the side of a rocky point, Whaler's Brew Pub has a panoramic ocean view. (Whaler's ad says, 'Come for the view - stay for a brew.') We prefer the view! As for the brew, you can't miss the shining brewery vats at the entry.

The scenery is best in daylight, so consider Whaler's for lunch, or an early dinner, especially if the moon is full. The dining room is comfortably informal, arranged in two tiers, with roomy booths along the walls. From tables on the lanai, you can sometimes see whales and more often, a jet approaching Lihue carrying a new load of eager tourists.

Whaler's offers reasonable prices and generous portions, like excellent seafood chowder ($4.50), piping hot and filled with fish. A large platter of grilled eggplant and cucumber ($7.95) is also tasty, as are oysters or mussels in a sampler plate, including two each of barbecue, teriyaki, and Rockefeller styles. Dinner entrées include fresh fish ($17.95) and NY steak ($17.50), or Whaler's signature twenty-ounce cheeseburger, as well as vegetarian dishes like stir-fry ($15.95). Fresh fish cleanly broiled is the best bet, with the plain sautéed ono and plain grilled ahi much tastier than the version crusted with ground pistachio nuts for $2 more. Vegetable lasagne ($12.95) is unique, the lasagne noodles rolled, stuffed with cheese, spinach, and zucchini, and set on end on the plate.

On grounds of Kauai Marriott, Lihue. 245-2000. Daily lunch & dinner 11 am - 10 pm. Oyster bar until 11 pm. Credit cards. Entertainment. Map 1

Vegetarian Ventures

Once upon a time, the best you could do on Kauai for vegetarian food was a salad bar, or in a pinch, some vegetable chow mein. Now that Kauai has entered a health-conscious age, vegetarian and natural food eateries are sprouting everywhere, including Hanalei's gourmet vegetarian restaurant, Postcards Café. In Kapa'a, Papaya's offers breakfast, lunch, and dinner choices, including garden burgers, tempeh burgers, grilled fish and chicken burgers, vegetarian sandwiches, pasta, salads, rice and stir fry dishes while neighbor Ba Le serves several creative vegetarian noodle selections. Caffé Coco offers a wide variety of tasty vegetarian/vegan dishes. Mermaids Café has tofu, chicken, or fish wraps and burritos. Next door, Blossoming Lotus serves 'international gourmet vegan and raw food cuisine,' including wraps, salads, soy and tofu creations, organic juices, great hummus, and delicious mango pie and healthful drinks. In Lihue, try Kalapaki Beach Hut's vegetarian sandwich or salad, and soups and sandwiches at Deli & Bread Connection at Kukui Grove Shopping Center.

On the north shore, *Hanalei Natural Foods* stocks vegetarian shelf foods, and across the street, *Neidie's Salsa & Samba* turns out distinctive vegetable dishes with a Brazilian accent.

In Kilauea, try *Kilauea Farmer's Market* for soup, sandwiches, salads and our favorite vegie sandwich on the island. *Healthy Hut Natural Foods*, 2430 Oka St. in Kilauea (call Monique at 828-6626), has local produce, organic dairy products, dried fruits and nuts. Hungry for fruit or a smoothie? Try the first rate *Moloa'a Fruit Stand* (Rt 56 in Moloa'a), which also offers vegetarian sushi, lots of fresh island fruits, smoothies, frosties, and juices, including fresh sugar cane juice. *Banana Joe's* and *Mango Mama's* (Kilauea), and *People's Market* (Puhi) have smoothies and local fruits. Try apple bananas and mangoes.

On the west side, *Hanapepe Café* serves vegetarian salads and sandwiches, as well as, occasionally, dinners. At *Wrangler's* in Waimea, try great vegetarian sandwiches, pizzas, vegie wraps, & salads.

Pizzerias are also catering to the health food crowd. *Pizza Hanalei* will make pizza with 'tofurella' cheese upon request, and a 'veggie special' pizza on whole wheat as well as white crust. In Kilauea, try *Pau Hana Pizza* for a whole variety of vegetable pizzas with excellent crust. *Brick Oven Pizza* in Hanapepe makes some of the best traditional cheese or 'vegetable' pizza you'll ever find anywhere. In Koloa, try *Pizzetta's* cheeseless vegetable pizza (742-8841).

For salad bars try *Duke's Canoe Club* and *Oki Diner* in Lihue; *Brennecke's Beach Broiler* and *Poipu Beach Broiler* in Poipu, *Wranglers* in Waimea; *CJ's Steak House* in Princeville. In Wailua, *The Bull Shed*, *Wailua Marina*, and *Pizza Hut*. Some of our favorite vegetarian meals on Kauai are the vegetable curries and stir fries at *Mema* and *King & I*; the vegetable plate at *Hukilau Lanai*, *A Pacific Café*, and *Aromas*; the wraps at *Mermaids* and *Blossoming Lotus;* and taro enchiladas at *El Café*.

Cheap Eats & 'Local Grinds'

EASTERN SHORE: In LIHUE, *Barbecue Inn* (245-2921) has one of the largest, most reasonably-priced lunch and dinner menus on Kauai, and it's air-conditioned. Try wonderful saimin at *Hamura's* on Kress St. or *Okazu Hale* across from Ace Hardware on Rice St. *Tip Top* is a Kauai tradition for breakfast, also lunch. *Borders Espresso Café* has excellent espresso and teas, sandwiches, and salads. Nearby at Kukui Grove, *Deli & Bread Connection* has delicious take-out sandwiches and tasty soups, or try *La Bamba* for inexpensive Mexican plates. *Quizno's* has made it to Kauai, also at Kukui Grove. Near Kalapaki Beach, *Kalapaki Beach Hut* makes great burgers, fresh fish sandwich, salads. Call ahead to save the wait (246-6330). Across from Wal-Mart, *Fish Express* (826-0026) is a local favorite for excellent bentos, plate lunches, and poki (marinated local raw fish). (245-7115).

In WAILUA, Coconut Plantation Marketplace's *Aloha Kauai Pizza* is a family favorite, and *Fish Hut* makes great fresh fish sandwiches, particularly ahi teriyaki with pineapple, fish tacos, wraps and dinner plates. Call ahead to save waiting time (822-1712). Try *Ba Le* in the Wailua Safeway Center for generous, tasty Vietnamese food. Just north on Rt 56, *The Big Kahuna* serves 'Kauai gyros,' and sandwiches a notch above Subways.

KAPA'A now has a cluster of small eateries with real personality. *Mermaids Café* (821-2026) makes healthful vegetarian/vegan dishes, and one of the best ahi wraps on Kauai, a spinach tortilla stuffed with fish, ginger infused rice and wasabi cream sauce ($8.95), as well as burritos, stir fry, salads ($7.95-$9.95) with tofu, chicken, or ahi. *Blossoming Lotus* (823-6887) next door has tasty wraps with hummus and fresh vegetables. *Java Kai* brews great coffee, with delicious mango cinnamon muffins, chai tea, bagels, steamed milk beverages, fruit drinks and smoothies, as well as breakfast waffles and eggs. *Ono Family Restaurant* offers bargain-priced breakfast and lunches. Down the street, *Bubba's* serves up tasty hamburgers, fries, rings; dine with a view of what's going down Rt 56.

Further north in ANAHOLA is a favorite family take-out spot on the eastern shore: *Ono Char Burger*, formerly Duane's. While service can be pokey, the burgers, french fries, onion rings, and fried chicken will seem worth the wait. Call ahead (822-9181) and take your order to the beach.

The inexpensive (around $5) 'plate lunch' with 'local grinds,' is a Kauai tradition. Try one at Kukui Grove's *Joni-Hana. Kauai Chop Suey* offers a "special plate" ($6.45) –enough to feed two. *Garden Island*

Barbecue & Chinese (245-8868) in Lihue has generous plate lunches and tasty saimin to go. *Ba Le* gives the plate lunch a delicious Vietnamese touch and a low calorie interpretation.

NORTH SHORE Near the Kong Lung Store in KILAUEA, *Kilauea Bakery & Pau Hana Pizza* (828-2020) features fragrant breads, rolls, cookies and fresh baked pizza with local vegetables. Great deli sandwiches, and a varied selection of fresh local fruits, vegetables, and salads, can be found at *Kilauea Farmer's Market* next door (828-1512). It's a great spot to fill up your picnic basket before heading to the beach.

In HANALEI, don't miss *Tropical Taco* (827-8226; tropicaltaco.com) for the best fresh fish burrito on the island, and other Mexican treats at reasonable prices. *Hanalei Gourmet* (826-2524) serves sandwiches on fresh-baked breads and rolls. At *Hanalei Wake Up Café* (826-5551), sample tasty home-cooked, inexpensive breakfasts and lunches daily (dinners Fri. and Sat.). *Subways* turns out sandwiches from inside Big Save, while across the street, *Bubba Burgers* fries up burgers within a reasonably short wait, and *Neidie's Salsa & Samba* makes wonderful Mexican lunches and dinners with a Brazilian accent. *Java Kai* serves a wide range of hot and cold drinks, and fresh bagels, muffins and snacks. In the Ching Young village, *Hanalei Mixed Plate* has a great ginger chicken combination plate for only $4.95. *Polynesian Café* has tasty Chinese/Polynesian lunch plates and wonderful ice cream. At *Pizza Hanalei* (826-9494) homemade crust is crispy and the cheese and toppings generous. *Hanalei Health & Natural Foods* (826-6990) has packaged foods; for small plates and wraps try *Zababaz.*

SOUTH SHORE, *Taqueria Nortenos* (742-7222) at Kukuiula, is a longtime local favorite for tasty, inexpensive Mexican delights. *Pizzetta* in KOLOA (742-8881) will deliver excellent pizza, as well as inexpensive pastas and calzones. *Sueoka's* has wonderful plate lunches. In POIPU, try *Puka Dog's* 'Hawaiian style' hot dogs. A hole (*puka*) made in the specially baked bun is filled with your choice of condiments, including relishes of star fruit, mango, banana, or papaya ,and then stuffed with your choice of sausage.

A few miles down Rt. 50 in KALAHEO you'll find great burgers and chicken at *Camp House Grill,* the island's best pizza and delicious sandwiches at *Brick Oven* (335-8561). Up early? *The Bread Box* bakes seven different breads, and also muffins, cinnamon buns, and pastries, each morning (T-Sat) from 4 am till *pau* (sold out). Call 332-9000 to check. A cup of coffee is still only a quarter! *Kalaheo Coffee Company* (322-5868) makes deli treats and gourmet coffees, while further west in ELE'ELE, try *Grinds* (335-6027) for coffees, breakfast and fresh-baked treats, and deli lunches, or *Toi's Thai Kitchen* for saimin and hamburgers. In WAIMEA, it's *Wrangler's* for sandwiches, plate lunches, pizza and calzones (338-1218).

View from Bali Hai Restaurant

North Shore Restaurants
'favor...eats'

Perched on the ocean bluff, some restaurants in PRINCEVILLE have unforgettable ocean views. From **Bali Hai Restaurant,** you can watch the sun set over Hanalei Bay, and the view from the restaurants at the Princeville Hotel, **La Cascata** and **Café Hanalei**, is simply breathtaking. Try **Café Hanalei's** breakfast buffet, excellent lunches, or sunset dinners, or come for tea or sunset cocktails at **The Living Room,** the hotel lounge overlooking the bay, and listen to Kauai's talented musicians. The hotel's Italian specialty restaurant, **La Cascata**, combines excellent food with an amazing view. Come early, enjoy the sunset, and bring your camera.

In nearby HANALEI, **Postcards Café** takes healthful foods into a whole new dimension, with wonderful pastas and fresh island fish. At **Neidie's Salsa & Samba**, tasty Mexican lunches and dinners come with a Brazilian flair at unbelievable prices. A favorite lunch and dinner spot for fresh island fish is the **Hanalei Dolphin. Zelo's Beach House** has reasonably priced breakfasts, lunches, (salads, sandwiches, burgers), and dinners. Try **Sushi & Blues** for fish dinners, sushi, music.

For inexpensive lunches, try **Hanalei Mixed Plate** for kalua pork many folks rave about, as well as tasty sandwiches, or **Tropical Taco's** wonderful Mexican fish specialties. **Bubba Burgers** offers hamburgers, and the **Hanalei Gourmet** next door makes deli sandwiches. **Old Hanalei Coffee Company** serves sandwiches on fresh-baked breads, and vegetarians can select from salads and sandwiches at **Hanalei Natural Foods** across the street. Pizza lovers can try **Pizza Hanalei's** homemade whole wheat crust. After lunch, try shave ice at **Wishing Well** in the silver trailer near Kayak Kauai. Nearby, **Princeville Golf Course Restaurant** creates excellent salads and sandwiches in a beautiful, relaxed setting.

In nearby Kɪʟᴀᴜᴇᴀ, **Pau Hana Pizza** serves home-baked pizza with imaginative combinations of delicious ingredients, and **Kilauea Bakery** serves delicious breads, rolls, and pastries. Just around the corner, **Kilauea Farmers' Market** makes first-rate deli sandwiches and vegetarian delights. Map 2

Bali Hai

Imagine dining as the sunset paints the sky all gold and orange above the magnificent angles of the dark and mysterious mountains, turning the ocean almost purple in Hanalei Bay. Sip a cocktail while the cool evening breeze, fragrant with tropical flowers, touches your skin like silk. At the Bali Hai Restaurant, you can find the Kauai of your imagination, the dream of an island paradise that haunts you in the dead of winter.

The dining experience could not be more relaxing, the food brought at a leisurely pace by polite waiters and served at large, elegantly appointed tables, on china painted in colors of the sea. Open to the air on three sides, the dining room's tall ceilings and two-tiered arrangement of tables make the room spacious and, even when full, remarkably quiet. Tables are angled and set to put each chair in the best position, while a wonderful salt water pool meanders through tropical gardens one level below, so that you can look out at the flowers and palm trees and listen to the sound of waterfalls. As we lingered over coffee to watch a sudden shower fill the air with shining drops, we felt more at peace than when we arrived.

For years, and through many changes in management, Bali Hai has struggled to find a cuisine to equal its view. In its newest incarnation, the restaurant seems to have found the right niche with an imaginative, yet practical, Pacific Rim cuisine. For example, fresh fish entrées ($27-$31) come in five styles: "Ha'ena Hanapa'a" (with crab, cheese and portobello mushroom), "Rock Jumping Fisherman" (Thai style, with coconut sauce), "Pele Goddess of Fire" (blackened), "Bali Hai Sunset" (sautéed with

View from the Bali Hai Restaurant

papaya ginger glaze), or "Tropical Breeze" (grilled with fruit salsa). We still prefer the fresh fish plainly grilled, though we enjoy having these sauces served on the side for a quick dip. Most entrées are expensive, like the tasty lamb chops ($30), and are accompanied only by vegetable and 'starch of the day.' Appetizers drive up the dinner price, though they are appealing, like blackened seared ahi with cabbage and wasabi cream, or superb crab cakes ($13) with curry corn sauce. Prix fixed menus ($55) are also available.

Bali Hai has a wonderfully romantic ambiance and unmatched view. Before dinner, listen to some of Kauai's favorite musicians who play nightly at *Happy Talk Lounge* next door (see p. 106), or enjoy a pleasant evening stroll. Head towards the cliff along the sidewalk between the tennis courts. From path's end, you can look down at Hanalei Bay, sparkling with beads of light and turning deep purple as the sun descends. A sailboat cuts silently across the water, the sails filling with the breezes which brush your face and fill your head with the fragrance of evening flowers. The dark craggy edges of the cliffs blend into soft purples and deep blues as the gold and orange sun sinks slowly towards the water, shining more brightly with each second, until flattened into a disk that shrinks to nothing before your eyes. A golden glow remains, burnishing the clouds, polishing the water, then fades to darkening dusk.

Princeville, Hanalei Bay Resort. Reservations: 826-6522. Credit cards. Breakfast 7 am -11 am; Lunch 11:30 am - 2 pm; Dinner 5:30 - 9:30 pm. Children's menu. Enter Princeville at the main gate, take the third left onto Liholiho Rd., then turn right onto Hono'iki Rd. Map 2

Bamboo Bamboo

In a space where three Italian restaurants have tried and failed, Bamboo Bamboo tries to offer a wider cuisine, spicing it with local and Pacific Rim flavors. You can dine on decks enclosed with ferns and plants (bring mosquito repellant and ask for a coil) with an informal picnic atmosphere complete with plastic chairs and tables, or inside the dining room, softly lit with candles, pleasant with breezes and relaxing music.

The menu features local ingredients and flavors in its fresh fish, chicken, steak and lamb entrées, at prices a bit on the high side. The least expensive entrées are ahi salad ($16.95) or chicken ($17.96). Fresh potato crusted mahi mahi was moist and tasty, accompanied by perfectly cooked local vegetables, but somewhat small for the price ($24.95). The clean grilled version we requested, however, tasted bitter from the grill, even after being sent back to be re-cooked. Fresh baked white bread is served immediately and cheerfully, and most of the wines on the well chosen list are available by the glass, a nice feature.

At Bamboo Bamboo, lunch is reasonably priced and tasty, with a variety of salads, pastas, and delicious sandwiches plates for less than $10.

Hanalei Shopping Center. 826-1177 for reservations. Credit cards. Map 2

Bubba Burgers

Bubba's began life on Kauai on main street, Kapa'a, with the philosophy that a decent hamburger should cost no less than a can of dog food. This idea, and the burger (2.5 oz. of 88% fat-free fresh-ground Kauai beef), caught on, and now the Bubba's in Hanalei is equally jammed.

Children will like the "frings" (a portion of fries topped off with a couple of onion rings), and the burgers are, to quote the teenage connoisseurs, "O.K. – sorta in-between McDonald's and Burger King." It's fast food, sorta cooked to order, and generally predictable.

Kapa'a and Hanalei 823-0069. 10:30 am - 6 pm daily. Kapa'a location closed Sundays. Cash only. Maps 1 & 2

Café Hanalei, Princeville Resort Hotel

You could not imagine a more spectacular spot for breakfast than Café Hanalei, with its panoramic view of a bay that in any weather has the romantic beauty of a fairy tale. Even in the rain, you can watch the mountains peek out from veils of mist like shy princesses. Or watch as the sun's sorcery transforms the landscape from smoky greys into blazing colors – vivid greens and golds, brilliant blues, and on the mountains rising majestically above the bay, the shining silver ribbons of waterfalls. In this land of enchantment, each moment reveals a new mystery, and under the spell of such beauty, you could enjoy breakfast with only a chair!

The breakfast buffet will draw you indoors, a generous array of fruits, juices, and fresh baked pastries, blintzes with sour cream, even an omelette bar where your eggs will be whipped into a colorful and tasty creation right before your eyes. This breakfast buffet ($23 or $16.50 for a 'continental' buffet) combines an incomparable setting with delicious food and friendly, polite service. Where else could you find such radiance in the rain?

At dinner, the setting sun kindles the sky to flame in orange and turquoise behind the darkening cliffs. Visit the lounge, appropriately called the 'Living Room' first, and enjoy a cocktail while you relax on one of the plush couches in the elegant room, with marble fireplaces and tall shelves filled with books. But who can stay inside at sunset? Outside, the terrace is enclosed by waist high panels of glass, so that you can enjoy the spectacular panorama of Hanalei Bay without a railing to obstruct your view. Boats glide silently; the only sound is the soft music of the waves. Mountains are shrouded in clouds, and the sky turns to gold as the sun slips slowly into the sea, and colors deepen the reflections in tall glass windowpanes. As Hanalei Bay recedes into the velvet darkness and the first stars appear, walk downstairs to Café Hanalei, where tall windows mirror dozens of dancing candle flames. Tables generously spaced are laid with elegant china and sparkling crystal and silver.

All this romance is expensive. Twelve entrées, priced above $30, reflect the flavors of the Pacific Rim. Try fresh island opakapaka presented like

View from the terrace, Princeville Hotel

a stir fry, with shiitake mushrooms and Hawaiian sweet potatoes ($30), very moist and tasty. The price of dinner goes up quickly with appetizers like spinach salad with fresh shrimp and lobster ($14.95), or crispy crab cake ($12). You could almost make a meal of two. Leave room for desserts – pineapple macadamia nut crunch with vanilla ice cream, or a superb lilikoi mousse cake with almond rainbow stripes ($7).

The Friday night Seafood Buffet is an island tradition. Try Salmon Wellington, a whole salmon filet topped with scallop mouse baked in a light, flaky pastry, shellfish of every stripe, ahi sashimi and ahi poki, snow crab and Dungeness crab, a tempura station, carved Prime Rib, and elaborate dessert bar. Everything is fresh, flavorful, and generous ($46).

Sunday Brunch is a similarly sumptuous display of hot and cold dishes as well as fruits and pastries. Visit the omelette station, or choose pancakes or waffles, blintzes, even sashimi.

At Café Hanalei, the presentation is attractive, the service friendly, and under the supervision of Rosemary Caldwell, professional. The best part of a wonderful dining experience remains the setting, which is spectacular enough to make dinner unforgettable. Walk around the hotel afterwards, take the elevator down to the beach and listen to the music of the waves and the melodies in the evening breezes.

Princeville, in The Princeville Hotel. Reservations 826-9644. 6:30 am - 9 pm daily. Sunday Brunch ($35) & Friday nite seafood buffet ($46). Children's buffet prices are calculated by age. Credit cards. Map 2. Enter Princeville's main gate and stay on this road until it ends at the hotel.

C J's Steak House

C J's Steak House replaces the popular Chuck's Steak House, which for years has served up countless steaks, chicken, and fish. C J's has taken over the space, given it a fresher look, while retaining the steak and salad bar menu that made Chuck's a local favorite.

Prices are reasonable and menu choices extensive. Dinners range from $15.95 (calamari) to $28.25 (rack of lamb), including rice, warm bread, and the salad bar ($8.95 by itself). Request pacing the dinner, or your entrée may arrive when you've barely finished your salad.

Dinners are reliably well-prepared. New York steak (12 oz. for $28.25) has great flavor and is very tender (ask for teriyaki sauce). Fresh fish is moist and cleanly sautéed. Wines are fairly priced.

Dinners at C J's will be reasonably priced and reasonably good. On the other hand, you don't get anything special either, in food or ambiance.

C J's offers no views of Hanalei's magnificent mountains or valleys to paint a memory for dark winter evenings back home.

Princeville Center, Rt. 56. 826-6211. Credit cards. Lunch: 11:30 am- 2:30 pm (M-F). Dinner 6 pm- 10:00 pm daily. Map 2

Hanalei Dolphin

For years, the Dolphin has had the reputation of serving the finest fresh fish on the north shore. Now, however, Dolphin has strong competition in the fish department from Postcards Café and Café Hanalei, and the drawbacks of its dining experience may seem more pronounced. The menu hasn't changed much over the years, and neither has the no-reservations policy, which can start your meal off with an irritating wait. The fresh fish dinners are expensive, and although service is often friendly, at times it can be harried, as the small restaurant is almost always crowded. If you choose a weeknight and arrive before 7 pm, you have your best shot at a quick seating. If there's a line, you can order wine and appetizers on the porch.

In the softly lit dining room, shutters are raised to let in evening breezes, and lanterns glow pleasantly on polished table tops. The menu features locally caught fresh fish with rice or hot, crispy steak fries. Depending on the season, you may find opah or moonfish, mon chung, as well the familiar ahi and ono. Two and sometimes three chefs alternate during the week, and so the cooking inevitably varies – sometimes excellent, sometimes needing more (or less!) doneness. On our last visit, the mahi mahi ($26 for an 8 oz. filet) was moist, tender, and flaky – cleanly broiled, with no taste of the grill. Ahi teriyaki ($26 for an 8 oz. portion) is one of the most delicious fish dinners on Kauai – juicy, tender, and full of spark. Non-fishy eaters can try 'Hawaiian' chicken ($20) or NY steak ($26/12 oz.). For $22, you can have a 'light dinner' of broccoli casserole or 'veggie tofu casserole.'

Some entrées are priced in a regular as well as a smaller, 'menehune' portion at about a 40% discount, and include fresh hot bread as well as Dolphin's signature 'family style salad,' a huge bowl of lettuce, cherry tomatoes, bean sprouts, and choice of oil and vinegar, or creamy garlic or Russian dressings (and you can request seconds). Seafood chowder ($6), is creamy, steamy, full of fish, scallops, and clams, and can be ordered as an entrée ($18), served with salad, rice or french fries, and bread.

The wine list offers good choices in the $25-$40 range, like a Kendall Jackson chardonnay. We were sad to discover that an old friend on the list

– the bottle of Chateau Lafitte Rothschild, which had survived Hurricane 'Iwa in 1982 even when the roof did not – hadn't made it through Iniki and was no longer available for $200. Suddenly, we felt older.

You can try Dolphin's fresh fish for lunch – an ono or ahi sandwich, as well as steak burgers, or chicken and vegetable sandwiches ($8-$9), and wonderful fish & chips made with swordfish – light, crisp, and flaky ($11). Dine at picnic tables next to the Hanalei River, or stop in at the Dolphin's fish market tucked behind the restaurant and cook your filet at home.

The Dolphin has been a local favorite for years. The riverside setting can be pleasant, though if mosquitoes tend to pick on you, bring Off and ask for a mosquito coil, for there are no screens. The fish is usually delicious, though warn the waiter that any overcooked fish will be thrown back, if not into the ocean, at least onto his tray!

Hanalei, on Rt. 560, just past Princeville and the one-lane bridge over the river. No reservations. 11 am - 10 pm. 826-6113. Children's dinners: chicken, steak, or shrimp. Smoking in bar only. Map 2

The Hanalei Gourmet

For years, on our way to the beach at Hanalei, we have wished for a first rate deli where we could buy sandwiches for picnics on the sand. The Hanalei Gourmet in the old Hanalei schoolhouse features home-baked breads and pastries, deli meats and salads, fine cheeses, soups, and a selection of gourmet foods and fine wines. Insulated backpacks are available for picnics. Order a sandwich ($7- $9) at the deli counter (or phone ahead), or take a table in the 'classroom' next door, converted into an attractive café cum bar for those who would prefer to avoid the sand altogether! In this 'tropical bar,' you'll find a large surprisingly large assortment of entrées ranging in price from $11 to $23, including pastas, salads, as well as chicken, fish, and steak. Try Big Tim's 1/3 pound hamburger ($8.95) or fresh ahi sandwich ($9.95).

Hanalei Center. 826-2524. Credit cards. 8 am to 10 pm daily. Custom picnic baskets. Kauai's musical entertainers play nitely. Map 2

Kilauea Bakery & Pau Hana Pizza

Some of the most imaginative pizzas on Kauai are created at Kilauea Bakery, whose small storefront displays crusty golden breads, cookies, macadamia nut sticky buns, as well as pizza by the slice at the counter. Don't leave without a bag of bread sticks – so popular that they are now distributed all over the island. When you arrive, you may find a pizza of goat cheese, sun dried tomatoes, and eggplant. Or perhaps one made with feta cheese, olives, zucchini, fresh mushrooms, and tomato slices. The crust, either white or whole wheat, will be very thin and crisp, and you'll find six different cheeses, including 'tofurella.'

About a dozen tables surround the counter, and outside, patio tables with umbrellas protect you from the sun as well as the sudden showers that can threaten to dampen your lunch. Service is friendly. You can order a salad of local organically grown lettuces, and organically grown coffee.

Kilauea, Kong Lung Center, on the Lighthouse Road. 828-2020. Open 6:30 am to 9 pm daily except Sundays. Pizza 11 am to 9 pm. Cash only.

La Cascata, Princeville Resort Hotel

A sunset dinner at La Cascata can be one of your most memorable island experiences. Even arriving at the Princeville Hotel is unforgettable. You drive up around a spectacular fountain, and then walk into an enormous lobby, where all along the western wall, giant windows which appear seamless reveal the spectacular colors of the cliffs beyond Hanalei Bay. In this wonderful spot is a beautiful lounge, called 'The Living Room,' where you can enjoy a glass of wine or a cocktail (or in the afternoons, enjoy afternoon tea and scones). Comfortable sofas invite you to relax and look out over Hanalei Bay, glistening in sunset's gold and orange, while you enjoy live music. Michaelle Edwards and Ken Emerson sing favorite Hawaiian melodies and play slack key and steel guitar (Th & Sun, 7 pm).

Walk down one level below the Living Room, and you will find La Cascata, with an equally dramatic and panoramic view of Hanalei Bay. At sunset, you can watch the sky break in brilliant gold and orange waves across the mountains, so bring your camera. Window screens slide open, and you may just capture that unforgettable moment, those matchless colors. The sunset views are more spectacular than the understated decor of the dining room itself, where the soft golden terra cotta color of the walls blends with the quarry tile on the floors to create an informal, comfortable ambiance. Tables widely spaced for privacy are set among arches painted with ivy to resemble an antique Tuscan garden, with picturesque looking chips in the plaster and water stains which are, we suspect, authentic souvenirs of Hurricane Iniki. Murals provide scenes of Italian landscapes. Candle lamps cast flickering golden light on the tables, dressed with white linen, decorated with tropical flowers in cut glass vases and elegant china, and surrounded with comfortable upholstered arm-

At sunset, an outrigger canoe glides silently across Hanalei Bay

chairs. A singer and guitarist provide pleasant, relaxing melodies.

Fresh bread arrives with a wonderfully soft extra virgin olive oil to put you in the best frame of mind to consider the menu, which changes monthly as the chef experiments. Because there is no longer a separate kitchen for la Cascata, one chef and one kitchen serve both La Cascata and Café Hanalei, so you can order from either menu at either dining room at comparable prices. Try a light and delicately flavored fish soup, or perhaps a salad of arugula, pear, and gorgonzola cheese with walnut vinaigrette ($12). Thin crust pizza with goat cheese, grilled mushrooms and arugula ($15) is another good choice. Fresh pasta is available each day ($24), as well as at least two fresh island fish, perhaps pan sautéed snapper with chanterelle-edamame succotash ($34) or fresh ahi, beautifully presented with salmon-artichoke lasagne ($34). The chef prepared a very fresh special vegetable salad for our vegetarian ($18). A prix fixe dinner ($51.95) includes 3 courses, coffee, cappuccino or espresso.

Service is polite, pleasant, and professional; every effort is made to be attentive to your needs. Do noodles leave your children cold? They may order a cheeseburger or grilled cheese sandwich from the children's menu in Café Hanalei. Not sure about a wine selection? You may be offered a taste before choosing from the extensive, and expensive, list.

At La Cascata, the food is not exceptional. But the setting truly is, and taken together, they can make a magical evening. When planning your dinner, try to set the time for sunset, when the dining experience is gilded with spectacular colors, particularly in summer when the angle of the sun allows it to sink right into the sea before your eyes. After dinner, stroll around the hotel, and take the elevator down to the beach and watch moonlight sparkle on the waves.

In the Princeville Hotel. 826-9644. Reservations recommended. Dinner nightly 6 - 9:30 pm. Credit cards. Enter Princeville at main gate and follow this road to the end. Map 2

Lighthouse Bistro Restaurant

The original Casa di Amici has moved to Poipu, and in the Kilauea location, chef Michael Moore has stayed on, bought the business, and continues the Italian cuisine he helped to develop, maintaining the same focus on local ingredients and the informal setting. The grey and white dining room is attractive, with sliding glass doors that open to evening breezes. In the candlelight, the tables, colorful with red ginger blossoms, look romantic, and the spare decor has its own charm.

Dinner begins with fresh wheat bread, which you can enjoy while you consider the menu and sip a tropical cocktail. Try a 'pineapple upside down cake,' or stolnichaya vanilla and pineapple vodkas with fresh fruit juice ($6.50). Delicious! And a more interesting alternative to the 30 or so wines on the menu, some of which are reasonable while others are overpriced, like this year's low cost red wine favorite, Australian Rosemont shiraz, expensive at $25. Macadamia nut crusted chicken ($17.95) is moist and tasty. The fresh fish was perfectly cooked, particularly the ahi with miso marinade over black lentils ($22.95) while the ginger crusted ahi arrived with a sauce too strong for the fish ($23.95). Lighthouse Bistro also offers pasta (from $12.95) and other entrées including chicken, veal and steak ($17.95-$24.95). We loved 'salad pomodoro' with tomatoes and fresh basil and olive tamponade and blueberry vinaigrette ($6.95). For dessert, try haupuna or lillikoi sorbet.

Entrées are served with rice and lightly sautéed vegetables. If you are really hungry, try the all-you-can-eat pasta bar ($13.95); one visit plus a salad is only $14.95. Service is friendly, and for the most part efficient. Lighthouse Bistro has excellent lunch sandwiches ($6-$11).

Kilauea, Kong Lung Center, on the Lighthouse Road. 11 am - 9:30 pm daily, lunch and dinner. Children's menu. 828-0480. Credit cards. Map 2

Hanalei Valley's fields of taro

Neidie's Salsa & Samba

On a back porch in Hanalei, with only a tiny sign out front, you will find a slight young woman cooking in a tiny kitchen just across a counter from a half dozen tables. Don't be fooled by appearances. Neidie makes magic in there, deftly blending Brazilian spices with Kauai's flavorful fresh vegetables and fruits.

You may have to wait for one of the tables, as there are only ten, and they are usually full. The reason is a combination of great food and great prices. Home-made chips and delicious fresh salsa start the meal, but save room for Neidie's wonderful Mexican and Brazilian cooking. She weaves Kauai's bountiful fresh fruits, vegetables, and fish into recipes from her homeland. Fresh island fish is cleanly grilled and tasty, with a delicious coconut milk sauce, served on a large platter with Brazilian rice and vegetable – at only $14.95, one of the best bargains on Kauai! Or try a vegetarian pancake with fresh island pumpkin, tropical squash and whatever vegetables have tempted Neidie at the market ($8.95). Demand for Neidie's pumpkin pancake has shifted a neighboring farmer into hyperdrive to keep her supplied. Service may be on the slow side but for the right reason – Neidie cooks everything to order. Spicing is subtle rather than flashy, so if it's not hot enough for your taste, you can add as many chilies as you want. Prices are amazing considering the generous size of the portions.

For delicious, carefully spiced and imaginative Brazilian dishes served with a pleasant, personal touch, don't miss Neidie's!

Hanalei Village. 826-1851. Credit cards. 11 am - 3 pm; 5 - 9 pm daily.

Postcards Café

As you round the last bend in the winding road into Hanalei, you'll see Postcards Café in the green Hanalei Museum. Despite its modest exterior, Postcards surprises you with a carefully crafted dining experience, an interesting, thoughtful cuisine served in a comfortably informal atmosphere. You enter Postcards from a small porch. Inside, you'll find an intimate dining room with open beamed ceilings and soft lighting that makes everything look at once clean and relaxing. Vintage Hawaiian postcards appear under glass table tops and in collages on the walls, along with black and white photographs of old Hanalei, even old-time ukuleles.

Dinner is café-style informal. Tables in this charming plantation cottage are set without linens, and windows, with the modern addition of screens, slide open for evening breezes, or close for occasional showers. The cuisine is exceptional, both in concept and execution, and everything is generous and fresh, prepared without meat, poultry, or chemicals. Taro fritters ($9) make a wonderful appetizer, the small patties deep-fried and served with a tangy home-made mango chutney. In salmon rockets ($10), tender slices of salmon are rolled in layers of lumpia and nori and quick fried. Summer rolls ($9) are delicious, as is homemade soup.

The dinner menu is small, only seven entrées featuring local, organically grown vegetables, or fresh island fish. Least expensive are pasta primavera or a Chinese vegetable dish with roasted tofu and a tamari ginger sauce ($15). Fresh ono was cleanly cooked, moist, flavorful and flaky, and although we sampled all four sauces on the menu and enjoyed each unique flavor, particularly the coconut, we preferred the fish cleanly grilled. Of the three pasta choices, two vegetarian, we liked 'Seafood Sorrento,' a combination of shrimp with medallions of all four fresh fish on the menu. It was delicious, gently seasoned in a sauce of mushrooms, tomatoes, bell peppers, and as requested, only light on garlic ($22). The portion was so generous that our son raved about the leftovers the next day. Children can choose pasta or quesadilla ($8). If you can't decide, the kitchen is ready to prepare your request, or you can opt for a beautiful local salad ($8 or $5).

Desserts, made without refined sugar, are elegant and delicious. Passion fruit mousse arrives in a lovely colored tumbler, and chocolate cake is amazingly light for its dense chocolate flavor. The wine list is small, though well-selected, and includes some delicious organic wines, or you can try organic smoothies and juices ($5), or organic Kona coffee ($3). Waitpersons are friendly, following the example of the owners who circulate among the guests, stopping to chat and give sound vacation advice to diners whom they treat as guests.

Postcards Café is a must stop on the north shore for excellent, imaginative cuisine served in an attractive, comfortably informal dining room. If you aren't a vegetarian, Postcards might even change your mind!

Hanalei. 8 am - 11 am and 6 - 9 pm daily. 826-1191 for reservations (at least a day in advance). Credit cards. Map 2

Princeville Restaurant

With a spectacular panoramic setting amid mountains, rolling fairways, and ocean, the clubhouse restaurant at the Prince Course is a great spot for a surprisingly inexpensive lunch or breakfast. The entry is all glass, and through enormous windows you can see all the way to the horizon as you walk downstairs, past the glass enclosed health club, to the dining room. The menu is small, offering fewer than a dozen sandwiches and salads priced around $9, but portions are generous and the choices well-prepared. The vegetarian sandwich ($8.75) is stuffed with carrots, lettuce and sprouts, and accompanied by first-rate, crispy french fries. Tangy Chinese chicken salad ($9.50) is full of crunchy vegetables and a tender grilled chicken breast. Ask for homemade papaya seed dressing. Fresh ahi salad is tasty and generous, the fish moist and tender ($8.95). A full bar is available, or you can enjoy smoothies and juice mixes ($4.50).

Princeville Restaurant offers an incredible view, pleasant servers, and tasty and generous portions. For the price, it's hard to find a more reasonable slice of ocean on seven grain bread!

Just east of Princeville on Rt. 56. 826-5050. Breakfast, lunch daily. Monday night Japanese buffet (5:30 - 8:30 pm). Air-conditioned. Map 2

Sabella's

Tucked away in Princeville's Pali Ke Kua condominium, Sabella's is pleasant in an understated way, with comfortable chairs and polished wood tables arranged in a two-tiered dining room. There is no view – the only

water you can see is in the swimming pool. But come early for a walk. Cross the parking lot to Pali Ke Kua and enjoy spectacular summer sunsets beforehand.

The menu features a mix of classic Italian cuisine with fresh island fish at fairly expensive prices. Appetizers may in fact turn out to be the most successful part of the meal. Soup of the day, a cold potato and leek, was excellent, light rather than overly creamy. Kauai goat cheese and tomato salad with Maui onion and balsamic vinaigrette ($12) arrived with four very large slices of ripe tomato, topped with delicious, fresh goat cheese and basil. Sashimi was another good choice, with excellent texture and flavor. As rather salty olive tapenade is served with the bread basket.

Entrées, on the other hand, were disappointing. The ahi steak was bland and overcooked, and not improved by the poorly flavored béarnaise sauce, which, fortunately, was served on the side. Instead, we dipped the fish in soy sauce and wasabi. Best on the plate were actually the wasabi mashed potatoes. Our vegetarian asked for an entrée of steamed vegetables, but what arrived was a small plate of carrots in butter and garlic. This kitchen seems reluctant to deviate from its set courses.

The wine list has some reasonably priced offerings, like Kendall Jackson chardonnay ($29), in a range of prices from $23 to $40. Service could be more attentive, but the attraction here is the convenient location.

In Princeville. Dinner nightly from 5:30 pm. 5300 Ka Haku Rd. at Pali Ke Kua. 808 826 6255 for reservations. Credit cards. Map 2

Sushi & Blues

On the second floor of Ching Young Village, not far from its parent, Zelo's Beach House, Sushi & Blues tries to be a happening place. The sushi bar takes up only a fraction of the space, and the signature elements are music and camaraderie. For decor, Sushi & Blues aims for industrial chic, with a silver ventilation system on the black ceiling as part of the decor, and a bubble lamp on the bar operating as the centerpiece.

The menu features a dozen entrées, including fresh fish, pasta, ribs, chicken (least expensive at $18) and steak. Dinner begins with edamame, and includes a first rate miso soup, stir-fry vegetables and either rice, wasabi potatoes, or a California roll. Service can be very slow, and when the food arrives, not all of it may arrive at the same time. Fresh mahi mahi could have been more cleanly broiled and was also on the small side, served with a tasty sake cream sauce. Seafood stir-fry was delicious though somewhat spicy, with lots of shrimp, fish, scallops and vegetables served sizzling on a fajita platter. The sushi bar offers 22 specialty rolls. Prices are at the upper end of the island sushi scale, though hand rolls are generously thick. Music begins at 9 pm, with dancing on weekends.

Ching Young Village, Hanalei. 826-9701 Dinner: Tues-Sun from 5:30 Credit cards. Call for entertainment details. www.sushiblues.com. Map 2

Tahiti Nui

Local people have enjoyed Tahiti Nui for years, ever since Louise Marston opened the doors and created its special character as a place where tourists could meet old timers and hear fascinating stories about the island over generous drinks in the bar. Even Tahiti Nui's famous 'family style luau' was not your typical Hawaiian extravaganza, but more like a local talent show, with Louise, her family, and large circle of musician friends providing the entertainment – occasionally even guests! Some evenings, Louise herself would stroll through the room singing 'Hanalei Moon,' spreading aloha from table to table, and guests would catch themselves grinning at perfect strangers across the room.

But Tahiti Nui never quite stayed the same from visit to visit. Today, the bar remains, but the dining room has become retail space, and the famous Wednesday night luau is being produced further west, at the Hanalei Colony Resort, in a dining room right on the water. The bar is still a favorite hang out for 'talking story.' Some things never change!

Hanalei village. Luau: Wednesdays /$52 adult) Fridays Steak & Seafood. 826-6277 for reservations. Credit cards. Map 2

Zelo's Beach House

Zelo's is popular for among local people and visitors alike for well-prepared meals at reasonable prices, with most lunch items around $6 - $12 and most dinner choices around $15 - $25. The lunch menu features Zelo's specialty fish chowder ($3.95/$5.95) – thick, creamy and tasty.

Hamburgers (from $5.25) are excellent, served on a sesame seed bun with fries, and other choices include wraps, salads, fish tacos, fish & chips, and sandwiches. Lunch salads and sandwiches, particularly fresh ahi, are excellent, as are seafood fajitas and fish tacos. Dinners range from pasta ($14) to prime rib ($24.95) and include a small salad, vegetable, bread, and rice or baked potato. The truly hungry can order the 'all-you-can-eat' spaghetti dinner for $9.95. With its full bar and espresso machine, Zelo's is equipped to provide you with almost any beverage you desire.

The dining room is cheerful and comfortable, the ceiling open to the rafters, and glass doors open to the outside. Service is sometimes friendly and efficient, sometimes not. Given the reasonable prices and main street location, it's often crowded. Expect to wait on line if you come at peak mealtimes, so go early if you plan to take the kids!

Hanalei. 826-9700. Open 11 am - 10:30 pm daily. Entertainment some evenings. Credit cards. www.zelosbeachhouse.com.

Some Useful Hawaiian Words

aloha – (a LOW ha) hello, good-bye, love, kindness, friendship
hale – (HAH lee) house
haole – (HOW lee) foreigner white man
heiau – (HEY ow) ancient Hawaiian temple
hui– (HOO' ee) club or group
kahuna– (ka HOO and) an elder, wise person
kalua– (ka LOO a) to roast underground
kai – the sea
kama'aina – (ka ma EYE and) a native
kane – (KA neh) man
kapu – (KA poo) forbidden, keep out
keiki – (KAY kee) child
kona– (KOH na) leeward side of the island

lani – (LAH nee) heavens, sky
lomilomi – (low me low me) massage
mahalo – (ma HA lo) thank you
makai – (ma KAI) ocean side
mauka– (MOW ka) towards the mountains
menehune– Kauai's legendary little people" & builders
nani – (NA nee) beautiful
ohana – (o HA na) family
ono – delicious
pali – (PA lee) cliff, precipice
paniolo – (pa nee O lo) cowboy
pau– (pow) finished, done
puka – (POO ka) hole
wahine – (wa HEE neh) woman, wife
wikiwiki – hurry up

South Shore Restaurants

Thousands of sugar cane tassels wave in the breeze near Koloa. Sugar plantations are closing, however, and tourism is now Kauai's main industry.

'favor..eats'

In Poipu, **Brennecke's Beach Broiler,** with a view of Poipu Beach, remains a local favorite for the best in fresh island fish, as well as a great salad bar. For a spectacular oceanfront setting, particularly at sunset, try the **Beach House Restaurant** near Spouting Horn. **Roy's Poipu Bar & Grill** features the signature Euro/Asian cuisine of Roy Yamaguchi, while next door at **Keoki's,** families and hearty eaters can enjoy generous steak and seafood dinners at reasonable prices. For pasta, try **Plantation Gardens,** with Italian cuisine in a romantic garden setting, local favorite **Casa di Amici** with reasonably priced, tasty pastas and entrees, or newcomer **Casablanca,** in a garden setting at the Kiahuna Tennis Club.

Wherever you dine, be sure to stroll through the beautiful **Hyatt Regency Hotel** afterwards, a treat which can be yours for the modest cost of the tip for the valet who parks your car. Enjoy Hawaiian melodies at the Seaview Lounge overlooking the gardens and ocean, or stop in at Stevenson's Library for an after dinner drink or game of billiards, or simply stroll the hotel's lovely grounds.

On a budget? Try Mexican take-out from **Taqueria Nortenos,** Kukui'ula Center, on the road to Poipu. But don't stay in Poipu! Take a short drive to Kalaheo for wonderful, reasonably priced restaurants – **Brick Oven Pizza,** a family favorite for the island's best pizza, or just down the road, **Camp House Grill** for outstanding hamburgers and milk shakes made in a genuine milk shake machine. **Pomodoro,** an intimate, family-owned Italian restaurant, offers a carefully seasoned cuisine and the professional service you'd expect at much higher prices, and don't miss **Kalaheo Steak House** for steaks, fresh fish, prime rib – one of the best dollar values on Kauai. Across the street, coffee still costs a quarter at **The Bread Box.** Seven fresh-baked breads, also muffins and pastries, from 4 am T-Sat until '*pau*' (sold out). Call 332-9000 to check.

The Beach House Restaurant

A longtime favorite of both residents and visitors, the Beach House once perched on a sea wall only inches from the waves, a great spot to watch the sun set into the ocean and enjoy dinner in a relaxed and casual setting. In fact, the tables were so close to the waves that when Hurricane 'Iwa struck Kauai in 1982, the entire restaurant was swept out to sea – leaving only the concrete slab to mark the spot where so many evenings had passed so pleasantly. Even though rebuilt at a more respectful distance from the waves, Beach House was again destroyed ten years later by Hurricane Iniki, and then re-opened once more in the same location, clearly in hopes that the third time is the charm.

The two-tiered dining room has sweeping ocean views and is beautifully detailed with paintings and elegant table dressings. But what comes to the table is even better, the signature Pacific Rim cuisine created by executive chef Linda Yamada, who has made Beach House the most popular restaurant on the south shore. Dinner begins with a basket of delicious oven-fresh breads, and on the appetizer menu, you'll find intriguing choices. A salad with fresh local asparagus, vine ripe local tomatoes, goat cheese, and a soy sherry vinaigrette ($9) is spectacular, and so is wild mushroom gnocci served with organic greens and smoked salmon ($8.50). Even the small dinner salad of greens from nearby Omao is special with a light sesame and orange vinaigrette ($6). Entrées, particularly fresh island fish, are delicious, like fire roasted fresh ahi, both flaky and tender ($27), or macadamia nut mahi mahi served with a delicious citrus miso sauce and accompanied by stir fried vegetables. The menu also features steak, salmon, and rack of lamb ($29), as well as chicken ($23) and seafood, with entrée prices averaging $24 – although two could make a light meal of several appetizers. Check the menu online (www.the-beach-house.com), buy gift cards, even make a reservation.

The setting is truly lovely. Tables are well-separated, and sliding glass doors open to the evening air and to spectacular views of surfers catching waves as the sun sets into the shimmering sea. It's lovely even after dark, as the last light of sunset fades, and you can linger over coffee and watch the waves begin to glisten with moonlight. It's such a special spot that you might emphasize to your server to *slow* the dinner pace, so you can take the time to enjoy so much of nature's splendor.

spectacular sunset dining & elegant cuisine!

Poipu, on Spouting Horn Road. 742-1424. Reservations at least a day in advance. Request a window table, but be prepared to wait for it. Credit cards. 5:30 - 10 pm nightly. Map 3

Brennecke's Beach Broiler

For almost twenty years, Brennecke's has been the front runner when it comes to the best reasonably-priced fresh fish dinners on Kauai. It offers a varied menu, a first-rate salad bar, friendly service, and a memorable dining experience for the whole family.

In this second-storey restaurant across the street from Poipu Beach Park, you'll find the atmosphere informal, so you'll feel comfortable no matter what you're wearing. But the informal ambiance is the result of the meticulous attention to detail which enhances every aspect of the dining experience. The decor, for example, looks very plain – a porch in soft grey and white tones – but everything is spanking clean, the paint shiny and fresh looking, the chairs and grey formica tables immaculate, the flowers in the window boxes bright and cheerful.

The food receives equal attention to detail. Clam chowder ($3.95) is creamy rather than thick, generous with clams, and delicately seasoned. Teriyaki chicken stix ($7.50) are tasty and sizzling hot. Tiger eye sushi, fresh ahi wrapped in rice and nori and quick fried, keeps the fish cool while the wrapper is hot. Dinner entrées include beef, pasta, poultry, even prime rib in three sizes ($17-$24), as well as a host of sandwich baskets and munchies, but fresh island fish is the reason to come to Brennecke's. Your fish, no matter which fin you choose, will be perfectly cooked, crisp on the outside, meltingly moist and delicious inside. The secret to Brennecke's flawless broiling is the grill, designed by owner Bob French and fueled by charcoal of kiawe wood. It burns hot and clean, sealing in juices quickly, leaving no aftertaste.

20 years of the best fresh island fish!

You can find fish you may not find in every restaurant, though even the old standbys, ahi and ono and mahi mahi, are cooked so perfectly that they seem extraordinary. Opakapaka, or snapper, could not be juicier or tastier, served with a wonderful papaya pineapple salsa. Grouper, or white sea bass, is also sensational, with a texture somewhat like lobster, garnished with homemade tartar sauce. Don't miss the onaga if it is on the menu. For a reasonable price ($23.95), you get a meal to remember! Dinners include rice or herb pasta, sautéed fresh vegetables, and a visit to a first-rate salad bar – fresh, colorful, ripe, and appetizing. Instead of rice, try Brennecke's pasta with your entrée, or as a side order ($3.95). Not hungry enough for a full dinner? Brennecke's offers more than a dozen reasonably-priced options, for example a huge platter of nachos ($9), burgers ($9) including a vegetarian variant, as well as several sandwich baskets, like an excellent chicken sandwich, cleanly grilled and served on a soft bun. Vegetarians will enjoy kiawe broiled seasonal vegetables ($16.25), or a delicious fresh fish sandwich ($11.50). Or stick with the salad bar ($9/multi-trip or $5/single visit) and add a cup of seafood chowder ($3). Though small, the wine list is fairly priced, with a Kendall Jackson chardonnay at about $25, or try an exotic drink from the full bar, served in a souvenir glass.

The 'under-12's' have a great menu, with pizza ($8), spaghetti or burger/fries ($5), fish sandwich ($9) or soup & salad ($5). They can have chocolate milk or a grown-up looking fruit punch. Kid's burgers, chicken, and fish are very successful, judging from the enthusiasm of six young-sters seated nearby. Order your coffee in a Brennecke's souvenir cup.

For the best in fresh fish, beautifully broiled and attractively served, it's hard to find a better spot than Brennecke's. The staff is friendly and professional, the dining comfortable and open to evening breezes. It may be noisy when full, but it's busy for all the right reasons. Since 1983, Brennecke's has been one of the most popular restaurants on the south shore. Be sure to phone ahead for a reservation if you don't want to stand in line, and you might check the fresh fish on the menu and reserve a portion of your favorite fin in advance.

Poipu, on Ho'one Rd. 742-7588 for the daily fish report & reservations (necessary). Credit cards. 11 am - 10 pm daily. Happy hour daily 2-5 pm. Reserve in advance: 888-384-8810. To order tee-shirts, Nukomoi surf wear, visit www.brenneckes.com. Map 3

Brick Oven Pizza

Ask just about any Kauai resident where to find the best pizza, and you'll probably hear, 'Brick Oven.' We agree! This family-owned operation in Kalaheo has been one of our most popular stops. And we're not alone, for tourists, as well as local families, have made Brick Oven a favorite for years. The cheerful dining room has red–checked tablecloths

*best pizza
on Kauai!*

and murals of pizza serendipity – a pizza shaped like the island of Kauai, for example, with "Garlic Grotto," "Mushroom Valley," "Grand Pizza Canyon," and "Port Anchovy." Friendliness is in the air.

But good as all this is, the pizza is even better, as fine as you'll discover anywhere. The homemade dough – either white or whole wheat – is delicious, crunchy without being dry and with a fluted crust like a pie, shiny with garlic butter. The sauce, in the words of the teenage judges, has "awesome spice, cooked just right." There is lots of cheese, the Italian sausage is made right in the kitchen, and tomatoes are red, juicy and fresh. Portions are generous and quality unbeatable. A family size (15 inch) starts at $18.35, but you may be tempted to try one of the outrageous special creations described on the menu, like the 'super.' Or consider a delicious sandwich on fresh baked roll, or a salad ($3 to $6). You can wash it all down with ice cold beer ($6 for 1/2 pitcher) or soda ($6/pitcher). A nice touch – the ice comes in the glasses, not in the pitcher. Kids will love to watch the dough spin into pizza during that hard, hungry time of waiting, especially at peak hours when it's jammed.

At Brick Oven, you'll find a smile and pleasant word for short persons no matter how cranky. When one child spilled coke, our waitress not only wiped her dry but brought her a new glass filled to the very brim. Each child can ask for a ball of pizza dough, which feels so good in the hands that it usually manages to stay out of the hair– all the way home.

Kalaheo, on Rt. 50. 332-8561. 11 am - 10 pm. Closed Mondays. Credit cards. Map 4

Camp House Grill

If you were able to find Kalaheo, a tiny blip on the line of Rt. 50 going west from Poipu, you would probably decide Camp House Grill looks too much like a greasy spoon, and drive right on by. Once inside, however, you'd be pleasantly surprised by the crisp, clean decor: the woodgrain formica tables are well-spaced, blue window frames make a nice contrast with whitewashed walls, and even the green plants look healthy and well-fed. A cheerful waitress will seat you with a smile, no matter how much sand you bring in from the beach, or whether everyone in your party has managed to come up with an even number of shoes.

Though you cut some corners for such reasonable prices, paper placemats and napkins, even paper cups, are a small price to pay for such tasty food and pleasant service. And the placemats with a drawing of a sugar plantation 'camp house' give hungry kids an opportunity to color, crayons courtesy of management. Another generous touch: sodas are served in a "bottomless cup" for $1.75. Better yet, try a milk shake. Camp House Grill makes kids feel welcome. Ten-and-unders can eat a "mene-hune special" cheeseburger $4, while bigger little people can choose junior quarter pound burgers, fish, hot dogs, and four types of chicken breast sandwiches from $5.50, with fries.

Everything is cooked to order, so you might have to wait a bit, but it will all seem worth while once you start eating. Waimea Burger ($5.75), a barbecue cheeseburger, is perfectly cooked medium-rare with tangy sauce and great cheese. In a Hanapepe Burger, broiled pineapple and teriyaki sauce make an ideal complement to the beef, Swiss cheese, lettuce, and tomato. Deep fried chicken ($9) comes to you hot, golden brown, and moist inside, a sure crowd-pleaser, while barbecue 'Huli' chicken ($9.75/half) is on the spicy side. To cool it all off, there's draft beer by the glass or pitcher. Note: there is a different chef on the dinner shift, so consistency varies. Steak, ribs, or chicken dinner plates include soup or salad, potato or rice and start at $9.

Camp House Grill is cheerful and sincere. What you see is what you get – and then some extras, including wonderful home-baked pies. A deer head and a stuffed rooster look out through the window at what is passing by on Rt. 50. Don't let that be you!

Kalaheo, on Rt. 50. 332-9755 for take-out orders. Daily 6:30 am- 9 pm. Breakfast special till 8 am. Map 3

Casablanca

Imagine walking down a torch-lit path, through the Kiahuna Golf and Tennis Club, and finding a little slice of the Mediterranean. The open air setting, wicker furniture, green plants, and cleverly recessed lighting create a comfortable, romantic atmosphere. And this restaurant has lofty ambitions: breakfast, lunch, dinner, tapas all day, as well as a full bar, and even a belly dancer on Thursdays!

Somehow, executive chefs Robin Goldstein and Adam Newman manage to pull this off, and at the same time transform local Kauai produce, fresh seafood, and big island grown beef into an exciting menu which varies seasonally. Dinner begins with fragrant, crusty bread still warm from the oven. On the server's recommendation, we tried 'Mozza-

rella Fresca' ($9), fresh mozzarella wrapped in proscuitto and served with a tasty port sauce over poached figs. 'Insalata Caprese' is also excellent, with roasted tomatoes, the tiny sweet cherry variety, a better choice than 'Panzella Salad,' a rather ordinary green salad with garlic dressing and croutons.

The menu offers a surprising variety of choices. Seared duck is a stand-out, perfectly cooked with a well seasoned balsamic sauce. Pork is also excellent, again with a sauce perfectly balanced and very light. In saucing entreés, the kitchen uses natural juices and vegetables to enhance the entrée's flavors rather than overpower them. Vegetarians have some wonderful choices, including vegetable couscous, made without garlic on request, a tasty combination of roasted root vegetables over couscous, so well-prepared you could distinguish the individual flavors.

Desserts are outstanding. Panna cotta is very light with a delicate boysenberry sauce. Blueberry noisetta, a tart chunky with blueberries, is very light and tasty, and a better choice than ricotta cheese cake. Prices are as high as at Plantation Gardens or Casa di Amici, with entreés averaging more than $20 and appetizers priced about $10.

2290 Poipu Rd. Kiahuna Swim and Tennis club. 742-2929. Tues-Sat 7:30 to 10 pm; Monday 7:30 to 6 pm; Sunday 8:30 until 3 pm. Happy hour 3-6 pm. Credit cards. Tapas, full bar, all day; well drinks $3.50. Map 3

Casa di Amici

Casa di Amici, once a Kilauea favorite, has refurbished a space once called the Aquarium, so named for the enormous aquarium which divided dining room from bar, whose fish population rose and fell with the restaurant's fortunes. The aquarium is still there, the fish are thriving, and Casa di Amici's updated dining room is more spacious and at the same time more intimate. Tables are well-separated, lit with candle lamps, and glass doors open to breezes.

Many of the entrées popular at the original Kilauea location are still on Casa di Amici's Poipu menu, including 'Tournedos Rossini,' with medallions of beef, paté de foie gras and fluted mushroom caps ($24). A nice feature for those who prefer small portions, entrées are priced as 'full' or 'light' portions, and include an impressive selection of veal and poultry, fresh fish, pastas, and some vegetable entrées. Prices range from $17/light or $21/full for chicken or eggplant casserole, to $26 for fennel crusted lamb loin (full portion). Most appetizers are $8, including 4 risotto dishes and 5 salads. The chef enjoys experimenting with flavors, and his combinations of spices and sauces usually add zest to his creations.

Of the variety of appetizers on the menu, the onion soup ($6) is rich and flavorful, topped with toasted bread and melted cheese. Salad of local greens is heaped with lettuces, perfectly flavored with a sesame ginger vinaigrette ($8). Lasagne fills a large bowl, layered with grilled eggplant and zucchini, ground sirloin, and spicy sausage ($19). Fresh ahi ($23 for the 9 oz. portion) was cleanly grilled and very tender, one of the best fish we sampled anywhere on the island. The large filet was served on linguini, though the sauce flavored with dill and 'scent of lobster,' was so too powerful we were glad we requested 'sauce on the side.' The wine list offers nice variety in the $20 - $30 range.

Everyone is friendly, as is appropriate in a restaurant which calls itself Casa di Amici, from servers to the hostess who ask you how you enjoyed your dinner and reminds you to drive safely. Friendly service, tasty food, and reasonable prices make dining at Casa di Amici an enjoyable experience. The parking lot is small; you may have better luck finding a spot on the street.

Poipu, 2301 Nalo Rd. Reservations 742-1555. Credit cards. Dinner nightly from 6 pm. Map 3

Dondero's, Hyatt Regency Hotel

Decorated in vibrant green and white, Dondero's is an elegant restaurant, designed to capture the more leisurely pace of the 1920's before jet-set timetables pushed life into permanent fast-forward. Dondero's dining room is attractively arranged on two levels, with tables comfortably spaced for privacy. Gracefully twining ivy vines painted on the walls complement the pattern of jade green and white tiles, some designed with seashells, so that the room seems poised on the edge of a seaside garden, with large windows and french doors opening to the terrace. During summer months, the colors of the setting sun make terrace dining beautiful. Tables set with china and silver are softly lit by crystal lamps with pleated shades, a golden glow in shades of darkness.

More than a dozen à la carte entrées range in price from $27 to $41, as well as pastas from $17. For appetizers, try porcini mushroom crêpes, with fontina and parmesan cream sauce, and balance this dish, substantial enough to share, with a salad of tomato, fresh mozzarella, roasted peppers, and fresh basil ($9.75). For entrées, a fresh local swordfish is perfectly cooked ($27.50), both moist and tender. Chicken parmiagiana served with fresh mozzarella was also tasty and tender ($27). The Hyatt wine list is expensive, most above $30, including a 'Captain's List' with *Wine Spectator* ratings, so you might consider one of the 14 vintage wines available by the glass. You'll love the desserts – chocolate mousse, an outstanding tiramisu, and strawberry flambeau with vanilla ice cream.

At Dondero's, prices are expensive, with the cost per person well over $40, but the hotel comes with the meal. Consider your dinner as a single course in your entire evening. For an aperitif, walk around the lovely hotel and listen to Kauai's musicians perform in the Seaview Lounge. After dinner, stroll the beautifully lit gardens and enjoy the breezes of evening.

Nature's disposable container

Poipu, Hyatt Regency Hotel. Reservations a must: 742-1234. Credit cards. Non-smoking section. Free valet parking. Children's menu.

Kalaheo Coffee Company

When you walk into this tiny eaterie on the main street of Kalaheo, you notice the fragrance. Sample specialty coffees grown on Kauai while you wait for your sandwich, salads, or cold and hot plates prepared with high quality ingredients. This little coffee shop offers a surprisingly large variety of breakfast and lunch options. Even though there is no table service, it's worth having to stand in line at the counter to order a tasty, inexpensive lunch on the way to the beach!

Try 'bulgar wheat and veggie salad' ($7.50) served with salsa and guacamole: the toasted bulgar wheat is crunchy, the salsa not too spicy, and the portion of greens, sprouts and onion reasonable ($4.25). Or add soup and foccacia to a plain green salad ($7.25). Local customers rave about 'bagel benny,' toasted with ham, turkey or grilled veggies, topped with a poached egg and hollandaise sauce (with rice or potatoes), croissant egg sandwich ($3.50), as well as a delicious wrap filled with tuna, bacon and melted cheddar and avocado. Don't miss the grilled vegetable sandwich (eggplant, zucchini, and lettuce and tomato), memorable for its unique spice and flavors, or grilled tofu and eggplant. On the children's menu, you'll find grilled cheese or PBJ ($3.50). For breakfast try delicious home baked pastries, or eggs, waffles, and pancakes and bagel creations.

For a beach picnic, call ahead to save waiting time, for a lot of local people like the place too. You can also buy Kauai coffee to take home.

Kalaheo, Rt. 50 at the traffic light. Open 6 am - 4 pm (M-F); 6:30 to 4 pm (Sat.); 7 am - 2 pm (Sun.). Credit cards. 332-5858 or 800-255-0137. www.kalaheo.com. Map 3

Kalaheo Steak House

For more than ten years, the Kalaheo Steak House has been serving some of the best, most reasonably-priced steaks on Kauai. The cozy, knotty-pine interior is both pleasant and informal, with comfortable booths along the wall and roomy tables set with fresh flowers and candles.

The restaurant prides itself on the finest of ingredients. Steaks are top-grade Midwestern beef. Bread is baked each day at the bakery across the street. Even the dinner salad is exceptionally attractive, served on a lovely glass plate with ripe tomatoes, white beans and red onions. Choose a delicious papaya seed dressing or a home made blue cheese vinaigrette with real cheese, topped with fresh ground pepper.

The menu offers steaks, seafood, and poultry dinners which include rice or baked potato as well as salad. Our waitress recommended the New York steak ($19.95) and the fresh island opah (10 oz. $21.95), and we were pleased with both. The generous portion of opah was flaky and tender, though you might have the butter sauce served on the side, unless you love garlic. When the steak arrived too well done to be 'medium rare,' the replacement was even larger, perfectly cooked, and accompanied by a second baked potato – well worth the wait! Prime rib ($27/12 oz. or $30/26 oz.), was both tender and tasty. Entrées are cooked with little salt, a nice feature. Service is friendly and efficient, and prices are extremely reasonable, with teriyaki chicken ($15.95) at the low end of the entrées. You can also choose a 'refillable salad plate' ($6.95).

Kalaheo Steak House offers one of the best values on Kauai, as two can dine in style for less than $50, including one of the 14 nicely selected wines on the almost unbelievably reasonable wine list. An excellent alternative to higher-priced Poipu restaurants, it's well worth the drive.

Kalaheo, 4444 Papalini Road. 332-9780. Credit Cards. Dinner nightly 6 pm - 10 pm. No reservations. Map 3

Keoki's Paradise

At Keoki's you might feel as if you've wandered onto the set of a commercial starring Tommy Bahama. Tables arranged on several levels surround a wandering stream, where taro grows among lava rocks, and a frog or two rest among the lily pads. Tropical plants grow everywhere, and the night is filled with the sound of crickets. Wooden tables are roomy and rattan chairs comfortably upholstered. Ask to be seated outside, where dining is cooled by evening breezes and you can watch the light of evening fade and the sky turn luminous with shining stars. Should a passing shower threaten to douse the table, waiters will set the awnings.

One of the most successful restaurants on the south shore, Keoki's offers reasonable prices as well as an atmosphere of South Pacific chic. In busy times, a line of hungry diners begins to form at about 7 pm.

To the right of the entrance is Bamboo Café, where you can eat pu pus, nachos, burgers, Mexican specialties from $5.95, and local style plates like BBQ chicken at $9.95. Come early and sit at one of the half dozen tables near the bar and you can put together an inexpensive dinner. Keoki's main dining room features a reasonably-priced, extensive menu offering fresh fish, chicken, steak as well as a huge portion of prime rib ($24.95), aptly named 'the Flintstone Cut' and available only "while it lasts." Entrées include salad, rice, and fresh bread. Many cost about $16, though you can spend less for a burger ($8.95), though fries are extra. Children have great complete dinners.

Some may find the fish chowder ($3.95) overly thick and salty. Dinners include homemade bran muffins and salad, a sharply seasoned Caesar salad with too much

Heliconia Parrot's Beak

cheese, too many croutons, and the limpness of bulk preparation. You might ask for romaine lettuce, oil and vinegar.

Fresh fish ($19.95-$23.95) can be ordered in 5 preparations, including 'simply healthy,' cleanly grilled with no butter or oil and served simply with pineapple salsa. This is the preparation of choice, as we have found the sauces and marinades to be of varying quality, like the strongly flavored wine and caper sauce which overwhelmed the fresh ono and should have been left on the side (or in the kitchen!). Fresh-baked opakapaka, on the other hand, was moist, generous, and fragrant with basil which complemented its flavor. Prime rib is moist, tender, and though a bit bland, its appearance, at 28 oz., was a show stopper ($24.95).

Entrées are accompanied by an adequate herb rice and vegetables, or you can have baked potato ($2.50), though only one of our order arrived in time for dinner. The small wine list offers a nice selection of California wines mostly in the $25 range. Don't miss the signature' hula pie' ($4.95).

Keoki's attracts a large clientele because of reasonable prices and generous portions. Service is friendly, though geared to the masses, so you may have to stand up to catch your waitperson's attention. Be prepared to enjoy what comes your way rather than trying to customize your order or change the way the kitchen prepares it. Enjoy Hawaiian contemporary music by some of Kauai's talented performers on Thursday and Friday nights, and Sunday afternoons. Call to see who's playing.

Poipu Shopping Village. 742-7534. Reservations a must. Credit cards. Bamboo Café menu: 11 am -11:30 pm; Dinner: 5:00-10 pm nightly.

Naniwa

Naniwa, the Japanese restaurant in the Sheraton Poipu Resort, won't whisk you away to an exotic world. The cuisine might be Japanese, but the restaurant was designed for western clientele, so you won't have to remove your shoes upon entering, and you won't be sitting on the floor.

Naniwa's dining room has been moved to the hotel's ocean side, which brings an advantage in location but the loss of much of its charm. Gone is the private room by the lagoon with its quiet location. Instead, you are seated in what can feel a bit like a cafeteria, a room surrounded by a sea of diners. You eat on paper place mats with disposable chopsticks at wooden tables. Prices are expensive. Entrées can be ordered either à la carte ($20-$30) or as complete dinners including rice, Japanese pickled vegetables and a delicately flavored miso soup (about $5 more). Beautiful sushi (à la carte $4-$13) is prepared by the chef. The menu features chicken, seafood, striploin, tempura and noodle entrées.

The dining room is attractive and comfortable, though you may find it noisier than you'd like because of its proximity to the main dining room.

Sheraton Kauai Resort, Poipu. 5:30 - 9:30 pm. 742-1661. Credit cards.

Pattaya Thai Cuisine

Pattaya looks like a dining room outdoors, its tile floor bordered with leafy green plants. Servers will greet you pleasantly and help you order

some of Pattaya's delicious Thai cuisine. Vegetarian spring rolls ($7) arrive crispy and hot. Ginger-coconut soup ($8) is delicately flavored and light, generous with chicken and the kaffir lime leaves which make the dish special.

Water lilies bloom at night in Moir Gardens.

'Evil Jungle Prince,' a wonderful coconut flavored curry dishes are served with chicken ($10), shrimp ($12) or seafood ($18). Eggplant with tofu appears in a tangy and flavorful brown sauce, and delicious curries start at only $9.95 (with chicken). Vegetables are carefully cooked and attractively served, and the sticky rice ($2.25) is first rate. Try a bowl of brown rice with some peanut sweet and sour sauce.

An offshoot of the very successful Mema Thai Cuisine in Wailua, Pattaya offers a pleasant evening at a very reasonable price.

Poipu, Poipu Shopping Village. 742-8818. Credit cards. Lunch: 11:30 am - 2:30 pm. (M-Sat). Dinner: 5 pm - 9:30 pm nightly. Map 3

Plantation Gardens

For more than 20 years, the lovely Moir Gardens have provided an especially romantic setting – a beautiful old plantation home, where you can dine outside on a veranda cooled by evening breezes fragrant with tropical flowers, and see water lilies glow in moonlit ponds like night-blooming stars. The newest resident of the old plantation home is by far the most elegant. China and crystal sparkle in candlelight on crisp linen cloths. At the same time, the decor is understated, so that the gardens, lit with subtlety and flair, draw the eye outside to a landscape brushed with shades of darkness. The dining room glows softly yellow and pink in the evening, like a plumeria blossom.

Although owned by Piatti, a chain of successful west coast Italian restaurants, Plantation Gardens presents an Italian cuisine Kauai style, incorporating island flavors, local vegetables, light sauces. Herbs, spices, greens, even eggplant, are grown in the restaurant's gardens. Crusty bread still warm from the brick pizza oven arrives immediately, along with a dish of olive oil pesto. While the wine list is not distinguished, there are some good choices at fair prices.

You'll find tasty home-baked pizzas from $11.95, salads and antipasti from $7-$14, and about 8 entrées ranging from lamb, veal, beef, pork, to chicken and seafood, pasta and risotto ($15 - $23). Many dishes feature local ingredients, like an appetizer of Kekaha shrimp ($10). Local green salad with tomatoes ($8) was rather ordinary, less interesting than the delicious grilled chicken salad, with local greens, almonds, feta cheese, with lilikoi vinaigrette ($10.95).

Entrées are artfully arranged and on the whole well-prepared. If you prefer the pure taste of island fish, you might ask to have the sauce served on the side. Our fresh ahi, though moist and tender, was covered in a

Hanalei Valley taro plants, source of poi

somewhat peppery sauce, as were the vegetables, while the fresh snapper, uku, was covered in a powerful soy-flavored sauce ($20). Best was 'Seafood Lau Lau,' fresh fish, shrimp, and scallops steamed in their own natural juices inside a ti leaf, a dramatic and tasty presentation ($18.95).

If you are looking for a romantic dinner with quiet conversation, Plantation Gardens is a good choice. You won't be hurried, and the setting, almost more than the menu, is a gorgeous centerpiece to your meal. Dine on the veranda, or if you prefer a more informal experience, on the porch near the bar, and see the gardens glimmering in candle light.

In Kiahuna Resort, Poipu. 742-2216. Request veranda. Credit cards. 5:30 10 pm daily. Take-out orders. FAX 742-1570. www.pgrestaurant.com

Poipu Bay Clubhouse

With its comfortable air-conditioned dining room and spectacular views, Poipu Bay Golf Course Clubhouse Restaurant has gone through several transformations trying to define its relationship with the Hyatt Hotel. At one time it was a Chinese restaurant; at another time, it presented a terrific soup, sandwich, salad bar for self-serve, speedy lunches. Now, the Clubhouse restaurant has finally been absorbed into the Hyatt Resort and offers Hyatt cuisine at hotel prices. You can still look out over the rolling green fairways of the Poipu Bay Golf Course, studded with palm trees. You can still see sand dunes and ocean waves smashing against the rocky cliffs in brilliant bursts of spray. But now you'll pay high prices and, if the dining room is crowded, wait a long time for rather ordinary food, especially irritating if you want to get to the beach!

The lunch menu offers a variety of sandwiches, including a half-pound hamburger served plain ($6.50) or with sautéed fresh mushrooms melted cheddar cheese ($7.50). The fresh fish sandwich ($9.50) is tasty if on the small side, and you have to request teriyaki sauce and pay extra for the pineapple ($1.50) that gives it flair. But servers are pleasant, tables comfortable, air conditioning welcome, and you can't beat the view.

Poipu, adjacent to Hyatt Regency Hotel. 742-1515. Breakfast 6:30 am - 11 am. Lunch 11 am - 3 pm. Credit cards. Smoking allowed at the bar.

Poipu Beach Broiler

The Poipu Beach Broiler has opened in the Poipu Kai resort complex, in the space once home to House of Seafood. The dining room has been decorated in a kind of coconut frond motif, like early Hawaiian church. Tables have a sponge painted top, and fly fans move cooling breezes from the open rafters. A focal point is the bar, where local people like to come for extensive, and delicious, pu pus during happy hour.

The steak and seafood menu features as its centerpiece the fruit and salad bar which occupies a long section of the restaurant's wall. You may be surprised, however, to find a $9 surcharge for the salad bar, or $5 for a single visit. You must also specify the single visit option when you order your dinner so that your server will give you the smaller plate, though your server may not get around to pointing that out. The salad bar by itself in unlimited trips is a good deal for $9, given the high cost of produce on Kauai; it's also available at lunch, a bargain ($9 for all you can eat).

If you don't buy the salad bar as an add-on, the dinner menu offerings are reasonably priced, including chicken ($16), prime rib ($22/14oz), as well as steak ($20) and fresh fish ($17) which can be prepared in several ways – blackened, spiced southwestern style, sautéed with macadamia nuts, or grilled. Our fresh ahi, described as "seared" arrived almost ocean-cold, and worse, the grilled ono tasted bitter from the grill. Even with the single visit salad bar, each dinner was close to $30 for a fairly ordinary meal.

Service is friendly, and the no reservations policy ensures that you come to know the reception staff by the time you are seated. The manager makes the rounds to ask how you are enjoying your dinner and your wine. He is very proud of the list, which has some excellent choices at good prices, particularly among the reds, like a La Crema pinot noir ($34).

Poipu Beach Broiler has a great concept, but be ready to buy an extra ticket to the main attraction.

1941 Poipu Road. 742-6433. 11 am –11 pm. Happy hour 2-5. Credit cards.

Pomodoro

Once upon a time, two hardworking brothers from Italy arrived on Kauai via New York City, where one found a wife, and opened the island's first Italian restaurant. Over the years, as Casa Italiana grew into a successful restaurant, they imported the island's first pasta machine from Italy. As time went by, other restaurants, including the specialty restaurants in the big hotels, began to order their pasta, and so they sold Casa Italiana and became full-time purveyors of fine noodle creations.

But long hours with eggs and flour were just not as interesting as working with people. A true New Yorker, Gerry missed all those midnight hours in the restaurant, the seven-day workweeks, the temperamental customers and frazzled servers. So the family sold the pasta company, opened Pomodoro Restaurant, and Gerry is once more in her element, bustling from table to table keeping her diners happy.

Pomodoro is both attractive and small, only ten tables. The dining room, filled with leafy green plants, is clean, comfortable, and informal; with a second room for small parties. Everything is prepared to order, with pastas from $10.50 and the most expensive dishes, the veal specialties, at $18.95. Add salad or soup, and the price goes up about $4. Children can eat spaghetti ($5.95), ravioli ($6.95), or small portions of some entrées.

What comes to the table is fresh, light, and tasty. Dinner begins with homemade foccacia served with extra virgin olive oil and balsamic vinegar instead of butter, a sign of the healthful times. Mixed greens ($4.95) look beautiful with purple and green spinach as well as various fresh organic lettuces. Minestrone ($3.75) arrives in a large bowl generous with noodles, beans, and still crunchy vegetables. Pomodoro's sauces are light and flavorful without being overpowering, for example in pasta primavera, where the vegetable broth perfectly complements fresh zucchini, carrots, tomatoes, green onions. Traditional pastas are more robust, like delicious manicotti, thin crepes generously stuffed with cheeses, or cannelloni, stuffed with meat and spinach ($13.95). Or try ravioli ($10.95) filled with ground beef or riccotta cheese, and even served with tasty meatballs ($12.95), or a delicious lasagne ($14.95). There's no fresh fish on the regular menu, but you'll find first- rate meatless choices like chicken cacciatore ($17.95), a skinless breast, and eggplant parmiagiana ($16.95). Kids can have spaghetti ($5.95) or ravioli ($6.95). There's a full bar (try an excellent chi chi) as well as reasonable wines.

great pasta in a friendly setting!

At Pomodoro, two can enjoy a first rate dinner for a remarkably small price, about $40. For excellent Italian cuisine and service at modest prices, Pomodoro is well worth the short drive from Poipu to Kalaheo.

Kalaheo, Rainbow Shopping Center. 332-5945. Children's menu (under 12). Credit cards. Dinner nightly. 5:30-9:30 pm. Closed Sundays. Map 3

Roy's Poipu Bar & Grill

Roy's is 'dining theater.' From the time you arrive (and you'll probably have to wait, even with a reservation), you're part of a performance. No matter where you stand, you'll feel like you're in the action, as waiters whoosh by, leaning like skiers into the turns in the pathways between tables, steaming plates in hand. Given Roy's long, narrow layout (it occupies several converted souvenir stores along one arm of the Kiahuna Shopping Center), each step, each turn counts, as servers maneuver through an obstacle course of patrons and supply stations.

The kitchen takes up a long slice of the restaurant, or it could be equally accurate to say that the dining room takes up a long slice of the kitchen. For at Roy's, the cookery is the main act, and the kitchen is center stage, just behind a wall of glass from the nearest tables. Chefs and servers hustle and bustle as if performing in a silent movie starring Charlie Chaplin. Watch one chef adorn plates with colorful greens and vegetables, another ladle steaming sauce, and a third flame pasta dishes in seeming defiance of fire safety rules. In a constant stream, servers enter the in-door, scoot along a narrow pathway picking up plates, and emerge from the out-door, while the executive chef surveys it all, smilingly serene.

At Roy's, what emerges from the kitchen is, for the most part, carefully crafted and delicious. Since most entrées can be ordered in appetizer portions for about half the price, you should sample as many dishes as possible. Try blackened ahi, high-grade, flash fried and outstanding ($13.50). Even a salad becomes an event, when granny smith apples are paired with cheese, walnuts, and sesame miso ($8.50). 'Hibachi salmon' ($9.95) is about as tender and moist as fish can be ($12.50).

For entrées, you may find as many as seven varieties of fresh island fish ($25-$29) in memorable preparations, like fresh thyme seared monchong with grilled asparagus and polenta ($28.50). Vegetarians can have kiave grilled mushrooms and vegetables ($14.50), the least expensive choice. Go before 6:30 pm and you can have the 'Sunset Prix Fixe Menu' (3 courses/$35). At any time, you can try the 'Sake Prix Fixe Menu' with 2.5 oz. sake servings with each course ($70/pp).

To keep prices under control, Roy's is organized for volume. One waiter takes your order, another serves bread and water, and food is delivered by runners. This system works well for the most part but is not foolproof, as some parts of our order arrived late, one never appeared at all, and sometimes dishes come so fast that there is no time to appreciate the presentation. The kitchen was out of five items by 8:30, and custom ordering, we were told, requires consent of the chef!

The first Roy's opened in 1988 on Oahu, and now has ten branches in Hawaii, Guam, Tokyo, and even Pebble Beach, California. All feature the same Pacific Rim cuisine, the same dining style. If you were to imagine the finest in dining, you might envision your table as a peaceful island,

imaginative Pacific Rim cuisine

where discrete waitpersons present each course unobtrusively, and the only sound you hear is the delicate tinkle of silverware and china. Well, not at Roy's! You won't find a quiet table, and you are never alone, for the plan, in the words of our waiter, is to 'attack the table' with a barrage of attention – serving and clearing, offering fresh baked rolls or ice-water, sweeping away crumbs from the granite-topped table or just asking how you are enjoying your meal. It's interactive dining. You're part of the performance, and everyone on the staff seems to be enjoying the show. This almost electric energy, as well truly delicious food, makes Roy's a unique dining experience on Kauai.

Poipu Shopping Village. 742-5000. Reservations. Nightly 5:30 pm - 9:30 pm. Credit cards. www.roysrestaurants.com (menus, recipes). Map 3

Shells

The main restaurant of the Sheraton Kauai Resort Hotel, Shells offers sweeping views of Poipu Beach in a large, comfortable dining room with a relaxed ambiance. Tables are spacious, and tall ceilings keep temperatures cool. However, a recent design decision has located all three hotel restaurants side by side, and resulted in what is unfortunately more like three contiguous compartments than separate dining spaces.

Shells menu offers à la carte entrées ranging from chicken ($18) to rack of lamb ($29). Appetizers quickly increase your dinner cost, but you can visit the extensive salad bar for only $7 ($12/as entrée). Dinners are of good quality but uneven. Rack of lamb is well-trimmed and tender, accompanied by garlic mashed potatoes and colorful vegetables.

Shells has a spectacular ocean view and a friendly feeling. On certain nights, Shells's offers theme buffets, and families have a great deal – one '12 & under' dines free with each adult. Listen to Hawaiian music played by Kauai's musicians next door at Point Lounge. Call for schedule.

Sheraton Kauai Resort, Poipu. Open daily, 7-11:30 am; 11:30-2 pm; 5:30-9:30 pm. 742-1661. Credit cards. Map 3

Taqueria Nortenos

When you drive by the Kukui'ula Center in Poipu, you often see a jammed parking lot and a small cluster of people on the sidewalk waiting for some of the best, most sensibly priced Mexican food on Kauai.

You'll have to wait on the take-out line by the tiny kitchen. (For those in a rush, there's an 'express window') and while you're being driven crazy by the wonderful aromas, you can calculate the price of your selections. The menu offers meat or vegetarian burritos, tacos, and tostadas at modest prices ($3-$4) with fillings and toppings priced separately ($.55 each). So you can skip the sour cream, say, and not pay for it. Beans, rice, and sauce come free, and inexpensive extras like tomatoes or onions will be cooked right inside your burrito or taco. Nachos have great cheese and plenty of everything, both fresh corn and flour chips. Guacamole is chunky with avocados. Your beef burrito will be filled with huge chunks of tender and tasty shredded beef, and covered with cheese, in a portion so large you will be hard pressed to clean your plastic plate ($6). Spices are mild, with plenty of hot sauce available.

Poipu, Kukui'ula shopping center. 11 am – 10 pm. Cash only. Closed Wednesdays 742-7222. Map 3

Tidepools, Hyatt Regency Hotel

Nestled at the bottom of the cliff in the center of the lovely Hyatt Regency Hotel, Tidepools combines an elegant ambiance with expertly prepared dinners, particularly fresh island fish. To get to Tidepools, you walk down from the hotel lobby, a spectacular marble perch built into the cliff and overlooking the sea. At the bottom, clustered near the edge of the hotel's wandering waterways, is the restaurant, a 'village' of connected Polynesian style huts. The dining room is comfortable, spacious, and attractive. Parquet tables with cloths of Hawaiian tapa design are well spaced for privacy (there's not a bad table in this restaurant). Candle

Tidepools Restaurant, Hyatt Regency Resort Hotel

lamps glow golden in the evening light, reflected in dark blue glassware.

Tidepools features steak and seafood flavored with contemporary versions of Hawaiian recipes and local spices and ingredients. On the appetizer menu, Kimo's crab cake is wonderful ($11), and you'll find several salads from $9. Entrée choices include prime rib, chicken ($26), and fresh island fish, which can be steamed, sautéed, grilled or even blackened. Try grilled ahi ($29), Hawaiian opah (moon fish), or onaga, our favorite snapper ($29). We like the unique flavor of the fish, and so usually order all sauces served on the side. Or you can choose lamb, chicken, prime rib or steak, while vegetarians can choose from 3 entreés or several local vegetables from the à la carte menu. Filet mignon ($36) is excellent, crisp on the outside, moist and tender inside. Children have a great menu – chicken nuggets, grilled cheese, fish, pasta, prime rib, or hot dog.

At Tidepools, portions are reasonably generous, presentation attractive, service polite and unhurried. Prices are high, but the hotel comes with the meal. Be sure to explore the lovely grounds, walk along the ocean and find one of the hammocks, lie back, listen to the sound of the waves, and look up into the bowl of stars.

Poipu, Hyatt Regency Hotel. Dinner nightly 6 - 10 pm. Reservations 742-1234. Valet parking. Credit cards. Map 3

Tomkats Grill

In a covered veranda at the rear of Koloa's historic Kawamoto Building, Tomkats offers informal, open-air dining at reasonable prices. About a dozen tables with cushioned rattan chairs cluster on the plank floor, and just beyond the railing is a small quiet garden, fringed with red ginger, and a small fishpond, where goldfish tuned in to 'Hawaiian time,' swim slowly enough to entrance the twelve-and-under set. Fly fans encourage breezes, and even in a sudden shower, this sheltered spot is peaceful, the rain beating a muffled tatoo on the tin roof.

Tomkats courts families, and features a special 'kittens' menu with hamburger or grilled cheese. The all-day menu offers a wide range of sandwiches, burgers, salads (from $7) and complete dinners (from $9.95 for 1/4 rotisserie chicken). Sandwiches are carefully prepared, and attractively served in baskets piled high with french fries. Turkey club on rye ($7.95) with avocado ($1.25 extra) was first rate, as was Cobb Salad ($8.50). Portions are generous, service friendly, and the hours make Tomkats a convenient stop after the beach, when some of your party may be hissing with hunger!

Central Koloa. 742-8887. 11 am -10 pm daily. Credit cards. Take-out. A full bar is adjacent, though not intrusive. Map 3

Espresso Kauai

Eastern Shore: LIHUE: *Border's Espresso Café* 246-0862, great bakery treats and sandwiches. WAILUA: *Papaya's* 833-0190 near Safeway also serves deli sandwiches, casseroles, and organic foods. KAPA'A: *Java Kai* 823-6887 has bakery treats. Lihue. *Starbucks* has arrived! Kukui Grove 241-7034, next to Jamba Juice. *Java Kai* has opened on Rice St downtown in what was once Dairy Queen. **North Shore**: PRINCEVILLE: *Hale O' Java* 826-7255. HANALEI: *Java Kai* 826-6717 (fresh-baked bagels). *Zelo's Beach House* 826-9700. *Old Hanalei Coffee Company* 826-6717. *Postcards* 826-1191. KILAUEA: *Kilauea Bakery* 828-2020 (organic to the filter paper!) **South Shore & Westside:** *Hanapepe Café & Espresso* 335-5011. *Kalaheo Coffee* 332-5858 has a bakery and deli. *Grinds* 335-6027 in Ele'ele has fresh baked bread, sandwiches. Stop at *Kauai Coffee* in Port Allen 335-0813 before your boat tour. *Lapperts* 335-6121.

Sunflowers in Waimea fields

Westside Restaurants

'favor...eats'

In Hanapepe, **Hanapepe Café & Espresso** serves wonderful vegetarian dishes, as well sandwiches and coffee drinks for lunch, and occasionally dinners. Nearby, the **Green Garden Restaurant** is a Kauai tradition for 'island style food' reflecting the multi-ethnic heritage of the island – Chinese, Japanese, Filipino, Portuguese, and American– and for lilikoi chiffon pie, all at reasonable prices. After lunch (or before) visit beautiful Salt Pond Beach Park, a great spot for family picnics. In Ele'ele, try **Toi's Thai Kitchen** for inexpensive, delicious, Thai food, and **Grinds** for tasty, generous sandwiches on homebaked bread.

Visiting Koke'e or the westside beaches? In Waimea, stop in at **Wrangler's Steakhouse** for excellent hamburgers and a salad bar; downstairs try great pizza, calzones, and first-rate sandwiches. **Waimea Brew Pub** has a terrific fresh fish sandwich. After the beach, stop in at **Jo Jo's Shave Ice** in 'downtown' Waimea for cold treat.

The Green Garden

There has been a Green Garden Restaurant for about as long as Kauai has been called the Garden Island. Owned and operated by Gwen and her family since 1948, its reputation is based on generous portions and inexpensive prices, and the menu features Chinese, Japanese, Filipino, Portuguese, and American complete dinners, many priced around $10. Even at lunch, meals include several courses and a beverage. Service is fast and friendly in a large dining room filled with plants and flowers.

You certainly get full value for your money. Where else could you find a hamburger platter with fries, a salad, dessert, *and* iced tea for under $6? At $7.95, fresh fish or shrimp tempura is another bargain. Club sandwiches at lunch cost about $6, and children's dinner/lunches cost $4. It may not win culinary awards, but remember: this price includes salad, lots of fries and a drink. Occasionally, a salad bar offers an assortment of fruits, vegetables, and great dressings for the amazing price of $5 at lunch and $7 at dinner. (To be sure it's 'on,' call ahead and ask). Combine it with soup, priced in three sizes; a 'medium' ($3.50) is actually large.

The Green Garden's pies would stand out at any price, and we recommend them all – chocolate cream pie is a child's favorite treat, and coconut cream pie has a light flaky crust filled with marvelously light egg custard topped with toasted coconut. Lilikoi chiffon pie, for which Green Garden is justly famous, has a light texture and a taste of passion fruit that will arouse your taste buds.

With dinner prices about a dollar or two higher than at lunch, the Green Garden is ideal for large families on small budgets, or anyone who wants a square meal and a fair deal. And aloha is in the air!

Hanapepe, on Rt. 50. Reservations suggested for dinner. 335-5422. 9 am - 2 pm and 5 pm - 9 pm. (Opens 8 am Saturdays and 7:30 am Sundays). Closed Tuesdays. Credit cards. Map 4

Hanapepe Café & Espresso

The sign to Hanapepe announces 'Kauai's Biggest Little Town,' and Hanapepe Café & Espresso is a major attraction for its vegetarian cuisine with an island flair. You'll find scones flavored with passion fruit, as well as a changing menu reflecting what's up with the chef and what's fresh at the local farmers' market. In the tiny restaurant, which has only a half-dozen tables, paintings by local artists brighten the clean white walls with color, and leafy plants, along with fresh flowers on white formica tables, provide the green and growing look. Dominating the dining area is the

On Kauai, poinsettia bloom along the road, and glisten in rain showers.

gleaming tiled counter, a remake of the 1940's curved lunch counter of the Igawa Drugstore, and now the home of Larry's espresso bar.

You don't have to be a vegetarian to enjoy this menu. A garden burger made from oats, carrots, cottage and mozzarella cheese is served on a cracked wheat roll with bright red local tomatoes, lettuce and a tasty spinach spread. Accompanied by an excellent potato salad, it's well priced at $6.75. Vegetable fritatta ($7.75) is stuffed with red and green peppers, zucchini, squash, mushrooms, mozzarella and topped with local tomatoes. Pasta of the day ($6.75) features fresh local vegetables with a light, delicious creamy tomato sauce. 'Healthnut' sandwich ($5.25) was spread with homemade hummus and served open faced so that we could assemble it ourselves, selecting just the right proportion of tomatoes, lettuce, sunflower sprouts, cucumbers and onions.

Dinner is served on an irregular basis, so call ahead. The dining room turns Cinderella-like into a lovely black and white café, with soft lighting and music. Entreés can include vegan lasagne, pasta with fresh mushrooms, or eggplant parmesan, as well as salads, soups and appetizers.

Afterwards, stroll the main street – it won't take you very long. You can try out the swinging bridge and sample some taro chips made at the Taro-Ka 'factory,' just around the corner. You'll love those chips!

Hanapepe, 3830 Hanapepe Road. 335-5011. Breakfast/Lunch: 8 am - 2 pm Tues. - Sat. Dinner (call). Credit cards. Map 4

Toi's Thai Kitchen

You can't get more underground that Toi's Thai Kitchen! It's original home was a carport semi-attached to a bar called 'Traveler's Den' in sleepy Kekaha, with a half dozen formica dinette sets, some with card table chairs. Now you'll find Toi's in a shopping center in almost-as-sleepy Ele'ele, or you'll try to find it, huddled under the arm of Big Save. Painted cinderblock walls are decorated by white lace curtains and plants, while fresh anthuriums brighten up the dozen formica tables. What comes out of the kitchen is much more special. Toi's has developed a loyal clientele who have spread the word, attracting newcomers who can't believe their eyes when they arrive – and are smiling when they leave.

We came in for lunch one afternoon, hungry and sandy from the beach. We loved Toi's saimin, Thai style – fresh white flat noodles float in a gently spiced broth colorful with vegetables, several varieties of bean sprouts ($5.95 for vegetarian) and because the fishermen had been lucky, fresh and delicious ono ($7.95). Rich and flavorful tofu soup ($7.95) was also terrific. The rest of the group ordered crispy spring rolls served with fresh lettuce, mint leaves, and a zesty peanut sauce ($6.95). The hot yellow curry pleased Jeremy, our spice enthusiast. Everyone loved Thai fried rice ($7.95), so colorful and tasty that it was devoured to the last grain. Those who prefer American food can try hot, crisp french fries ($1.50/$3), sandwiches, or burgers (about $5).

Dinners include green papaya salad, dessert, and brown, jasmine, or sticky rice. Try Pad Thai ($7.95), the tender chicken and fresh Thai noodles sweetened with coconut milk and fresh basil. Fresh eggplant sautéed with tofu and huge fresh mushrooms offers a marvelous contrast, both pungent and spicy ($7.95). Be sure to try Toi's Temptation, a sweet curry made with your choice of chicken, beef, pork, or fish simmered in coconut milk and flavored with lemon grass, lemon and basil leaves, and served with either potatoes or pineapples.

With prices so reasonable and food quality first-rate, Toi's Thai Kitchen makes great family fun!

Ele'ele Shopping Center, Rt. 50. 335-3111. Lunch 10:30 - 2:30 pm. Dinner 5:30 - 9:30 pm daily. Closed Tuesdays & Sunday for lunch.

Waimea Brew Pub

Waimea Brew Pub serves a modest lunch and dinner menu in the living room and on the porch of a restored planation house in Waimea. You can order sandwiches, burgers (a third pounder for $6.75), or salads

($4.95-$9.50). At dinner, try steak ($18.95), fish ($18.95) and chicken ($15.95), or pastas ($15.95). Best is the fresh fish sandwich ($8.95), which is juicy, tasty, attractively served in a basket with fries and spicy peanut cole slaw, one of the great lunches on Kauai! Children can choose a hot dog, PBJ or grilled cheese for $3.50. As for home brew, four beers are typically on tap, two ales, a porter, a stout, and a wheat.

The comfortable old planation house has wonderful wide verandas which would make an elegant dining setting (as once they did, in the days before Iniki). The restaurant occupies a small part of the house, and the adjacent bar is a smoking area. Dining on the patio outside can be quite pleasant, but at mid-day, the awnings provide only partial shade.

Just west of Waimea Town, 9400 Kaumuali'i Hwy. 11 am - 9 pm daily. 338-9733. www.wbcbrew.com

Wrangler's Steakhouse

Wrangler's dining room retains the outlines of its historic building, where you expect to see Matt Dillon amble in and take a chair. Ceilings are open to the rafters, fly fans keep the air moving, large windows bring in light. Tables are roomy and well separated, arranged on two levels for quiet and privacy, and there's a veranda for open air dining. The decor has a plantation flavor – saddles and tools from the Hawaiian cowboys, the paniolos. On the lower level, you can try calzones ($4-$5), a terrific turkey wrap, home baked pizza with crispy crust (from $9) and

deli sandwiches.

    With most lunches, Wrangler's offers a salad bar, with a variety of fresh greens, tasty pasta salad, and even home made chips and salsa. (Soup and salad bar alone: $7.95). Sandwiches and plate lunches include a 'plantation worker special' with beef teriyaki and tempura served in a traditional three tiered 'kau kau' pot ($8.95). 'Wrangler Burger' is a juicy half-pounder on a sesame seed roll, with bacon, mushrooms and cheese, served with crispy, piping hot steak fries ($8.95). Fresh ono sandwich is also first rate.

    Service is friendly, prices reasonable, and Wrangler's gift shop features lovely items from local artists, including Hawaiian quilts, dolls, and stuffed animals. Deborah Tuzon of Waimea weaves placemats and jewelry of lauhala; Caz creates wonderful sunflower barrettes and headbands of colorful woven plaid paniolo cloth, and you can try Dennis Okihara's local grown 'Black Mountain' coffee. On your way to Koke'e or to Polihale, you'd be hard pressed to find a better spot. Across the street from Wranglers, at the Waimea Hawaiian Church, circa 1820, Hawaiian language service is held at 8:30 am.

Downtown Waimea, on Rt. 50. 328-1218. Lunch 11 am - 4 pm M-F. Dinner 4 pm - 9 pm M-S .Closed Sundays. Credit cards. Map 4

Cyber Cafés

Check e-mail, download photos from digital cameras, burn CDs. Expect to pay about $5/half hour for internet access.
Eastern Shore: KAPA'A: *Akamai Computers:* Windows. ADSL. Rentals. 823-0047. 9 am -5:30 pm (M-F). 4-1286 Kuhio Hwy Suite A., next to Ono Family Restaurant.
Aloha Dude: Windows. ADSL. 822-DUDE. 9 am-7 pm (M-Sat), next to Olympic Restaurant. Map 1
North Shore: HANALEI: *Discount Activities Internet Portal.* Windows. 826-9117. 8 am - 8 pm daily. Across from Zelo's.
Bali Hai Photo, Ching Young Village. 826-9181. Map 2
South Shore: *Koloa Country Store.* Windows. ADSL. Espresso & pastries. 8 am - 8 pm (M-Sat); 9 am - 5 pm (Sun.). 742-1255. Behind Crazy Shirts. Map 3
Westside: Wireless on Kauai? Check e-mail while you have lunch or dinner at *Waimea Brew Pub.* It's free! 338-9733. Map 4

234

Index

Kauai Underground Guide 'Campaign for Kids'

A portion of the sales price of each book benefits these outstanding non-profit agencies helping Kauai's children:

* **The YWCA Family Violence Shelter** (808-245-6362) needs money for books, toys, clothes, writing materials and art supplies, paper and paint, puzzles and learning games, and child car seats. The YWCA can help you buy a car seat to use on Kauai, have it ready at the rental car agency, then pick it up as a donation when you leave. "We have almost no money in our regular budget for the special needs of individual children." – Director, Nancy Peterson. 3904 Elua St., Lihue HI 96766.

* **Friends of the Children's Advocacy Center** helps young victims of abuse and neglect. "Sometimes it's money for summer camp to get a child out of an abusive situation; sometimes it's books, or school supplies. Such small things, though they seem trivial, can have a huge impact on a child's life." –Director, Sara Silverman. 4473 Pahee St.-M. Lihue HI 96766

* **Hale 'Opio** (808-245-2873) helps children referred by the Family Court. "We need help for after- school tutoring, and special learning programs in art, Hawaiian culture, and photography. That's why Lenore's project is so important." – Director, Mary Lou Barela. 2959 Umi St., Lihue HI 96766

* **Kauai Children's Discovery Museum** (808-823-8222) brings hands-on educational activities to Kauai's children, involving science, computer studies, nature studies, photography, art, videography and more. These programs help children develop learning and leadership skills. – Director Robin Mazor, 6458 B Kahuna Rd., Kapa'a HI 96746

* **Ambassadors of Aloha** provides scholarship aid for children gifted in the arts. According to founder and President, former Mayor Maryanne Kusaka, "Our children need our help to develop their special talents, and to be able to benefit from opportunities beyond the island." – Director Sharon Agnew, 4121 Rice Street, #2506, Lihue, HI 96766

Tax-deductible contributions can be sent directly to these fine agencies.

www.explorekauai.com

Start planning your Kauai adventure today!

Name
_____

Address
_____

City _____ State _____ zip code _____

e-mail address
_____

$12.95 includes a CD of beautiful Hawaiian music by Keali'i Reichel. A portion of the proceeds will be donated to the organizations helping Kauai's children, listed at left.

_____ Number of copies @ $12.95

_____ Shipping ($1.50/bookrate or $3/priority)
free with orders of 2 or more copies

_____ Total enclosed by check or money order

Mahalo!
Lenore

Papaloa Press
362 Selby Lane
Atherton CA 94027
(650) 369-9994
50) 364-3252 FAX
aloa@pacbell.net

Keep Up-to-Date on Kauai!
r the latest updates, visit our web site
ww.explorekauai.com